1988

PSYCHIATRIC PATIENT RIGHTS AND PATIENT ADVOCACY

THE COMMUNITY PSYCHOLOGY SERIES
SPONSORED BY

THE DIVISION OF COMMUNITY PSYCHOLOGY OF THE AMERICAN PSYCHOLOGICAL ASSOCIATION

The Community Psychology Series has as its central purpose the building of philosophic, theoretical, scientific, and empirical foundations for action research in the community and in its subsystems, and for education and training for such action research.

As a publication of the Division of Community Psychology, the series is particularly concerned with the development of community psychology as a subarea of psychology. In general, it emphasizes the application and integration of theories and findings from other areas of psychology, and in particular the development of community psychology methods, theories, and principles, as these stem from actual community research and practice.

TITLES IN THE COMMUNITY PSYCHOLOGY SERIES UNDER THE EDITORSHIP OF DANIEL ADELSON, FOUNDING SERIES EDITOR
(1972–1979)

Volume 1: Man as the Measure: The Crossroads, edited by Daniel Adelson
Volume 2: The University and the Urban Crisis, edited by Howard E. Mitchell
Volume 3: Psychological Stress in the Campus Community: Theory, Research, and Action, edited by Bernard L. Bloom
Volume 4: Psychology of the Planned Community: The New Town Experience, edited by Donald C. Klein
Volume 5: Challenges to the Criminal Justice System: The Perspectives of Community Psychology, edited by Theodore R. Sarbin

UNDER THE EDITORSHIP OF BERNARD L. BLOOM (1980–)

Volume 6: Paraprofessionals in the Human Services, edited by Stanley S. Robin and Morton O. Wagenfeld
Volume 7: Psychiatric Patient Rights and Patient Advocacy: Issues and Evidence, edited by Bernard L. Bloom and Shirley J. Asher

PSYCHIATRIC PATIENT RIGHTS AND PATIENT ADVOCACY

Issues and Evidence

Edited by

Bernard L. Bloom, Ph.D.
Shirley J. Asher, Ph.D.

University of Colorado
Boulder, Colorado

Volume VII, Community Psychology Series
American Psychological Association,
Division of Community Psychology
Series Editor: Bernard Bloom, Ph.D.

HUMAN SCIENCES PRESS, INC.
72 FIFTH AVENUE,
NEW YORK, N.Y. 10011

Library of Congress Cataloging in Publication Data

Main entry under title:
Psychiatric patient rights and patient advocacy.

  (The Community psychology series; v. 7)
  Includes index.
  1. Psychotherapy patients—Legal status,
laws, etc.—United States. 2. Mental health
laws—United States. 3. Insanity—Juris
prudence—United States. I. Bloom, Bernard L.
II. Asher, Shirley J. III. Series. [DNLM:
1 Patient advocacy. 2. Mental disorders—
United States—Legislation.   WM 29.5 P974]
KF3828.P76   344.73'044   LC 81-13165
               347.30444   AACR2   ISSN   0731-0471
  ISBN 0-89885-056-8

CONTENTS

CONTRIBUTORS

SHIRLEY J. ASHER received her Ph.D. in clinical psychology at the University of Colorado, Boulder. She recently completed her internship at Denver General Hospital. Her major interest is in community mental health. A graduate of Brandeis University, she worked at Massachusetts General Hospital and at the Weld Mental Health Center in Greeley, Colorado prior to beginning her graduate education.

SUSAN MAKIESKY BARROW, an anthropologist, is research scientist in the Community Support Systems Monitoring and Evaluation project at the New York State Psychiatric Institute. She has examined social networks and schizophrenia, and is now studying the community experiences of deinstitutionalized schizophrenic patients.

BERNARD L. BLOOM has been a professor in the Department of Psychology at the University of Colorado, Boulder since 1965. He received his Ph.D. from the University of Connecticut in 1952 and Master of Science in Hygiene from Harvard School of Public Health in 1962. In the intervening decade he worked in a number of clinical settings, including the Veterans Administration Out-patient Clinic in Boston, and as the director of Psychological Services and Training at the Hawaii State Hospital. Between 1962 and 1965 he was a mental health consultant for National Institute of Mental Health (NIMH) at the Denver Regional Office of the U.S. Public Health Service.

CLAUDIA COWAN was trained in social psychology at Stanford University and is working on a law degree at the University of California at Berkeley. In working toward a career in applications of psychology to criminal law, she pursues interests in mental health law and sentencing procedures. Her most recent work is on jury selection in capital trials.

PAUL P. FREDDOLINO is currently an assistant professor of social work at Michigan State University. He recently completed a two-year post-doctoral fellowship in mental health evaluation research in the Department of Sociology at the University of California, Los Angeles, during which he conducted an evaluation of a private mental health advocacy project. He is a consultant to NIMH and is the project director of an evaluation of a state mental health advocacy program.

RICHARD J. GRANDISON was trained in social psychology at the University of Georgia. His professional activities have included counseling youthful offenders, alcoholics, and inpatient schizophrenics, and the assessment of client improvement. He is currently investigating the cognitive and behavioral consequences of the mental illness label.

LINDA GUTWIRTH, an anthropologist, is research scientist in the Child Psychiatry Department at the New York State Psychiatric Institute. She has participated in research on social networks and schizophrenia, on the community experience of deinstitutionalized schizophrenic patients in northern Manhattan, and on the role of social networks in child and family health.

JOHN MONAHAN is Professor of Law at the University of Virginia, and was formerly in the Program in Social Ecology at the University of California, Irvine. He received his Ph.D. in clinical psychology from Indiana University in 1972. He has been the president of the American Psychology-Law Society, the chair of the American Psychological Association's Task Force on Criminal Justice, and a member of the Panel on Legal Issues of the President's Commission on Mental Health and the Panel on Offender Rehabilitation of the National Academy of Sciences.

JOHN O. NOLL is professor and director of the clinical program in the Department of Psychology, University of North Dakota. He has been interested in patient rights for a decade and has offered an annual seminar in patient-client rights since 1972. He received the Ph.D. from the University of Pittsburgh in 1955.

MARK D. PASEWARK is an attorney practicing with the St. Louis, Missouri firm of Sidel, Sandweiss, & Kaskowitz. He graduated from Washington University School of Law in St. Louis.

RICHARD A. PASEWARK has been professor and director of clinical psychology training at the University of Wyoming since 1961. Prior to that time, he served as director of the Wyoming Division of Mental Health. His interests are primarily in the areas of training and the interfacing of the mental health and legal systems.

STEVEN R. PERRY is in private practice in Boulder, Colorado. He attended Antioch College (B.A., 1966) and San Diego State University, and received the Ph.D. in clinical psychology from the University of Colorado in 1980. The producer of several films, he also coauthored *Interpersonal Communications* (Charles C. Thomas, 1971). He has taught psychology and political science at Kauai (Hawaii) Community College and was the first director of the Antioch experimental television facility.

JUDITH GODWIN RABKIN is a research scientist at New York State Psychiatric Institute, a position she has held for 12 years. She received her Ph.D. in clinical psychology from New York University and a Master's in Public Health (Epidemiology) from the Columbia University School of Public Health, where she was a postdoctoral fellow in the Psychiatric Epidemiology Training Program. She has an appointment as adjunct assistant professor of Public Health (Epidemiology) in the Department of Psychiatry at Columbia University.

CATHERINE E. ROSEN was trained in psychology at the University of Michigan and the University of Georgia. She is currently affiliated with the University of Georgia and is also in private practice. Her research, ranging from the study of children's play to the evaluation of mental health programs for the elderly, has typically evolved from her experiences in clinical settings.

JAMES SPENSLEY is an associate clinical professor at the University of California, Davis, School of Medicine. During his association with Davis, he has directed a community mental health center. He has just completed a study of interdisciplinary training for mental health professionals.

HENRY J. STEADMAN is director of Special Projects Research Unit of the New York State Office of Mental Health, and adjunct associate professor in the Department of Sociology at the State University of New York, Albany. His most recent book, *Beating a Rap: Defendants Incompetent to Stand Trial,* reflects his long-standing research interests in the wide range of issues at the interface of mental health and criminal justice.

PAUL H. WERME is currently a private consultant in the area of hospital and mental health administration. He was formerly assistant director for mental health administrative services at the University of California, Davis, Medical Center in Sacramento, where he served as administrative officer for three comprehensive community mental health centers. A graduate of Clark University, he received his master's degree in experimental psychology from the University of Denver in 1966.

ARTHUR ZITRIN is a professor of psychiatry at the New York University Medical Center, and a practicing psychiatrist and psychoanalyst. For 13 years, until 1968, he was director of psychiatry at Bellevue Hospital, and his interest in outcome studies of hospitalized psychiatric patients stems from this experience.

PREFACE

During the past 15 years, there has been a dramatic increase in the volume of litigation, court decisions, legislative statutes, and administrative regulations affecting the rights of psychiatric patients. Courts, legislatures, and mental health agencies are in the process of establishing, reevaluating, and redefining virtually all policies relating to the care of psychiatric patients. Paralleling this increase has been a proliferation of conceptual, ideological, and empirical writing on every aspect of the complex of issues pertinent to the clinical as well as the civil rights of psychiatric patients.

Position papers written by attorneys and mental health professionals on the care and rights of the psychiatrically disabled population generally reveal that these groups approach the issues from vastly differing ideological positions. All sides claim to represent the best interests of patients, yet until recently there has been little empirical evidence to draw on in choosing among differing ideological points of view. This volume represents an attempt to bring together, review, and analyze critically empirical research studies relating to a number of important aspects of the ongoing debate. We hope that it will provide some common ground for those professionals whose points of view might seem irreconcilable in spite of their shared interest in enhancing the quality of care of psychiatric patients.

This volume pertains only to the rights of psychiatric patients. There is equally voluminous literature on the rights of the developmentally disabled and of medical and surgical patients that we hope will someday also receive a critical analysis. It was not possible for us to include a section dealing with the important issue of determination of grave disability as it relates to involuntary commitment statutes because of the dearth of empirical studies in this area. International developments regarding the rights of psychiatric patients were also beyond the scope of this volume, although those developments are taking place rapidly in numerous countries around the world.

The volume begins with an overview of the patient rights movement that includes the identification of some of the most critical issues and some of the related judicial decisions that have been promulgated. The major portion of the book involves a review and analysis of the empirical research literature relating to these issues. Two original studies on attitudes toward patient rights are presented, followed by an epilogue that provides a special perspective on this literature and its ideological implications.

We wish to acknowledge our indebtedness to the following persons, all of whom gave generously of their time in a series of conversations about patient rights and patient advocacy with the senior author —Herbert M. Silverberg, Commission on the Mentally Disabled, American Bar Association, Washington, D.C.; Thomas Dixon, American Bar Association Monitoring and Advocacy Project, Norristown State Hospital, Norristown, Pennsylvania; Melvin Sabshin, American Psychiatric Association, Washington, D.C.; Serena Steier, Fred Strassburger, and Carolyn Suber, American Psychological Association, Washington, D.C.; Michael L. Perlin, Division of Mental Health Advocacy, Department of the Public Advocate, Trenton, New Jersey; David Ferleger, Mental Patients Civil Liberties Project, Philadelphia, Pennsylvania; James W. Ellis, Paul R. Friedman, Joel Klein, and Patricia M. Wald, Mental Health Law Project, Washington, D.C.; and Thomas K. Gilhool, Public Interest Law Center of Philadelphia, Philadelphia, Pennsylvania. We also wish to thank Jonathan D. Asher for keeping us abreast of legal developments in the field of patient rights.

Bernard L. Bloom
Shirley J. Asher
Boulder, Colorado
March 15, 1980

Part I

OVERVIEW

Chapter 1

PATIENT RIGHTS AND PATIENT ADVOCACY:
A Historical and Conceptual Appreciation

Bernard L. Bloom
Shirley J. Asher

For the first 175 years of this country's history, courts maintained a hands-off policy regarding our major social institutions. On those rare occasions when grievances were brought to the attention of the court, whether concerning prisons, schools, hospitals, or other care-giving settings, courts almost invariably deferred to the presumed expertise of the professionals operating these institutions. The court was unwilling to substitute its judgment for that of the staff of long established institutions, and lacked the confidence and competence to review or fashion remedies affecting the quality of life, programming, or treatment within these institutional settings.

Starting about 1955, this state of affairs began a process of dramatic and accelerating change, and, as most institutionally based human service providers will attest, the courts are now increasingly involved in the day-to-day operations of a wide variety of settings (McGarry & Kaplan, 1973). The reasons for this profound change in the role of the court in the evaluation of social services and social policies are multiple and interactive. Firstly, a series of atrocities within prisons were brought to the attention of the public and the courts. Graves of decapitated prisoners were dug up in the pasturelands of prison farms in Arkansas. California prison strip cells were exposed to the public eye, and a variety of torture devices used on prisoners were discovered. Factual accounts of such blatant cruelty and an outraged public made it impossible for the courts to continue deferring to the expertise of institutional staff. While courts could continue to assert that they were not expert in the identification of high quality care, they now felt no hesitancy in making assertions about unacceptably low quality care (Mitford, 1973).

Secondly, the activist posture of the Warren Court permitted cases to be argued that the Supreme Court had previously refused to consider. Out of these arguments came the initial decisions regarding school desegregation, and decisions protecting the civil rights of members of the armed forces, rights of the poor and of welfare recipients, rights of draftees and draft evaders, tenants and landlords, parolees, debtors, and, most recently, environmentalists. The general impact of these decisions was to assert that constitutional liberties and legislated services were not a privilege—they were a right (Curran, 1968).

Thirdly, changes were beginning in the practice of law and in the character of new lawyers. Federal funds, mainly through the Office of Economic Opportunity, became available for the practice of public interest law and for the provision of legal services to the poor, a group which had historically been denied adequate legal representation. Well-trained young attorneys became attracted (and continue to be attracted) to this new and expanding arena of legal practice. State and national bar associations, along with a number of private foundations, became interested in and supportive of the practice of public interest law.

Finally, long-standing practices of authority figures were challenged. The general erosion of the status of authority figures—including institutional directors, teachers, physicians, husbands, and parents—along with the reaction against paternalism, altruism, and benevolence, which had begun in the 1960s, constituted another aspect of the historical context of the civil rights movement.

Interest in the protection of the civil rights of psychiatric patients developed rather late in this sequence of events. Because psychiatric patients are in a treatment setting (sometimes under involuntary civil commitment for such treatment), issues related to the protection of their civil rights are unusually complex. And because psychiatric patients are sometimes not fully rational, protection of their civil rights is doubly complex.

In the past 15 years, a rapidly expanding literature has been appearing on the topic of psychiatric patient rights and patient advocacy. The vast majority of these writings have come from psychiatrists and attorneys. The *Mental Health Court Digest,* a monthly summary of the reported state and federal court decisions relating to mental health, began publication in 1957. Four journals are now published that deal virtually exclusively with legal and civil rights issues of psychiatric patients. The *Journal of Psychiatry and the Law* began publication in 1973. The *Bulletin of the American Academy of Psychiatry and the Law* began publication that same year. The *Mental Disability Law Reporter,* a publication of the American Bar Association Commission on the Mentally Disabled, began in 1976. Finally, *Advocacy Now: The Journal of Patient Rights and Mental Health Advocacy* began publication in 1979. A fifth journal, the *Journal of Law and Human Behavior,* started publication in 1977.

Interest in the topic of patient rights and patient advocacy is worldwide. Articles dealing with patient rights have been published in most Western European countries, as well as in Australia, China, Japan, Iran, and the Soviet Union (see, for example, Gharagozlou, 1974 and Singer, 1974).

The social work profession has had a long and active interest in the area of patient rights. Judging by articles that have appeared in *Social Work,* the official publication of the National Association of Social Workers (NASW), the major concern in the past decade has been with the social worker as patient or client advocate. An Ad Hoc Committee on Advocacy was established by the NASW in 1968, and in addition to the report of that committee, other publications consider the role of the social worker as social or political activist, or as advocate for welfare clients, for the poor, and for consumers. A secondary interest on the part of the social work profession is concerned with confidentiality of client records (see Ad Hoc Committee on Advocacy, 1969; Brager, 1968; Dickson, 1976; Eisman, 1969; Gilbert & Specht, 1976; Grinnell & Kyte, 1974; Kelley & Weston, 1974, 1975; Miller, 1968; Orlin, 1973; Panitch, 1974; Pratt, 1972; Scherrer, 1976; and Wineman & James, 1969).

The current situation with respect to the profession of psychology is somewhat different. There are no American Psychological Association (APA) policies or statements in the area of patient rights or patient advocacy (Stier, 1976), although the APA (through its Board of Social and Ethical Responsibility) has joined with other organizations in the preparation of a number of *amicus* briefs. There is a specific interest in issues related to child advocacy (Hyman & Schreiber, 1974; Knitzer, 1976; Lewis, 1970). As is the case with social workers, psychologists have a clear concern with confidentiality of client records, particularly in the case of school-aged children (see Boruch, 1971; Trachtman, 1972; also see Cardon & Kuriloff, 1975). Finally, psychologists have expressed particular concern about issues of rights that intersect with the conduct of human research (see Baumrind, 1971; Cox & Sipprelle, 1971; Epstein, Suedfeld, & Silverstein, 1973; Gergen, 1973; Kelman, 1972; Nikelly, 1971; and Silverman, 1975; see also Nelson & Grunebaum, 1972).

The area of concern, loosely called patient rights, is burgeoning so rapidly that it threatens to expand beyond intellectual grasp, and yet mental health professionals have little alternative other than to become more knowledgeable and involved with the issues being raised. This admonition is aimed not only at those mental health professionals who are employed in public sector inpatient facilities. In our judgment, issues pertaining to patient rights are no less pertinent to private sector facilities and to outpatient settings such as community mental health centers. Furthermore, to the extent that psychologists, social workers, and psychiatric nurses become part of a reimbursable health service delivery system, it will be even less appropriate than it now is to leave the debate in the hands of the professions of psychiatry and the law.

While the debate is still primarily ideological, clear progress is being made in strengthening the empirical foundations of the patient rights and patient advocacy movement. Our primary objective in this introductory chapter is to provide an overview of this multidimensional area. Only secondarily does a particular perspective emerge. We introduce the concept of *substitute judgment* as a way of understanding an important aspect of the debate between mental health professionals and attorneys; discuss the key words, *rights* and *advocacy;* and then attempt to identify the major issues that make up most of this rapidly developing field. The chapter concludes with a discussion of its implications for further conceptualization and study.

THE MENTAL HEALTH PROFESSIONAL AND THE ATTORNEY: ALTERNATIVE STYLES OF SERVICE

In reviewing the literature on the rights of psychiatric patients, it is not difficult to conclude that attorneys and mental health professionals (mainly but not exclusively psychiatrists) are often in an adversarial relationship (see Kumasaka & Gupta, 1972; Kumasaka & Stokes, 1972; Rachlin, Pam, & Milton, 1975; Sehdev, 1976; and Wenger & Fletcher, 1969). The so-called antipsychiatry literature itself is already so voluminous that it has been possible for the Mental Patients Association of Vancouver to prepare an annotated bibliography of nearly 400 items (Frank, 1974). The now-famous letter by Treffert, written to the *American Journal of Psychiatry* while he was the superintendent of a Wisconsin state hospital, referred to patients "dying with their rights on" (1973, p. 1041). Treffert wrote, "It seems to me that if there is a right to drown, for example, there must also be a right to be rescued" (p. 1041). Clearly, from his point of view, the mental health professional is the rescuer.

There do appear to be fundamental differences, both in theory and in practice, between the role of physician and the role of attorney. Neither attorneys nor mental health professionals are a monolithic group, however, and there is substantial current debate within both groups regarding the proper balance between so-called *civil* and *clinical rights.*

Disagreements between attorneys and mental health professionals seem to arise out of a fundamental difference in orientation to the services delivered to people—a difference highlighted by the use of the words *patient* and *client.* Mental health professionals have tended to adopt the traditional physician's orientation to service. A patient seeks relief from a set of symptoms. The physician diagnoses and prescribes a set of remedies. If appropriate, those remedies are provided by the physician in the form of medical care. The physician seeks to determine what is best for the patient and asks only that the patient comply with those treatment recommendations. In essence, physicians are accustomed to and, indeed, are trained to provide what might be called *substitute judgments* for their patients. Mental health professionals see the attorney's actions as reducing their own discretionary activities and flexibility of treatment approaches, that is, their own freedom to make substitute judgments.

In contrast, the traditional operating style of the attorney is to determine what the client wants, try to persuade the client to adopt other wants or other strategies, if indicated, and then either attempt in good faith to attain the wishes of the client or withdraw from the case. Not only are substitute judgments not made, but they are in theory contrary to the principle of legal advocacy. Attorneys often see mental health professionals as too ready to sacrifice the patient's civil rights in the service of the mental health professional's efforts to do what is believed to be best for the patient clinically. In an oft-quoted opinion, Justice Louis Brandeis of the U.S. Supreme Court was moved to say: "Experience should teach us to be most on our guard to protect liberty when the government's purposes are beneficent. Men born to freedom are naturally alert to repel invasion of their liberty by evil-minded rulers. The greatest dangers to liberty lurk in insidious encroachment by men of zeal, well-meaning but without understanding" (*Olmstead* v. *U.S.,* 1928).

The consequences of these differing styles of service are further complicated in the psychiatric arena by the fact that the treatments are often of limited effectiveness. Attorneys find it difficult to justify depriving a person of his or her liberty by means of civil commitment to a psychiatric facility so that a treatment of limited or unproved effectiveness can be administered. The informed patient may be unwilling to comply with the mental health professional's recommended course of action for the same reason. A further complexity facing both mental health professionals and attorneys is that it is sometimes difficult to disentangle the rational from the irrational components of a psychiatric patient's wishes, thus making strictly defined legal advocacy less clearly defensible.

THE KEY WORDS: RIGHTS AND ADVOCACY

Before identifying some of the major issues that are of concern to the legal and mental health professions regarding patient rights and patient advocacy, it is first necessary to make some general comments about the two key words, *rights* and *advocacy.* Jorgensen and Lyons (1972) have discussed the concept of rights from a philosophical point of view. They introduce the concept of moral or natural rights as those rights that the law *ought* to recognize and then discuss whether there are any circumstances under which such rights might justifiably be suspended or forfeited.

From a more legalistic point of view, four categories of rights can be identified with respect to psychiatric patients. Firstly, one thinks of *constitutional rights,* those rights explicitly protected by the U.S. Constitution. These explicit constitutional rights include the right to the free practice of religion, to assemble peaceably, to petition for redress of grievances, to freedom of speech and of the press, the right to due process, the protection from self-incrimination, the right to counsel and to trial by jury, freedom from cruel and unusual punishment, freedom from involuntary servitude, and right to equal protection under the law. These rights are not lost simply because a person is a psychiatric patient, either voluntarily or by civil commitment (see Kemper, 1974).

The second group of rights are often referred to as *common law* or *fundamental rights,* that is, rights implicitly and, in some instances, explicitly protected under the general constitutional concepts of liberty and privacy. Included in this category are the right to interstate travel, to live wherever one chooses, to work in a job one has freely chosen, to leave a job at will, to marry, and to use contraceptive devices. In general, these implicit rights protect one's right to come and go according to one's own choice, and to decide one's own fate. Obviously, many of these rights are seriously attenuated under civil commitment.

The third groups of rights, sometimes called *entitlements,* are those provided by federal and state statutes or regulations. Since statutes vary from state to state, there is no universal or uniform set of entitlements. Examination of currently applicable laws regarding civil commitment or the insanity defense in criminal commitment procedures, for example, may identify a set of rights that are protected under state statutes.

Finally, certain rights are accorded by reason of *professional standards* to which an institution subscribes. In order to be accredited by the Joint Commission for Accreditation of Hospitals, for example, a hospital must provide access to a room where one can be alone, a locked storage space, bathroom privacy, physical exercise, and a private place for meeting with visitors. These requirements constitute rights in the sense that failure to provide for them will jeopardize a hospital's accreditation.

Unfortunately, rights are not self-executing. Statements of rights do not include guarantees that such rights will be implemented and enforced, and advocacy generally involves the implementation and enforcement of rights. The concept of *advocacy* is broadly defined by Lourie as "a device for increasing pressures against the social structure to achieve social equity and justice" (1975a, p. 69). Most writers on the subject agree that advocacy means defending or promoting a cause and pleading a cause on behalf of another (see Ad Hoc Committee on Advocacy, 1969; Neufeld, 1974; and Panitch, 1974). As will be seen, however, the term advocacy is used to describe a very broad range of activities, so broad, in fact, that without specification it is not safe to assume what is meant. In some settings, the term appears to be used as a synonym for case management or even for psychotherapy, as in the phrase "child advocacy team" to mean that group of interdisciplinary staff in a community mental health center charged with the responsibility for providing treatment services to clients under age 16.

A distinction can be made between advocacy provided to individual patients on a case-by-case basis, which might be called *service advocacy,* and advocacy programs, usually of state, regional, or national scope, which advocate on behalf of psychiatric patients in general, or a class of patients, activities that might be called *policy advocacy.* These two types of advocacy activity are interdependent. Service advocacy programs frequently identify issues of general importance requiring effort to change policies or statutes (see Kopolow, 1978). Decisions arising from policy advocacy programs inevitably have implications for the lives of individual psychiatric patients.

Lourie (1975a, 1975b) proposes a distinction between *legal advocacy* and *operational advocacy.* Legal advocacy programs involve "the use of the law to achieve social purposes and redress current social wrongs" (Lourie, 1975a, p. 77). Attorneys take individual and class action cases into the courts in an effort to implement and enforce the rights that psychiatric patients have been accorded. Operational advocacy, on the other hand, is concerned with human service delivery systems. The right to receive certain services is meaningless unless

130,185

those services are accessible and meet the needs of individuals and the community. Operational advocacy seeks to assure that community needs are accurately assessed, that services are coordinated but not duplicated, and that the service needs of the community are met.

Advocacy programs, in addition to including many diverse activities, vary according to their objectives, modes of operation, and relationships with the institution or group of institutions within which they function (see Annas, 1975; Cohen, 1974; Ferleger, 1975; Knitzer, 1976; and Neufeld, 1974). These variations are crucial to our understanding of the potential role and effectiveness of patient advocacy programs, and there are strongly held opinions regarding the optimal characteristics of such programs. An inductive understanding of the spectrum of uses of the word advocacy, can be developed from the consideration of the following vignette descriptions of programs that use the term advocacy in their title.

1. A staff social worker in a public institution for the mentally retarded inaugurates a volunteer program whereby persons living in the community are each assigned one mildly retarded child. The activities of these volunteers include visiting with the child, taking the child shopping or to the movies in the city, and helping the child improve his or her reading and writing skills. The citizen volunteer is not paid for participation in the program, and the contractual relationship with the program is such that volunteers may terminate their involvement with the program at any time. Some limited supervision is provided by the social worker, who refers to these volunteers as "child advocates."

2. Because of some pressure from patients and staff, the medical director of a public psychiatric hospital issues a directive to the effect that all social workers assigned to wards will assume, as an added duty, the role of "patient advocate" on their wards. The directive indicates that patients may bring their grievances to the social worker, who is empowered to investigate the grievance and attempt to resolve the problem. The social worker has no authority to impose a solution and, in the event that the problem cannot be solved to everyone's satisfaction, the directive requires that the social worker write down the facts of the case, the results of the investigation, and any recommendations, and forward this document to the clinical director of the hospital for possible action.

3. Pursuant to an order from the director of a state Department of Mental Health, each community mental health center and

institution for the mentally ill is required to establish a standing Human Rights Committee. This committee is to be composed of two employees of the institution, a current patient of the institution, and two members of the community who serve without pay, all selected by the institutional director. Members of the Human Rights Committee are referred to as "patient advocates," and patients are directed to the committee in the event that they have grievances regarding their care and treatment. Limited staff assistance is provided to the committee by the director's office, and the committee is instructed to relay its deliberations and recommendations to the institutional director.

4. A community mental health center employs a mental health professional in the full-time position of "patient advocate." Whenever clinical staff find that they are not able to obtain services for their patients in other community agencies, or that desirable services do not appear to exist, they are instructed to refer that patient or that problem to the patient advocate. The patient advocate functions aggressively to obtain services in other agencies to which the patient is entitled and helps generate new or expanded community resources when they appear to be needed. The "power" of the patient advocate comes from his or her general and specific knowledge of agency programs and regulations, personal relationships with other agency staff, and moral persuasion.

5. As a consequence of an exposé in the local press, the legislature has appropriated funds to employ one ombudsperson in each of the state's institutions for the mentally ill and mentally retarded, and in each of the state's correctional facilities. These ombudspersons, who are also referred to as patient advocates, report to the state director of the Department of Institutions, and are not in a line relationship to any employees within individual institutions. These ombudspersons are all mental health professionals (either psychologists or social workers), and one part-time psychiatrist is employed to provide consultation to them regarding grievances around overmedication and other forms of alleged medical mismanagement. The Director of the Department of Institutions is required to investigate cases brought to his or her attention by ombudspersons, and may discharge, for cause, any employee on the basis of this investigation.

6. A state Department of Institutions enters into a time-limited contract with the state bar association to provide legal services

for patients in its institutions. The bar association hires a small number of attorneys who are then placed within the state institutions. Their office is called the Patient Rights Office and the staff are called patient advocates. In addition to attempting to mediate grievances brought by patients, these patient advocates are specifically permitted to litigate on the behalf of patients.

7. Whenever a patient is committed to an institution for the mentally ill, the court is required to appoint a local attorney as the patient's "advocate." This attorney, whose fee is paid by the court, is specifically charged with the responsibility to protect the civil rights of his or her client, but may, in addition, perform legal duties exactly the same as if the patient were a regular client of the attorney. The practice of the court is to rotate this appointment among all eligible attorneys in the community.

8. A state legislature creates a Department of the Public Advocate, headed by a cabinet-level official appointed by the governor. Within this department is a Division of Mental Patient Advocacy. This division employs 10 attorneys as well as a small staff of paralegals and mental health professionals as patient advocates. All patients who are under civil commitment are automatically referred to this division for study, and the staff of the division are empowered to act in the protection of the civil rights of these patients. They are specifically permitted to bring suit against the State Department of Institutions if no other remedy appears to be successful in the protection of these rights.

9. A free-standing patient advocacy project exists, supported by contributions from several private foundations. This project provides no direct-service advocacy, but is in the full-time business of bringing class-action suits against institutions or groups of institutions when, in its opinion, the civil rights of a class of psychiatric patients are being violated. In addition, the organization publishes a monthly newsletter and maintains an active collaborative and consultative relationship with a large number of other patient advocacy programs throughout the country.

While these examples do not exhaust the variety of patient advocacy programs that currently exist, they are sufficiently illustrative to indicate the major dimensions along which the concept of advocacy varies. As can be seen, programs can be run by unpaid volunteers or appointees or by paid staff. The advocates can report to a number of different levels within the institution or to an authority outside of the institution. Advocates can be full-time or part-time, and advocacy programs can be thought of as experimental and possibly short-lived or as a permanent part of a mental health program. Advocates may or may not be legally trained and may or may not be permitted to bring litigation against a state department of government or a public institution. Advocacy programs may be limited to issues directly related to mental illness and the procedures involved in institutionalization, or may be broader in scope and purpose. Advocacy may be concerned with challenging existing services, increasing the availability of existing services, or attempting to generate new services. Advocates may engage in this activity as part of other responsibilities, or may do nothing other than patient advocacy. Advocates who are paid may be employees of a specific institution, of a cabinet-level state governmental department, or of a private organization that has a contractual agreement with the state.

Most generally, patient advocacy programs can be viewed in political terms as efforts to resolve fundamental conflicts between institutions and the people they are designed to serve. The historical roots, basic assumptions, and general parameters of the political view of patient advocacy have been most ably reviewed by Knitzer, 1976; see also McDermott, Bolman, Arensdorf and Markoff, 1973; and Womack and Sata, 1975.

PATIENT RIGHTS AND PATIENT ADVOCACY: A DESCRIPTION OF THE ISSUES

With this background orientation, it is now appropriate to comment on what appear to be the major issues of concern to persons involved in or responsible for the protection of the civil rights of psychiatric patients. A general issue in the protection of the civil rights of psychiatric patients concerns the role of patient advocacy in that process. Can patients' civil rights be adequately protected by an educational program or by administrative regulations, or must an adversarial relationship be fostered with its accompanying threat of court action? Is there any alternative to patient advocacy, in the sense of the ability to litigate, in the protection of patients' civil rights? If the ability to litigate is necessary but not sufficient, what are the other necessary components in a well-functioning patient advocacy program (see Cohen, 1974; Greenblatt, 1975; Kopolow & Bloom, 1977; Meisel, 1975; Murray, 1975; Silverberg, 1974; Slovenko & Luby, 1974; Smith, 1973; and Yale Law Journal, 1975).

Behind this general issue lie a series of specific concerns that are debated with varying degrees of intensity. The most important of these specific concerns follow.

Rights of Society

In the move to assure the protection of the rights of psychiatric patients, have the *rights of society* and *the rights of families* been forgotten? What are the rights of emotionally disturbed individuals? Should society be protected against the possibly dangerous mentally ill person, or against the discomfort or inconvenience occasioned by the presence in the community of persons previously in institutions for the mentally ill? Given the inability to predict dangerousness accurately, particularly when no previous antisocial acts have been committed (see Steadman, this volume), how can one justify the deprivation of personal liberty by means of involuntary hospitalization on the grounds of what a person might do in the future?

Abramson (1972) believes that as it becomes more difficult to commit patients involuntarily, community pressure will force mentally disturbed persons into the criminal justice system. Thus, while societal rights will be protected, the rights of the mentally ill may continue to be violated. Society may find itself returning to the imprisonment of the mentally ill, just as was the case a century ago prior to the establishment of public psychiatric facilities (see Modlin, Porter, & Benson, 1976).

Several writers (Abramson, 1972; Deasy & Steele, 1976; Modlin, 1974; and Rachlin, 1974) have commented on the dilemma posed by new involuntary commitment statutes that incorporate the criterion of dangerousness, thus making it more difficult to get a person committed than did older statutes that often used the criterion of "being in need of hospitalization." These new statutes, while designed to protect the rights of potential patients, may instead have the effect of violating the rights of families and other individuals in the community who come into contact with these potential patients.

Stone (1975) comments at length on the inability of mental health professionals to predict dangerousness or violence accurately. Attempts to predict violence invariably lead to overprediction, since violent behavior among the mentally ill is so infrequent (also, see Peszke, 1975). Sadoff (1978) contends that dangerousness is a legal concept that has been foisted upon the psychiatric profession. Since psychiatrists do not know how to predict or treat dangerousness, they should not be responsible for involuntary commitments. Judges should take responsibility for determining when an involuntarily committed patient is no longer dangerous and may return to the community.

Rights of Children

What are the *rights of parents with regard to their children?* Under what circumstances, if any, may a parent commit a child to a mental institution without due process protection for the child? What are the special issues associated with child advocacy?

Gottesman (1975) has noted that the juvenile law has evolved in a peculiar way: "Rather than recognizing that children are citizens, and therefore entitled to exercise their rights under the constitution, and then placing limitations upon these rights, the law has evolved from the premise that children have no constitutional rights and that society must always act on their behalf" (1975, p. 14). Until the late 1960s, cases in the area of the rights of parents vis-à-vis their children assumed that the interests of the child and the interests of the parents were indistinguishable. Parents, guardians, and the courts had almost total control over the lives of children. In 1967, in the *Gault* decision, the Supreme Court granted juveniles in delinquency cases the same 14th Amendment due process rights that are accorded adults, such as the right to notices of charges, right to counsel, and the right against self-incrimination. This case marked a turning point in juvenile law. In *Wyman* v. *James* (1971), a case in which the Supreme Court found that a welfare mother could not refuse to permit a home visit by a welfare department worker, the rights of the child were distinguished from those of the parent.

The right of parents to commit their children to residential treatment facilities is currently being questioned. Children voluntarily committed to such an institution cannot leave without the consent of their parents. Many authorities believe that when parents want to commit their child "voluntarily," such a procedure should be treated as an involuntary commitment proceeding, and that under such a proceeding a child would be accorded the due process rights that an adult would have in such a situation.

It is specifically regarding the competing rights of parents and guardians to control their childrens' unbringing and the rights of children to due process that a number of mental health and mental retardation-related organizations joined forces to prepare a statement for consideration by the Supreme Court in the case of *Kremens* v. *Bartley* (1977), which challenged a Pennsylvania law that permitted parents and guardians to commit juveniles to mental institutions without benefit of counsel or other due process procedures. The organizations included the American Psychological Association, the National Association of Social Workers, the American Orthopsychiatric Association, and the two largest volunteer organizations in the field, the National Association for Mental Health and the National Association for Retarded Citizens (Wald & Friedman, 1976).

The position of these groups is that, except for short (less than two weeks) institutionalizations in the case of children under age 12, all children being considered for institutionalization should be granted procedural due process protections, including an impartial hearing. These organizational representatives have argued that institutionalization of children can result in loss of family and community ties, can stigmatize them, and threaten their intellectual and emotional development, and that in the process of deciding on institutionalization, parents are often unaware of alternative solutions available to them and often have conflicting interests that make the decision to institutionalize a child suspect. Finally, it is argued that children are not sufficiently protected by procedures generally in effect in institutional admitting services (see also *Mental Disability Law Reporter,* 1978; Teitelbaum & Ellis, 1978).

In 1976, Pennsylvania passed a new state law repealing the law challenged by the plaintiffs, thus rendering the case moot. In addition, the class of patients in whose behalf *Kremens* v. *Bartley* was instituted was judged by the Supreme Court to be too fragmented in that it included both the mentally retarded and the mentally ill.

The U.S. Supreme Court has recently ruled, however, in *Parham* v. *J. L. and J. R.* (1979) into which a Pennsylvania case similar to *Bartley* was incorporated. The Court held that a minor is not entitled to a formal adversary hearing during a commitment proceeding, but that an independent medical decision-making process is sufficient in protecting the due process rights of the child. The Court ruled in this manner because it believed that, in most instances, parents act in the best interest of the child, and that "the statist notion that governmental power should supercede parental authority in *all* cases because *some* parents abuse and neglect children is repugnant to American tradition" (p. 4744).

Involuntary Commitment

Has the procedure of *involuntary civil commitment* outlived whatever usefulness it might once have had? Can the circumstances under which civil commitment remains indicated be specified in order that its inappropriate use be minimized? If civil commitment is ever indicated, what procedures must be included to assure the protection of the prospective patient's civil rights? If these procedures include hearings, the right to cross examine, the verbatim recording of testimony, and the right of the prospective patient to introduce opposing psychiatric testimony, how will mental health professionals find the time for court appearances without reducing the provision of mental health services for which they were trained and are being paid? Is involuntary commitment justified if effective treatments are not known or not available for the diagnosed condition? How are a prospective patient's rights to avoid self-incrimination to be protected?

There is much debate and controversy both within and between the legal and mental health professions as to the usefulness of involuntary commitments (see Chodoff, 1976; Peck, 1975; and Rachlin et al., 1975). A number of psychiatrists and lawyers have called for the abolition of all provisions for involuntary mental hospitalization. Szasz stated: "We should value liberty more highly than mental health no matter how defined. . . . No one should be deprived of his freedom for the sake of his mental health" (quoted in Chodoff, 1976, p. 497; also see Ennis & Siegel, 1973).

Chodoff (1976), Rachlin (1974), Rachlin et al. (1975), and Treffert (1973) disagree with this abolitionist position. Rachlin states that "the liberty to be psychotic is no freedom at all" (1974, p. 410). Chodoff sets forth criteria he believes would not upset the balance between humane and legal concerns. He suggests that, in order to be involuntarily committed, a person should have a mental illness, exhibit disruptive functioning, *and* need care and treatment. Peck (1975) believes that "the best possible solution might be to limit involuntary commitment to those who are considered dangerous in terms of a rigorous definition of danger as overt acts or threats, or to those adjudicated incompetent" (p. 315).

Numerous courts and legislative bodies have come to recognize that involuntary civil commitment constitutes a deprivation of liberty comparable to that of prison commitment. As a result, persons involved in commitment proceedings have gradually been granted the same due process rights as those afforded criminal defendants. In *Lessard* v. *Schmidt* (1972), a landmark case concerning due process protection for mental patients, a Wisconsin court ruled that persons involved in commitment proceedings are entitled to an attorney and a full hearing and that adequate notice for the hearing must inform the patient of the basis for detention, the right to a jury trial, the names of the persons to testify in favor of commitment and the substance of their testimony. This case further held that the privilege against self-incrimination applies in commitment proceedings and that statements made to a psychiatrist cannot be used as the basis for commitment unless patients are informed that statements made might be used against them and that they need not respond.

While there are now many similarities between civil commitment and criminal proceedings, the U.S. Supreme Court ruled in *Addington* v. *Texas* (1979) that a less stringent standard of proof in commitment proceedings does not violate the due process protection of patients. The standard of "clear and convincing" evidence will apply to commitment cases while the "beyond a reasonable doubt" standard will apply to criminal prosecutions and delinquency proceedings. The Court declined to adopt the "beyond a reasonable doubt" standard to commitment proceedings because "given the lack of certainty and the fallibility of psychiatric diagnosis, there is a serious question as to whether a state could ever prove beyond a reasonable doubt that an individual is both mentally ill and likely to be dangerous" (p. 4476).

The concept of *grave disability*, defined as the inability to provide for basic personal needs of food, clothing, or shelter, was introduced in California in 1969 as part of a modernization of its involuntary commitment procedures. Grave disability, danger to self, and danger to others are the three legal justifications for the removal of an individual's civil rights and the imposition of involuntary psychiatric treatment. Wilbert, Jorstad, Loren, and Wirrer (1976) have attempted to develop and evaluate a procedure for objectively determining grave disability.

Their study took place in the context of an occupational therapy program, and subjects included 51 patients, a representative sample of all patients for whom the designation of gravely disabled was being sought. The procedure included having the patient plan a budget and a menu, shop for food, and prepare a meal and clean up afterwards. A total of 17 out of the 19 patients in the sample with diagnosis of organic brain syndrome (89%) failed the evaluation procedure. Of the 27 schizophrenics in the sample, 19 (70%) failed the test. Of the remaining five patients, one failed the test. The authors suggested that seeking the designation of grave disability was sometimes inappropriate and an indication that the staff were desperate as to how to make an appropriate disposition of the patient.

Epstein and Lowinger (1975) conducted brief interviews with 50 recent admissions (average length of hospitalization at the time of the interviews was 36 days) to a Michigan state hospital in an effort to learn about their perceived needs for legal counsel. All but two of the 50 patients were able to answer the interview questions meaningfully. About one-third of the patients felt the need for legal assistance at the time of admission; one-half or more would want counsel in future dealings with the court. Of the total sample, 41 were involuntarily committed and they were generally more interested in legal counsel than were the voluntary patients. Patients with prior histories of psychiatric hospitalization were substantially more interested in legal counsel than were first admissions. The authors concluded that a need for legal aid, particularly regarding civil commitment proceedings, was demonstrated, and speculated that if such aid were to be provided, there would be fewer commitments, more regular review of commitment status, increased confidence of the patients in the mental health services being delivered, and the development of a better image of the mental hospital in the eyes of the public, since a larger proportion of patients would be voluntary.

Jansen (1974) contrasted 35 psychiatric patients and 20 alcoholic patients, all of whom made use of a part-time patient rights office in a Minnesota state hospital during a 10-month period in 1973 with similar patients who did not make use of the office on a variety of demographic characteristics and on MMPI scores. Visitors were generally comparable to nonvisitors demographically, but the committed patients were far more likely to complain about denial of rights than were voluntary patients. Numerous significant personality differences between patients rights office visitors and nonvisitors were found, all indicating that visitors displayed far more psychopathology than nonvisitors. In comparison with nonvisitors, visitors appeared significantly more dependent, bizarre, hypomanic, and sociopathic.

The risk of significant abridgement of civil liberties is most obvious in the case of petitions for involuntary commitment, and a significant beginning has been made in the empirical examination of the commitment process. Albers and Pasewark (1974) examined 300 consecutive petitions for involuntary commitment of prospective patients to a Western state hospital to determine the degree of agreement between psychiatric recommendation and court disposition. These prospective patients were apparently not represented by counsel. These authors found a 98% agreement rate. Psychiatric recommendations were virtually always followed. In a sample of 21 of these 300 hearings, mean length of time required for the court procedure was eight minutes. The authors argue that while it has sometimes been asserted that the court is qualified to render decisions regarding psychiatric hospitalization, in fact, courts may have surrendered this decision-making process to psychiatrists.

Wenger and Fletcher (1969) observed commitment hearings for 81 potential patients over a four-and-a-half-month period. These hearings were held on the grounds of a Midwestern state mental hospital and the procedure was designed to decide whether the prospective patient was in need of treatment. If the finding was affirmative, the patient would be committed for a period not to exceed 90 days. Hearings were short (average of eight minutes per case) and tended to be about twice as long when legal counsel was present as when there was no legal counsel. More importantly, however, there was a strong association between the presence of legal counsel and the finding of the court. Of the 66 hearings without counsel, 61 commitments were made; of the 15 hearings with counsel present, only 4 commitments were made. When prospective patients were grouped ahead of time according to the degree to which their behavior met the legal criteria for commitment, and when separate analyses were made within each group, prospective patients represented by an attorney consistently were at lower risk of being committed regardless of which group they were in. The authors suggest that: "psychiatrists possess something less than ultimate authority in the decision to admit patients. . . . More than psychiatrists might care to perceive, lawyers influence their [the court's] decisions" (p. 71).

The extent to which an attorney can influence a court's decision may depend on the role the attorney sees as appropriate during commitment proceedings. Hiday (1977), in observing 64 contested commitment hearings, found that in cases where attorneys representing prospective patients assumed an advocacy role, actively challenging adverse testimony of psychiatrists and family members, 45% were committed. When counsel assumed a more passive role and allowed damaging testimony, 88% were committed. In-depth interviews with the attorneys revealed considerable role confusion. Neither legal tradition, statutes, case law, nor the American Bar Association Code of Professional Responsibility provide clear guidelines for the role of counsel in commitment cases.

Kumasaka and Stokes (1972) interviewed a sample of 30 psychiatrists and 26 laywers in New York to determine their attitudes toward involuntary commitment and toward using an assessment of dangerousness as a criterion for involuntary hospitalization. The 26 lawyers were divided into two groups according to whether they represented patients in court or whether they served as court officers whose responsibility to patients was limited to informing them of their rights. Psychiatrists differed dramatically from attorneys who represented patients in their attitudes toward involuntary hospitalization. All psychiatrists considered involuntary hospitalization to be indispensable; less than half of attorneys felt the same way. Attorneys who did not represent patients in court and who had no direct professional interaction with the psychiatrists in the study agreed with psychiatrists that involuntary hospitalization was indispensable. About half of psychiatrists and of nonrepresenting attorneys believed dangerousness to be a valid criterion for long-term involuntary hospitalization. None of the attorneys who represented patients in court agreed with this belief. The striking differences of opinion between psychiatrists and attorneys functioning as advocates is clear in this study insofar as involuntary hospitalization is concerned.

It thus appears that, when prospective patients are not represented by counsel in commitment proceedings, decisions rest primarily on psychiatric recommendations. When prospective patients are represented by counsel, commitment rates drop sharply regardless of the apparent degree of psychopathology exhibited by the person in whose behalf the commitment petition has been introduced.

First Amendment Rights

To what extent are the *First Amendment rights* to send and receive mail, to see or refuse to see visitors, to request visitors, to make or receive phone calls, to have free access to one's own clothing or money, to practice one's own religion, and to vote, subject to protection? How are sufficient monetary and staff resources to be guaranteed to psychiatric facilities to make it possible to protect these constitutional rights?

There is little case law that specifies the First Amendment rights of involuntarily committed mental patients. Bass (1973) points out, however, that since it was ruled in *Rozecki* v. *Gaughan* (1972) that involuntarily committed mental patients charged with a crime but not yet convicted are entitled to be treated as well as, if not better than, convicted prisoners, it should be possible to transpose these favorable prisoner's rights precedents into the mental health field. The regulations of most states guarantee committed patients the full spectrum of First Amendment rights and specify those conditions under which such rights may be abridged. As in all areas of patient rights, whether or not patients are in reality able to exercise these rights depends on the attitudes of staff of the institution, adequate monitoring, and other mechanisms to ensure compliance (see Clayton, 1976; Meisel, 1975).

At least one First Amendment right has been examined empirically. Klein and Grossman (1967) studied the voting behavior of 325 primarily schizophrenic, open-ward patients at Bronx State Hospital in the New York City mayorality race in 1965, and found remarkable similarity between the proportion of votes received by each candidate from the hospitalized sample, from the voters in the hospital district in the borough of the Bronx, and in New York City in general. The winner of the election, for example, had a total overall margin of victory of 4.1%. Among the hospitalized psychiatric patients, his margin of victory was 2.9%. The authors, noting that only 4.8% of ballots were invalid, suggested that the patients understood the task of voting and were able to carry it out accurately. In their conclusion, the authors urged that hospitals support this basic patient right and asserted that "there would be no significant effect upon the election results if all psychiatric patients in a community hospital were permitted to vote" (p. 152).

Least Restrictive Alternative

How is the concept of *least restrictive alternative* to be implemented in the case of psychiatric disability? Most of the rulings on the principle of the least restrictive alternative have derived from *Shelton* v. *Tucker* (1960) in which the Supreme Court declared that in judging governmental actions, "even though the governmental purpose be legitimate and substantial, that purpose cannot be pursued by means that broadly stifle personal liberties when the end can be more narrowly achieved." (Quoted in Chambers, 1973, p. 993.) In *Lessard* v. *Schmidt* (1972) it was ruled that, prior to involuntary hospitalization of the mentally ill, the Constitution requires a demonstration that there are no suitable, less restrictive alternatives. In *Wyatt* v. *Stickney* (1971), an Alabama court held that a mentally retarded person should not be committed to an institution unless a prior determination has been made that the setting is the least restrictive alternative feasible for that person (see Chambers, 1973, for these and related cases).

A more recent case involving the least restrictive alternative is *Dixon* v. *Weinberger* (1975) (see *Mental Health Law Project Summary of Activities,* March, 1976). The decision held that the residents of the federally supported St. Elizabeth's Hospital have the right to receive treatment in the least restrictive, most appropriate facilities. This decision is important because, firstly, the right to treatment in a less restrictive setting is viewed as an aspect of the right to treatment itself. Secondly, the case translated into legal theory the psychological principle that unnecessary institutionalization is debilitating. Thirdly, this case marks the first time that the government has been ordered to finance alternatives to hospitalization (also, see Rachlin, 1974).

How less restrictive alternative settings are to be assessed, who will assess them, and what criteria will be used for determining which patients are eligible for care in less restrictive settings are issues that are yet to be resolved (see Armstrong, 1979). The court may not have a staff to perform such a function and the mentally handicapped may be unaware of available alternatives to hospitalization. New Mexico recently passed a regulation requiring that alternatives be examined through community mental health centers (Chambers, 1973, p. 1006). Under the Community Mental Health Amendments of 1975, Public Law 94–63, community mental health centers are required to screen residents of the center's catchment area who are being considered for referral to a state mental health inpatient facility to determine if treatment can be appropriately provided in the center as an alternative.

Empirical studies pertinent to the issue of the legal rights to the least restrictive form of psychiatric treatment include, of course, those studies evaluating alternatives to hospitalization for psychiatric patients. Fairly successful alternatives have been reported by Langsley, Machotka, and Flomenhaft (1971) and by Pasamanick, Scarpetti, and Dinitz (1967), for example, and Glick, Hargreaves, Raskin, and Kutner (1975) have identified some of the parameters that make short-term hospitalization superior to long-term hospitalization. The methodological issues in this research domain are complex, however, and some of them have recently been addressed by Erickson (1975).

An issue related to least restrictive alternative in that it involves the release of patients into the community is that of periodic review. What procedures need to be instituted to assure that patients are not retained in treatment settings longer than necessary? If periodic review of records is indicated, how frequently should such reviews take place and what should the role of the patient be in that review process?

The right to periodic redetermination of the basis for confinement was granted in the *O'Connor* v. *Donaldson* decision (*Mental Health Law Project Summary of Activities,* September, 1975; see also Crane, Zonana, & Wizner, 1977). The Supreme Court held that even if the original confinement under a mental health law was found on a constitutionally adequate basis and was permissible, it could not continue once the basis no longer existed. Since the assumption underlying involuntary commitment is that the mentally ill person can be cured, there must be periodic evaluations to determine whether or not the person has recovered.

The Donaldson decision seems to put the burden on the state to establish, from time to time, that continued confinement is necessary. It is probably not enough that a state grant a patient the right to a periodic review. Rather, the state must initiate such reviews at reasonable intervals.

Deasy and Steele (1976), after reviewing the new mental health law in Florida, conclude that periodic review will result in the release of many confined persons and might create hardships for the patient and for professionals in the community. The catchment area to which over 300 patients will probably be released, for example, has one mental health center and four nursing homes. These resources are obviously inadequate to meet the needs of these patients, nearly half of whom have been diagnosed as suffering from organic brain syndromes, and another 40% from schizophrenia or a major affective disorder. While the release of these patients is in compliance with the new state law, it can be construed that the release violates the human rights and dignity of the patients also guaranteed by that same law, since adequate care in the community may not be available.

Right to Treatment

Does a psychiatric patient have a *right to treatment?* Is the failure to provide treatment adequate grounds for release? What justification exists for asserting that institutionalization itself constitutes treatment?

Although the right to treatment was first publically advanced in 1960 (see Birnbaum, 1974), it was not until 1966 in *Rouse* v. *Cameron* that a court affirmatively recognized the existence of such a right. Rouse was found innocent by reason of insanity of a misdemeanor charge and committed to St. Elizabeth's Hospital. Four years later, Rouse attacked his continued confinement on the grounds that he was not receiving treatment and he was no longer insane. The court ruled that the right to treatment was contained in the District of Columbia 1964 Hospitalization of the Mentally Ill Act, and that there might also be a constitutional right to treatment based on due process, cruel and unusual punishment, and equal protection. Furthermore, the ruling specified that treatment must be "adequate" and that lack of resources could not justify the lack of treatment (see Friedman & Halpern, 1974; Stone, 1975).

The decision in *Wyatt* v. *Stickney* (1971) goes substantially beyond that of previous decisions in the area of the right to treatment (Dix, 1976). The case was filed against the mental health commissioners and the hospital administrators of the State of Alabama when large numbers of employees were terminated from Bryce Hospital because of budget cuts (see Simon, 1975). It was charged that the staff cut threatened the quality of care and denied patients the right to treatment. The decision in *Wyatt* holds that there is a constitutional right to effective treatment, that this right also pertains to the mentally retarded, and, most importantly, "*Wyatt* is the first case in which a court has promulgated objectively measurable and judically enforceable standards by which the abstract right to treatment can be practically implemented" (Friedman & Halpern, 1974, p. 227). The standards include minimum staff-patient ratios, nutritional requirements, the abolition of peonage, provisions to insure a humane psychological environment, and treatment plans and programs. In *O'Connor* v. *Donaldson* (1975), another major case in the area of the right to treatment, the plaintiff was awarded damages totaling $20,000 because he was involuntarily confined to a state hospital without treatment (see *Mental Health Law Project Summary of Activities,* September, 1975).

Right to treatment issues, while they may seem clear and logical, are far from resolved (see Peck, 1975; Schwitzgebel, 1973). A major issue raised by Schwitzgebel concerns the effectiveness of treatment. It is generally assumed that the purpose of psychiatric hospitalization, voluntary or involuntary, is to alter behaviors or improve an individual's mental condition so that confinement is no longer necessary. Many psychotherapy outcome studies, however, particularly those focusing on the more traditional psychoanalytically oriented psychotherapies, show few significant differences between treated and untreated groups. If treatment is not effective, then certainly involuntary treatment is very difficult to justify. Schwitzgebel believes that the right to treatment must include realistic goals and objective critieria for determining whether these goals have been met. He concluded that "only the fulfillment of the therapeutic promise in fact can justify the deprivation of fundamental human liberties" (p. 535).

Peck (1975) sees the right to treatment as posing several additional problems. The first is that judgments must be made as to the appropriateness of treatment and whether confinement alone can be considered therapy. The second problem involves the patient who is either untreatable or not amenable to treatment. A third problem involves the patient who refuses treatment and then seeks release from an institution on the basis that he has been denied his right to adequate treatment.

Right to Refuse Treatment

Does a psychiatric patient have the *right to refuse treatment?* May a patient refuse treatment on religious grounds? Does a mental health facility have the right, and perhaps the obligation, to discharge a patient who refuses treatment?

The right to refuse treatment is controversial and remains unresolved (see Peck, 1975; Stone, 1975; and Wing, 1977). One basis for the right to refuse treatment, the right to be left alone, was first articulated by Justice Brandeis in *Olmstead* v. *U.S.* (1928). Brandeis stated that the makers of the Constitution "conferred as against the government the right to be let alone—the most comprehensive of rights and the right most valued by civilized man." In 1971, *Wyatt* v. *Stickney*, a case most widely known for its right to treatment provisions, made specific reference to the right to refuse treatment: "Patients have the right not to be subjected to treatment procedures such as lobotomy, electro-convulsive treatment, aversive reinforcement conditioning, or other unusual or hazardous treatment procedures without their express and informed consent after consultation with counsel or an interested party of the patient's choice." (Quoted in Scott, 1977, p. 372).

A second basis for the right to refuse treatment is the First Amendment freedom to generate ideas. Since therapy may have the power to control a person's mind or regulate his/her thoughts, a person should have protection against it and be able to refuse it. This right, together with the constitutional right to privacy, were the bases of the decision in *Kaimowitz* v. *Michigan Department of Public Health* (1973), in which a court ruled that an involuntarily committed psychiatric patient is legally incapable of consenting to undergo experimental surgery designed to change behavior by irreversibly destroying abnormal brain tissue. Medical patients have tried to exercise the right to refuse treatment on religious grounds protected by the First Amendment. In *Winters* v. *Miller* (1972), it was ruled on appeal that a Christian Scientist did have the right to refuse medication since she had never been adjudicated incompetent. The Eighth Amendment, prohibiting cruel and unusual punishment, provides another justification for the right to refuse treatment. In *Knect* v. *Gillman* (1973), a court ruled that the involuntary administration of apomorphine, which induces vomiting and is used in aversive conditioning, was prohibited by the Eighth Amendment.

Related to the concept of the right to refuse treatment is that of *informed consent.* How is that concept to be defined? One element in the issue of informed consent is whether a legally committed person is competent to decide to accept or refuse treatment. Stone (1975) suggests that competency be evaluated anew in each context with regard to the specific task or procedure to be performed. A second element with respect to consent is the informed nature of the consent. Informed consent means that the person has adequate information about the therapy and is aware of possible risks as well as alternative forms of treatment. Under the Wisconsin case, *Lessard* v. *Schmidt* (1972), a psychiatrist is required to identify himself or herself to every patient examined and inform the patient that any information that is divulged might be used to hospitalize the patient involuntarily. This type of informed consent impresses some psychiatrists as being comparable to reading the *Miranda* (1966) warnings to criminal defendants (Sadoff, 1977). Most definitions of informed consent presume adequate or expert knowledge on the part of the informer, in this case the physician. Gottlieb, Nappi, and Strain (1978) administered a questionnaire designed to test the knowledge of medical students, interns and residents in internal medicine and psychiatry with regard to drugs commonly used to treat anxiety and depression. While residents in psychiatry scored significantly higher than residents in internal medicine, psychiatrists did show significant deficits in knowledge. This issue is further complicated by the fact that the courts have suggested that physicians are not obligated to inform patients about certain side effects of a treatment if that very information would be detrimental to the health of a patient (see Stone, 1975, p. 103). As can be seen, the concept of informed consent may be antagonistic to the concept of substitute judgment presented earlier.

Some state statutes provide for a third party (relative, guardian, or physician appointed by the court) to make a decision about treatment in the event that a patient refuses a suggested treatment or is not competent to exercise the right to informed consent. Stone (1975) believes that such a regulation is not acceptable, as the third person might be in conflict with the patient. Such a provision does not insure protection of the patient's civil liberties. A more acceptable alternative might be a judicial hearing at which the patient would be represented by counsel. In *New York City Health and Hospitals Corporation* v. *Stein* (1972), a court ruled that an involuntarily committed patient could refuse electroshock treatments in spite of a valid commitment and in spite of the fact that her mother had given consent for the treatment. The judge himself spoke with the patient and held she was competent to make decisions regarding treatment.

In a more recent New Jersey case, *Scott* v. *Plante* (1976), it was held on appeal that an involuntarily committed person could refuse the administration of psychotherapeutic substances. The person may be commitable but has never been adjudicated incompetent, unable of giving informed consent. Thus, the finding that a person is not competent to remain outside a psychiatric hospital does not imply legal incompetency to participate in treatment decisions.

Institutional Peonage

What is the *role of work* in the therapeutic process? May patients be required to work within institutions if they are not paid? May they be required to work if they are paid? If patients are willing to work, must they be paid the minimum legal wage?

The issue of patient work or institutional peonage is discussed by Friedman (1973), Stone (1975), and Safier (1976). Uncompensated patient work, the benefit of which accrues only to the institution, has been termed peonage. This practice has been justified on the grounds that work is therapy in that it may counteract passivity and depression, it contributes to a sense of community within the institution, it brings the patient into contact with reality and may be helpful in making the transition to the outside world.

In spite of these justifications, patient labor has been attacked on the grounds that it violates the Fair Labor Standards Act; that it violates the Thirteenth Amendment, which prohibits involuntary servitude; and that it may violate a person's right to treatment if nontherapeutic labor depresses the patient and results in postponing release. In 1966, the Fair Labor Standards Act, which set the minimum wage, was amended to include any person working in a mental institution. The law does not distinguish patients from nonpatients or the sane from the insane. Wage systems were established for handicapped persons who are less productive than nonhandicapped persons. The Department of Labor was lax in implementing these standards and, as a result, a number of suits were brought, including *Souder* v. *Brennan* (1973; see Friedman, 1973). In this case it was ruled that as long as the institution derives any economic benefit from a patient's work, an employment relationship and not a therapeutic relationship exists. In *National League of Cities* v. *Usery* (1976), the Supreme Court ruled that the wage and overtime provisions of the 1974 amendments to the Fair Labor Standards Act could not be constitutionally applied to state and local governments. This decision seems, in part, to be a contradiction of the *Souder* ruling, which held that minimum wage laws apply to patients and residents of state hospitals and institutions. As a result of the *Souder* decision, work programs at some institutions were terminated. There is now a move to have these programs reinstated on the grounds that their termination caused patients' conditions to deteriorate, and lack of work opportunities makes deinstitutionalization of some patients more difficult (see *Mental Disability Law Reporter,* 1978).

There are still some unresolved issues in distinguishing between work and therapy. If an institution asks someone to wash dishes in preparation for being a dishwasher, is that work or job training? In *Dale* v. *State of New York* (see Friedman, 1973) it was asserted that in order for work to be regarded as therapy, it should be assigned after a thorough evaluation of the patient's condition; it should benefit the patient not the institution; it should be part of a larger treatment program and assigned by a physician or other professional; it should be performed voluntarily; and the patient should be paid.

Restraints

Under what circumstances and with what limitations should *physical or chemical restraints or seclusion* of patients be permitted? What process must be established to assure that such restraints are not used punitively or otherwise inappropriately?

The use of seclusion and restraints has been limited under the Eighth Amendment, which provides protection against cruel and unusual punishment. Most of the cases in this area have involved the use of solitary confinement in prisons, but generally can be extended to mental institutions (see Burt, 1973). Some hospital administrators, however, have argued that solitary confinement is different from hospital seclusion because the latter is part of a larger treatment plan. Standards for the proper therapeutic use of seclusion were set forth in *Wyatt* v. *Stickney* and permitted seclusion only for brief emergencies to restrain a person from doing harm. In institutions for the retarded, residents may never be placed alone in a locked room (see Burt, 1973).

Most states have regulations covering the use of seclusion and restraints. In Texas, for example, the use of physical or drug restraint and seclusion is prohibited except to protect the patient from doing injury to himself or others or as part of a written behavior modification plan or in other specified exceptions (see Texas Department of Mental Health and Mental Retardation, 1975). The use of restraint and seclusion is prohibited if used as punishment.

Confidentiality

How is the *confidentiality* of the therapeutic relationship to be maintained? Under what circumstances may patient's records or the fact of the existence of such records be released? May a patient request a court hearing to protect the release of records? After some period of time, may a patient petition for the destruction of his or her records? Under what circumstances, if any, may a prospective employer appropriately ask about the history of prior psychiatric treatment of a job applicant?

The issue of confidentiality is becoming more critical since medical records are often stored in centralized computers. The Mental Health Law Project filed a case, *Volkman* v. *Miller* (1976), asking that a practice requiring a patient's name, address, social security number, symptoms, and diagnosis and then placing that information into a central computer bank, be declared illegal and unconstitutional in that it constitutes an infringement of the doctor-patient relationship and the right to privacy. The degree to which such information was confidential was unknown. There was some indication that any physician or government employee could gain access to the information simply by dialing a specific phone number and making a request. The court ruled that the New York Department of Mental Hygiene could maintain such a data bank because no one's rights had been violated. One judge in a dissenting opinion asserted that is a denial of justice to wait until a leak of information occurs before ruling on the issue.

Currently, the most controversial case with regard to confidentiality is *Tarasoff* v. *Regents of the University of California* (1976). The case involves a student who was a patient at a university psychiatric clinic and told his therapist that he was going to kill a coed who had rejected him. The therapist asked the campus police to keep the patient under observation and attempted to institute a 72-hour hold, but was overruled by his supervisor. Two months later, when the patient was no longer in treatment, he killed the woman. In a suit brought by the parents of the victim against the therapists and the police for failure to warn of the patient's stated intention, the California Supreme Court ruled that a therapist is obligated to do whatever is necessary to protect an intended victim against danger. In the only other case to date concerning the issue of whether therapists have a duty to warn potential victims that a patient presents a danger to them, the New Jersey Supreme Court in *McIntosh* v. *Milano* (1979) agreed with the precedent set in *Tarasoff*. The duty of a therapist to warn a potential victim was seen as analogous to the obligation a physician has to warn third persons of infectious or contagious diseases.

Stone (1976), in criticizing the *Tarasoff* decision, believes that, while the decision was designed to increase public safety, it may have the opposite effect. A breach in confidentiality will damage the therapeutic alliance. Psychotherapists, already reluctant to treat dangerous patients, may become more so for fear of being sued for negligent failure to predict dangerousness and protect the public. At this point it is not known whether other states will follow the precedent set in *Tarasoff* and *McIntosh* or whether they, like Stone, will view commitment as the more appropriate and effective means of protecting the public from dangerous individuals.

The Voluntary Patient

In reviewing state and federal legislative and judicial actions over the past two decades, one cannot help but be impressed with the inexorable progress being made toward the full protection of the civil rights of psychiatric patients. Ironically, these rights now seem better protected in the case of public sector services than in the case of the private sector, and better protected in the case of inpatients than outpatients (Hare-Mustin, Marecek, Kaplan, & Liss-Levinson, 1979). While it may seem that patient rights issues arise only when there is an involuntary civil commitment, significant concerns in the case of voluntary patients exist and have yet to be resolved.

Is the threat of civil commitment used to force patients to enter psychiatric facilities voluntarily? Do outpatients have free access to independent consultation and the right to request a change in therapist or treatment modality without prejudice? Are there special problems with the protection of civil rights of patients in the case of the solo practitioner or in the case of the patient hospitalized in a private psychiatric hospital or psychiatric ward of a general hospital?

Persons who are voluntarily committed may not actually be in a mental institution of their own volition and may not feel free to leave. The voluntary patient may have been pressured, threatened, or coerced by relatives or friends. Even if the potential patient has not been threatened, admission into a hospital cannot be said to be on a voluntary basis unless the person is fully informed about conditions at the institution, alternatives to institutionalization, and the probable difficulties in reintegration into the outside world. That is, voluntary patients' rights to the least restrictive treatment setting and to informed consent may not be protected.

Chambers (1973) and Lewis (1975) point out that in many instances the plight of the voluntary mental patient is no better and may be worse than that of the involuntarily committed patient. The attitude toward such patients is that if they dislike their treatment or wish a less restrictive setting, they can walk away from the institution. But although voluntary patients have the right to leave treatment or seek alternative forms of therapy or another therapist, they may not feel they have this freedom and may, in fact, be subjected to subtle pressure that discourages such action.

Perhaps the most fundamental question regarding voluntary psychiatric patients is to what extent they understand the conditions under which they have been admitted. Olin and Olin (1975) interviewed a sample of 100 patients who admitted themselves voluntarily into either a public or a private psychiatric inpatient facility in Massachusetts in order to determine their comprehension of the conditions of their admissions. In Massachusetts, applicants for voluntary admission must sign a statement indicating that they understand that they are free to leave any time by giving written notice "provided, however, that the superintendant may, at his discretion, delay my departure for at least three days from the time of my notice, and also may petition the district court for my further retention if it appears necessary to him" (Olin & Olin, 1975, p. 941). The applicant must also agree to accept care and treatment, which may include the injection of medicines.

Only eight of the 100 patients interviewed were found to be fully informed concerning the terms of their admissions and, in general, private patients did not appear to be any better informed than public patients. More than half of the sample admitted not understanding the terms of their admission at all, or their understanding was in error (also, see Szasz, 1972).

CONCLUSIONS AND IMPLICATIONS

There seems little question but that the relationship between the health care provider and the patient is undergoing profound change, a change in no sense limited to mental health services. But because the civil rights of psychiatric patients have been abridged for so long, in their case one can see the general issues in magnified form. The challenge for the coming decade for all mental health professionals will be to organize mental health services in a manner that protects both civil *and* clinical rights. For the moment, however, it does seem that sides are drawn and that the major protagonists appear to be choosing between the protection of civil *or* clinical rights.

Much remains to be done if patients are to achieve full protection of their civil rights. Legislation and judicial decisions are not enough. Attorneys and mental health professionals need to join forces wherever possible and need to develop greater understanding of each other's ideologies and operating styles. They can work together to see that adequate funds are appropriated and responsibly expended for the provision of desirable community-based alternatives to hospitalization, for program and patient care quality control, and for the expansion of needed institutional mental health and legal services. Mental health dollars do not appear to be appropriated in relationship to where patients are being treated, with far too little money being available to fund community-based programs.

Attorneys and mental health professionals can work together to identify issues about which there is little if any conflict (for example, the protection of First Amendment rights) and to spell out the disagreements and strategies for their resolution where conflict is identified. They can collaborate in developing efficient procedures for implementing judicial decisions. And they can provide a viewpoint to help deal with the understandable frustration of the public faced with the discrepancy between its expectations for adequate human services, on the one hand, and the limitations of existing resources and programs, on the other hand. Public expectations for expanded services have been rising rapidly during the past two decades, and society can no longer accept the principle of *caveat emptor* in mental health and general health services. Attorneys and mental health professionals can join forces in the development and enforcement of the highest possible standards of mental health care.

Zeal and lack of understanding are a destructive combination, whether practiced by mental health professionals or by attorneys. The last two decades have witnessed a reaction against the excessive practices of mental health professionals, but one must guard against similarly excessive legal practices. Conflict between these two professionals is easy to identify in the abstract, away from mental health service settings, and often diminishes dramatically when there is a common interest in providing optimal care for a specific patient or group of patients. The mental health professional, particularly in the public setting, is often the last resort for the desperate human being, and the collaborative task for the attorney and mental health professional is to provide care that represents the highest level of competence and social responsibility.

A great many questions posed by attorneys and by mental health professionals lend themselves to prompt empirical study. Since the issues are in part a consequence of differing ideological perspectives, research data cannot be expected to play a critical role alone, but the quality of the debate can surely be enhanced by empirical evidence. As has been shown, the likelihood of a petition for involuntary commitment being granted is dramatically reduced when the prospective patient is represented by counsel. Less is known about the long-term and short-term consequences of involuntary civil commitment upon the psychological well-being of patients. It seems clear that the behavior of mental health service personnel changes when legal patient advocacy services are inaugurated. Less is known about the consequences of these behavior changes for the psychological well-being of psychiatric patients.

Furthermore, little is yet known about the psychological consequences of relatively recent judicial and legislative decisions—the requirement of periodic case review; restrictions on the use of chemical as well as mechanical restraints; the promulgation of patients' bills of rights, for example. It would be important to demonstrate that these decisions and policy changes had no negative consequences, and more impressive to show that these changes actually brought with them demonstrable positive effects upon the patient's institutional course and subsequent history. Staff with research training and responsibilities employed in the mental health service delivery system might well examine how their own clinical and research activities could accelerate the development of therapeutic programs and procedures that meet the requirements of both the socially responsible mental health professional and the clinically responsible attorney.

Recent empirical studies have begun to counteract the past failure on the part of mental health professionals to provide an adequate empirical base to the legal deliberations currently underway. That failure has been clearly recognized:

> The lack or minimal amount of material on the therapeutic effects . . . of long-term hospitalization cries out for correction. Similarly, while charges are made that the process of a hearing is detrimental to the patient's mental health and future treatment, these have been refuted by others who feel that the hearing process is, in fact, beneficial therapy for the patient. Neither side has proven its case through any scientific study. The effect of the availability of independent medical expertise on behalf of the patient at the hearing requires exploration. These issues are currently being litigated and the dearth of research is appalling. (Brown, 1972, p. 41)

As the remainder of this volume shall attest, a far stronger empirical base now exists. That base forms an invaluable resource in the continuing social policy debate.

REFERENCES

Abramson, M. E. The criminalization of mentally disordered behavior. *Hospital & Community Psychiatry*, 1972, *23*, 101–105.

Addington v. Texas, 47 U.S. Law Week 4473, 4476 (May 1, 1979).

Ad Hoc Committee on Advocacy. The social worker as advocate: Champion of social victims. *Social Work*, 1969, *14*, 16–22.

Albers, D. A., & Pasewark, R. A. Involuntary hospitalization: Surrender at the courthouse. *American Journal of Community Psychology*, 1974, *2*, 287–289.

Annas, G. J. *The rights of hospital patients: The basic ACLU guide to a hospital patient's rights.* New York: Avon Books, 1975.

Armstrong, B. St. Elizabeth Hospital: Case study of a court order. *Hospital & Community Psychiatry*, 1979, *30*, 42–46.

Bass, S. A. First, Sixth, and Fourteenth Amendment rights in mental institutions. In B. J. Ennis, P. R. Friedman, & B. Gitlin (Eds.), *Legal rights of the mentally handicapped* (Vol. 2). New York: Practicing Law Institute, 1973.

Baumrind, D. Principles of ethical conduct in the treatment of subjects: Reaction to the draft report of the committee on ethical standards in psychological research. *American Psychologist*, 1971, *26*, 887–896.

Birnbaum, M. The right to treatment: Some comments on its development. In F. J. Ayd (Ed.), *Medical, moral, and legal issues in mental health care.* Baltimore: Williams and Wilkins Co., 1974.

Boruch, R. F. Maintaining confidentiality of data in educational research: A systematic analysis. *American Psychologist*, 1971, *26*, 413–430.

Brager, G. A. Advocacy and political behavior. *Social Work*, 1968, *13*, 5–15.

Brown, I. Lawyers and psychiatrists in the court: Afterword. *Maryland Law Review*, 1972, *32*, 36–41.

Burt, R. A. Eighth Amendment rights in mental institutions. In B. J. Ennis, P. R. Friedman, & B. Gitlin (Eds.), *Legal rights of the mentally handicapped* (Vol. 2). New York: Practicing Law Institute, 1973.

Cardon, B., & Kuriloff, P. *Law and the school psychologist: Challenge and opportunity.* New York: Human Sciences Press, 1975.

Chambers, D. Right to the least restrictive alternative setting for treatment. In B. J. Ennis, P. R. Friedman, & B. Gitlin (Eds.), *Legal rights of the mentally handicapped* (Vol. 2). New York: Practicing Law Institute, 1973.

Chodoff, P. The case for involuntary hospitalization of the mentally ill. *American Journal of Psychiatry*, 1976, *133*, 496–501.

Clayton, T. O'Connor v. Donaldson: Impact in the states. *Hospital & Community Psychiatry*, 1976, *27*, 272–281.

Cohen, R. E. Interface teams as an integrating agent in mental health services. *International Journal of Mental Health*, 1974, *3*, 65–76.

Cox, D. E., & Sipprelle, C. N. Coercion in participation as a research subject. *American Psychologist*, 1971, *26*, 726–728.

Crane, L., Zonana, H., & Wizner, S. Implications of the *Donaldson* decision: A model for periodic review of committed patients. *Hospital & Community Psychiatry*, 1977, *28*, 827–833.

Curran, W. J. The revolution in American criminal law: Its significance for psychiatric diagnosis and treatment. *American Journal of Public Health*, 1968, *58*, 2209–2216.

Dale v. State of New York, 335, N.Y.S. 2d 485 (3rd Dept. 1974).

Deasy, L. C., & Steele, C. I. An analysis of a state hospital population subject to release under Florida law. *Hospital & Community Psychiatry*, 1976, *27*, 42–44.

Dickson, D. T. Law in social work: Impact of due process. *Social Work*, 1976, *21*, 274–278.

Dixon v. Weinberger, 405 F. Supp. 974 (D.D.C. 1975).

Eisman, M. Social work's new role in the welfare-class revolution. *Social Work*, 1969, *14*, 80–86.

Ennis, B., & Siegel, L. *The rights of mental patients.* New York: Avon Books, 1973.

Epstein, L., & Lowinger, P. Do mental patients want legal counsel: A survey. *American Journal of Orthopsychiatry*, 1975, *45*, 88–92.

Epstein, Y. M., Suedfeld, P., & Silverstein, S. J. The experimental contact: Subjects' expectations of and reactions to some behaviors of experimenters. *American Psychologist*, 1973, *28*, 212–221.

Erickson, R. C. Outcome studies in mental hospitals: A review. *Psychological Bulletin*, 1975, *82*, 519–540.

Ferleger, D. A patients' rights organization: Advocacy and collective action by and for inmates of mental institutions. *The Clearinghouse Review*, 1975, *8*, 597–604.

Frank, K. *Anti-psychiatry bibliography and resource guide.* Vancouver, British Columbia: Mental Patients Association, 1974.

Friedman, P. R. Thirteenth Amendment and statutory rights concerning work in mental institutions. In B. J. Ennis, P. R. Friedman, & B. Gitlin (Eds.), *Legal rights of the mentally handicapped* (Vol. 2). New York: Practicing Law Institute, 1973.

Friedman, P. R., & Halpern, C. R. Rights of the mentally handicapped in mental institutions—the right to treatment. In B. J. Ennis, P. R. Friedman, & B. Gitlin (Eds.), *Legal rights of the mentally handicapped* (Vol. 1). New York: Practicing Law Institute, 1974.

Gault, In re, 387 U.S. 1 (1967).

Gergen, K. J. The codification of research ethics: View of a Doubting Thomas. *American Psychologist*, 1973, *28*, 907–912.

Gharagozlou, H. The rights of the mentally ill in Iran. *Mental Health and Society*, 1974, *1*, 62–64.

Gilbert, N., & Specht, H. Advocacy and professional ethics. *Social Work*, 1976, *21*, 288–293.

Glick, I. D., Hargreaves, W. A., Raskin, M., & Kutner, S. J. Short versus long hospitalization: A prospective controlled study, II: Results for schizophrenic inpatients. *American Journal of Psychiatry*, 1975, *132*, 385–390.

Gottesman, R. *Children's legal rights in counseling: Rights and responsibilities of mental health professionals.* Washington, D.C.: U.S. Government Printing Office, 1975.

Gottlieb, R. M., Nappi, T., & Strain, J. J. The physician's knowledge of psychotropic drugs: Preliminary results. *American Journal of Psychiatry*, 1978, *135*, 29–32.

Greenblatt, M. Psychiatry: The battered child of medicine. *New England Journal of Medicine*, 1975, *292*, 246–250.

Grinnel, R. M., Jr., & Kyte, N. S. Modifying the environment. *Social Work*, 1974, *19*, 477–483.

Hare-Mustin, R., Marecek, J., Kaplan, A. G., & Liss-Levinson, N. Rights of clients, responsibilities of therapists. *American Psychologist*, 1979, *34*, 3–16.

Hiday, V. A. The role of counsel in civil commitment: Changes, effects, and determinants. *Journal of Psychiatry and Law*, 1977, *5*, 551–569.

Hyman, I., & Schreiber, K. The school psychologist as child advocate. *Children Today*, 1974 (March–April), *3*, 1–4.

J. L. and J. R. v. Parham, 412 F Supp. 112 (M.D. G.A. 1976).

Jansen, D. S. Personality characteristics of state hospital patients' rights office visitors. *Journal of Clinical Psychology*, 1974, *30*, 347–349.

Jorgensen, G. T., & Lyons, D. D. Human rights and involuntary civil commitment. *Professional Psychology*, 1972, *3*, 143–150.

Kaimowitz for John Doe v. Michigan Department of Mental Health, Civ. No. 73–1943–4 (Cir. Ct. Wayne County, Mich., May 10, 1973).

Kelley, V. R., & Weston, H. B. Civil liberties in mental health facilities. *Social Work*, 1974, *19*, 48–54.

Kelley, V. R., & Weston, H. B. Computers, costs, and civil liberties. *Social Work*, 1975, *20*, 15–19.

Kelman, H. C. The rights of the subject in social research: An analysis in terms of relative power and legitimacy. *American Psychologist*, 1972, *27*, 989–1016.

Kemper, G. W. Rights of patients/residents in mental health facilities. *Journal of the Tennessee Medical Association*, 1974, *67*, 1004–1005.

Klein, M. M., & Grossman, S. A. Voting pattern of mental patients in a community state hospital. *Community Mental Health Journal*, 1967, *3*, 149–152.

Knecht v. Gillman, 448 F. 2d 1136 (8th Cir. 1973).

Knitzer, J. E. Child advocacy: A perspective. *American Journal of Orthopsychiatry*, 1976, *46*, 200–216.

Kopolow, L. E. Patients' rights and psychiatric practice. In W. E. Barton & C. J. Sanborn (Eds.), *Law and the mental health professions: Friction at the interface.* New York: International University Press, 1978.

Kopolow, L. E., & Bloom, H. (Eds.), *Mental health advocacy: An emerging force in consumer rights.* Washington, D.C.: U.S. Government Printing Office, 1977.

Kremens v. Bartley, 402 F. Supp. 1039 (E.D. Pa. 1975) reversed on other grounds, 431 U.S. 119 (1977).

Kumasaka, Y., & Gupta, R. K. Lawyers and psychiatrists in the court: Issues on civil commitment. *Maryland Law Review*, 1972, *32*, 6–41.

Kumasaka, Y., & Stokes, J. Involuntary hospitalization: Opinions and attitudes of psychiatrists and lawyers. *Comprehensive Psychiatry*, 1972, *13*, 201–208.

Langsley, D. G., Machotka, P., & Flomenhaft, K. Avoiding mental hospital admissions: A follow-up study. *American Journal of Psychiatry*, 1971, *127*, 1391–1394.

Lessard v. Schmidt, 349 F. Supp. 1078 (E.D. Wis. 1972).

Lewis, T. The patient is responsible. *Nursing Times*, 1975, *71*, 434–435.

Lewis, W. W. Child advocacy and ecological planning. *Mental Hygiene*, 1970, *54*, 475–483.

Lourie, N. V. The many faces of advocacy. In I. N. Berlin (Ed.), *Advocacy for child mental health*. New York: Brunner/Mazel Publishers, 1975(a).

Lourie, N. V. Operational advocacy: Objectives and obstacles. In I. N. Berlin (Ed.), *Advocacy for child mental health*. New York: Brunner/Mazel Publishers, 1975(b).

McDermott, J. F., Bolman, W. M., Arensdorf, A. M., & Markoff, R. A. The concept of child advocacy. *American Journal of Psychiatry*, 1973, *130*, 1203–1206.

McGarry, A. L., & Kaplan, H. A. Overview: Current trends in mental health law. *American Journal of Psychiatry*, 1973, *130*, 621–630.

McIntosh v. Milano, 48 U.S. Law Week 2040 (July 17, 1979).

Meisel, A. Rights of the mentally ill: The gulf between theory and reality. *Hospital & Community Psychiatry*, 1975, *26*, 349–353.

Mental Disability Law Reporter. Mental health treatment for minors. 1978, *2*, 460–472.

Mental Health Law Project Summary of Activities: September, 1975. Washington, D.C.

Mental Health Law Project Summary of Activities: March, 1976. Washington, D.C.

Miller, H. Value dilemmas in social casework. *Social Work*, 1968, *13*, 27–33.

Miranda v. Arizona, 384 U.S. 436 (1966).

Mitford, J. *Kind and unusual punishment: The prison business*. New York: Alfred A. Knopf, Inc., 1973.

Modlin, H. C. Balancing patients' rights with the rights of others. *Hospital & Community Psychiatry*, 1974, *25*, 474–475.

Modlin, H.C., Porter, L., & Benson, R. E. Mental health centers and the criminal justice system. *Hospital & Community Psychiatry*, 1976, *27*, 716–719.

Murray, J. E. Assuring accountability for the poor: Patient advocates. *Journal of Psychiatric Nursing and Mental Health Services*, 1975, *13*, 33–37.

National League of Cities v. Usery, 426 U.S. 833 (1976).

Nelson, S. H., & Grunebaum, H. Ethical issues in psychiatric follow-up studies. *American Journal of Psychiatry*, 1972, *128*, 1358–1362.

New York Health and Hospitals Corporations v. Stein, 70 Misc. 2d 944, 335 N.Y. 2d 461 (Sup. Ct. 1972).

Neufeld, G. R. Council as advocate: The advocacy role and functions of councils for the developmentally disabled. In J. L. Paul, R. Wiegerink, & G. R. Neufeld (Eds.), *Advocacy: A role for DD councils.* Chapel Hill, N.C.: Developmental Disabilities Technical Assistance System, 1974.

Nikelly, A. G. Ethical issues in research on student protest. *American Psychologist*, 1971, *26*, 475–477.

O'Connor v. Donaldson, 422 U.S. 563 (1975).

Olin, G. B., & Olin, H. S. Informed consent in voluntary hospital admissions. *American Journal of Psychiatry*, 1975, *132*, 938–941.

Olmstead v. U.S., 277 U.S. 438, 478 (1928).

Orlin, M. A role for social workers in the consumer movement. *Social Work*, 1973, *18*, 60–65.

Panitch, A. Advocacy in practice. *Social Work*, 1974, *19*, 326–332.

Parham v. J. L. and J. R., 47 U.S. Law Week 4740, 4744 (June 19, 1979).

Pasamanick, B., Scarpetti, F. R., & Dinitz, S. *Schizophrenics in the community.* New York: Appleton-Century-Crofts, 1967.

Peck, C. L. Current legislative issues concerning the right to refuse versus the right to choose hospitalization and treatment. *Psychiatry*, 1975, *38*, 303–317.

Peszke, M. A. Is dangerousness an issue for physicians in emergency commitment? *American Journal of Psychiatry*, 1975, *132*, 825–828.

Pratt, M. Partison of the disadvantaged. *Social Work*, 1972, *17*, 66–72.

Rachlin, S. With liberty and psychosis for all. *Psychiatric Quarterly*, 1974, *48*, 410–420.

Rachlin, S., Pam, A., & Milton, J. Civil liberties versus involuntary hospitalization. *American Journal of Psychiatry*, 1975, *132*, 189–192.

Rouse V. Cameron, 372 F. 2d 451 (D.C. Cir. 1966).

Rozecki v. Gaughan, 459 F. 2d 6 (1st Cir. 1972).

Sadoff, R. L. Changing laws and ethics in psychiatry. *Bulletin of the American Academy of Psychiatry and the Law*, 1977, *5*, 34–40.

Sadoff, R. L. Indications for involuntary hospitalization: Dangerousness or mental illness. In W. E. Barton & C. J. Sanborn (Eds.), *Law and the mental health professions: Friction at the interface.* New York: International Universities Press, 1978.

Safier, D. Patient work under Fair Labor Standards: The issue in perspective. *Hospital & Community Psychiatry*, 1976, *27*, 89–92.

Scherrer, J. L. How social workers help lawyers. *Social Work*, 1976, *21*, 279–283.

Schwitzgebel, R. K. Right to treatment for the mentally disabled: The need for realistic standards and objective criteria. *Harvard Civil Rights—Civil Liberties Law Review*, 1973, *8*, 513–535.

Scott, E. P. The right to refuse treatment: A developing legal concept. *Hospital & Community Psychiatry*, 1977, *28*, 372.

Scott v. Plante, 530 F. 2d 939 (3rd Cir. 1976).

Sehdev, H. S. Patients' rights or patients' neglect: The impact of the patients' rights movement on delivery systems. *American Journal of Orthopsychiatry*, 1976, *46*, 660–668.

Shelton v. Tucker, 364 U.S. 479, 488 (1960).

Silverberg, H. M. Protecting the rights of mental patients: One lawyer's experience in a world of psychiatrists. *Barrister*, 1974 (Fall), 46–49; 60.

Silverman, I. Nonreactive methods and the law. *American Psychologist*, 1975, *30*, 764–769.

Singer, K. Society and rights of the mentally ill: A historical perspective of the Chinese. *Mental Health and Society*, 1974, *1*, 49–55.

Slovenko, R., & Luby, E. D. From moral treatment to railroading out of the mental hospital. *Bulletin of the American Academy of Psychiatry and the Law*, 1974, *2*, 223–236.

Smith, R. T. Health and rehabilitation manpower strategy: New careers and the role of the indigenous paraprofessional. *Social Science and Medicine*, 1973, *7*, 281–290.

Souder v. Brennan, 367 F. Supp. 808 (D.C. Cir. 1973).

Steier, S. Personal communication, Sept. 7, 1976.

Stone, A. A. *Mental health and the law: A system in transition.* Washington, D.C.: U.S. Government Printing Office, 1975.

Stone, A. A. The *Tarasoff* decisions: Suing psychotherapists to safeguard society. *Harvard Law Review*, 1976, *90*, 358–378.

Szasz, T. S. Voluntary mental hospitalization: An unacknowledged practice of medical fraud. *New England Journal of Medicine*, 1972, *287*, 277–278.

Tarasoff v. Regents of the University of California, 551 P. 2d 334 (1976).

Teitelbaum, L. E., & Ellis, J. W. The liberty interest of children: Due process rights and their application. *Mental Disability Law Reporter*, 1978, *2*, 582–603.

Texas Department of Mental Health and Mental Retardation. Rules of the Commissioner of Mental Health and Mental Retardation (MHMR) Affecting Client (Patient) Care, 302.04.06.001–010 (Restraint and Seclusion). Austin, Texas: 1975.

Trachtman, G. M. Pupils, parents, privacy, and the school psychologist. *American Psychologist*, 1972, *27*, 37–45.

Treffert, D. A. Dying with their rights on. *American Journal of Psychiatry*, 1973, *130*, 1041.

Volkman v. Miller, 383 N.Y.S. 2d 95 (App. Div., 3rd Dept. 1976).

Wald, P. M., & Friedman, P. R. *Brief of American Orthopsychiatric Association, American Psychological Association, Federation of Parents Organizations for the New*

York State Mental Institutions, National Association for Mental Health, National Association for Retarded Citizens, National Association of Social Workers, and National Center for Law and the Handicapped as Amici Curiae in Support of Appellees. Washington, D.C.: Mental Health Law Project, 1976.

Wenger, D. L., & Fletcher, C. R. The effect of legal counsel on admissions to a state mental hospital: A confrontation of professions. *Journal of Health and Social Behavior,* 1969, *10,* 66–72.

Wilbert, D. E., Jorstad, V., Loren, J. D., & Wirrer, B. Determination of grave disability. *Journal of Nervous and Mental Disease,* 1976, *162,* 35–39.

Wineman, D., & James, A. The advocacy challenge to schools of social work. *Social Work,* 1969, *14,* 23–32.

Wing, K. R. The right to refuse treatment: Legal issues. *Bulletin of the American Academy of Psychiatry and the Law,* 1977, *5,* 15–19.

Winters v. Miller, 446 F. 2d 65 (2nd Cir. 1971) *cert. denied,* 404 U.S. 985 (1971).

Womack, W. M., & Sata, L. S. The first year of a child advocacy project. *Hospital & Community Psychiatry,* 1975, *26,* 819–822.

Wyatt v. Stickney, 325 F. Supp. 781 (M.D. Ala. 1971); 334 F. Supp. 1341 (M.D. Ala. 1971) enforced by 334 F. Supp. 373, 344 F. Supp. 387.

Wyman v. James, 400 U.S. 309 (1971).

Yale Law Journal. The role of counsel in the civil commitment process: A theoretical framework. 1975, *84,* 1540–1563.

Part II

THE KNOWLEDGE BASE

Chapter 2

THE STIGMA OF PATIENTHOOD

Catherine E. Rosen
Claudia Cowan
Richard J. Grandison

Implications of current research on the mentally ill leave mental health personnel facing a dilemma. Some studies suggest that once people are treated for mental illness, society reacts negatively to them. The failure to treat people, however, for fear of stigmatizing them is to withhold needed help. Often the mentally ill are hurting, are troubled, and are unwanted. What recourse do they have when their most direct source of help is a mental health system that provides stigma-engendering treatment?

Cases of maltreatment, injustice, and discrimination against patients or ex-patients of the mental hospital system (cf., Rachlin, Pam, & Milton, 1975) are well-known to people who identify with the mental health movement. For the discharged patient, finding housing, jobs, or school placements involves the possibility of discrimination. The label "emotionally unstable" may preclude many opportunities. Advocates of civil liberties have long recognized the stigma of mental hospitalization and have fought against the designation of an individual as potentially, if not currently, "crazy" that stems simply from contact with the mental health system.

Bruce Ennis (1972), in *Prisoners of Psychiatry*, recounts the story of Henry Mercer, a dramatic example of the ex-mental patient and bureaucratic injustice. At age 13, Henry was committed to Rockland State

Mental Hospital. Doctors recognized that the boy was not psychotic, but a foster home placement was not available. Finally released, after four years, to the custody of his brother, Mercer settled down, earned his high school diploma in night school, and worked his way up from nurse's aide to a trusted ambulance attendant at a local hospital. Fifteen years after his commitment, Mercer applied for a taxi driver's license in New York City, and was denied it because of his mental hospital record. A year-long court battle ensued during which six psychiatrists unanimously agreed that Mercer showed no signs of mental disturbance and was capable of holding a hack license. Indeed, he had never evidenced any psychotic behavior. Three court appearances, numerous letters, petitions, and recommendations testified to Mercer's stability and competence. The Hack Bureau offered to settle out of court. Henry Mercer was granted a hack license, but there was a provision that he furnish psychiatric evaluations every six months. Unfortunately, no favorable court decision or precedent was established thereby for dealing with discrimination against former mental patients.

If all the mentally ill were merely victims of stereotyping and prejudice, the problem would be simple, but rarely are they simply society's ill-treated. Instead, they may be hurting and in personal crisis; they may live daily in intolerable family situations; they may be eccentric and nuisances; their behavior may be odd and disturbing.

Often the public views the mentally ill with an anxious mixture of fear, sympathy, and rejections. When Goldstein and Blackman (1975) asked college-age respondents to pick adjectives most descriptive of someone "mentally ill," their results showed a surprising combination of terms. While the mentally ill were characterized as unreliable, grasping, quick-tempered, and evasive, they were also described as more imaginative, sensitive, and meditative. Perhaps this study indicates that attitudes have changed since the time when folk belief in demonic possession was common. Perhaps the mentally disturbed individual is no longer perceived as a criminal, to be locked up or burned at the stake.

This chapter is an attempt to comprehend, from a research framework, the experience of the ex-mental patient on returning to the community. Indeed, this summary is designed to reconcile the need to help with the negative consequences of helping. Perhaps by recognizing the dimensions of the problems the mentally ill encounter, the reader may become aware and, through such enlightenment, help to create a societal climate that best serves the interests of the mentally ill, the community, and the mental health profession.

Research on the Situation of the Former Mental Patient

Experimental work on people's reaction to the former patient's return to society can be conceptualized in terms of increasing personal contact with the person labeled as mentally ill. Consider a man about to leave a mental hospital who is wondering what impact his hospitalization might have on his future life.

Attitudes Toward the Mentally Ill.

The ex-patient will probably be anxious about the public's attitude toward those who have been institutionalized. S/he will question: Does this information have any effect on how people feel about her/-him? How much do people know about mental problems? Is it possible that the community's reaction will affect feelings and behaviors of former friends and acquaintances? Can it influence prospective employers? We might note, parenthetically, that it is the community's attitudes that determine the amount of support for ongoing local mental health programs.

Expectations of the Public Regarding Ex-patients.

What do friends and family think will happen when the ex-patient returns? Will it make any difference? Expectations of dangerous or disturbed behavior may lead to the avoidance of contact, a social isolation that proves to be an additional burden. On the other hand, a warm and sympathetic reception by friends and family can greatly ease the transition to everyday work and sociability.

Reactions to the Ex-patient.

Ex-patients will want to know how people will in fact react to them. How will others behave when they come in face-to-face contact with an ex-mental patient? Will others treat them with special care, thereby making them feel ill-at-ease and uncomfortable?

Self-perception.

Finally, the experience of mental hospitalization could change a person's feelings about himself. Goffman, in *Asylums* (1961), has theorized that the label of "mental patient" or "mentally ill" can give the individual a *master status*, i.e., a blueprint for how he and others are to view his past life and interpret his present behavior. Crucially, this master status may change the person's view of himself. Believing he is "sick," he comes to perceive himself as helpless, weak, disturbed, as basically different and apart from other people.

In the sections that immediately follow, the research pertaining to these four areas is considered in greater detail. some areas were heavily investigated, others have scarcely been touched, but all provide glimpses into the perceived world of those who have been labeled mentally ill.

ATTITUDES TOWARD THE MENTALLY ILL

In an early study, J. C. Nunnally (1961) found that the general public sees the mentally ill as dangerous, dirty, unpredictable, and worthless. The mental health community, taking note of studies such as these, has carried on a campaign to educate the public to the nature and consequences of mental illness.

Has this campaign succeeded? Currently, debate exists among researchers in regard to improvements, if any, in public attitudes toward the mentally ill over the last three decades. Some scholars conclude that the society of the 1970s accepts the mentally ill, with the stigma of mental illness existing more in the awareness of the professionals than in the *modus operandi* of the public (Crocetti, Spiro, & Siassi, 1971; Spiro, Siassi, & Crocetti, 1974; Herbert, 1978).

Despite this optimism, anecdotal reports of discrimination continue, and other scholars (Sarbin & Mancuso, 1970, 1972) argue persuasively that the public's fundamental fear and rejection of the mentally ill has not changed. Rather, they believe that the major impact of the mental health education campaign has been to increase knowledge of the current "medical model" without changing basic feelings toward people already identified as mentally ill.

Early Research on Attitudes Toward Mental Illness

One of the earliest studies of public recognition of the symptoms of mental illness was the survey carried out by Shirley Star (1955) of the National Opinion Research Center. She presented a nationwide sample of 3,500 adults with six case histories, namely, vignettes describing classical stereotypes of paranoid schizophrenia, simple schizophrenia, alcoholism, anxiety neurosis, juvenile character disorder, and compulsive phobia. Her findings indicated that only the most extreme case description (paranoid schizophrenia) was identified as mentally ill by a majority (75%) of the respondents, and correct recognition of the other vignettes ranged to a low of 7% for the compulsive phobic description. Star concluded that people will tolerate all but the most deviant behavior, resisting employing the label of mental illness as much as possible. Cumming and Cumming (1957) repeated the study in Canada and came to the same conclusion.

Asking such social-distance questions as, "Would you let your daughter marry a man who had been to see a psychiatrist about mental problems?" Watley (1959) found that 64% would oppose such a union, and only 15% would consider as a babysitter a woman who had seen a psychiatrist. Despite these rejections of persons with the relatively innocuous stigma of merely consulting a psychiatrist, more than 80% of the sample disclaimed the notion that "it is best not to associate with people who have been in mental hospitals." Apparently the sample was willing to be compassionate and accepting in very abstract situations, but responded with rejection when the suspicion of mental illness came closer to home.

Early studies present a fairly consistent picture of public attitudes toward the mentally ill. The 1950s public failed to recognize symptomatic behaviors, but once a person had been associated with mental illness, had in effect been labeled, he or she was disliked and avoided. Results of studies conducted in the sixties and seventies have moderated this uniformly negative picture.

Recent Studies

Generally, recent studies indicate that the public's knowledge about traditional psychiatric diagnostic categories has improved dramatically. This is evident from D'Arcy and Brockman's (1976) review of the findings of 10 studies conducted over two decades. These studies used the Star vignettes to assess recognition of mental illness. The public seems increasingly open about mental illness and optimistic about its treatment (Bentz & Egerton, 1970; Spiro et al., 1974).

Despite this increased verbal acceptance of the mentally ill and the medical model of mental illness, some recent studies continue to report negative public reactions, although not at the extremes of dislike indicated by the Whatley (1959) and Cumming and Cumming (1957) surveys.

Tringo (1970) had 500 people rate various types of disabilities and found that the physically and sensorially disabled received the highest ratings. The mentally ill were given the lowest ratings, falling in the same group with the mentally retarded, the ex-convict, and the alcoholic. Wilkins (1978) has demonstrated that negative attitudes toward the mentally ill can be acquired during childhood.

Grandison (1978) asked 165 male psychology students to rate four kinds of male peers: Best friend, a complete stranger, a former mental patient, and an ex-convict. Raters said the ex-mental patient's conversation and behavior were less predictable, and they felt more ill-at-ease and less physically safe with the ex-patient than the stranger. Nevertheless, the stranger, ex-patient, and ex-convict were rated as equally likeable.

Olmstead and Durham (1976) directly addressed the issue of the changing of attitudes toward mental illness over a decade and concluded that the basic attitudinal reference system toward the mentally ill had not changed. College students accept psychiatric labels, and consequently reject such classes of people as mental patients and insane persons. However, they seemed to accept the former mental patient as cured, and negative feelings were substantially reduced.

From Saying to Believing

One note of caution is offered by epidemiologist Judith Rabkin (1975) concerning the view that the public now accepts the mentally ill. Rabkin contends that the mental health education campaign may have changed the public's rejection of the mentally ill less than it has changed its willingness to admit to it. In other words, "candid rejection of the mentally ill seems to be less socially acceptable than it used to be" (p. 450).

In support, she cites the puzzling findings of a 1963 New York City survey (Elinson, Padella, & Perkins, 1967). While the survey showed widespread belief in the medical model and great optimism for mental health treatment, it also found that people still see the mentally ill as a despicable group. More than three-quarters of those surveyed felt that physical illness makes most people sympathetic, but mental illness tends to repel most people. In self-serving fashion, the respondents attributed more enlightened views to themselves, with only 16% admitting that they were personally repelled. Studies by Page and Yates (1975) and D'Arcy and Brockman (1976) demonstrated that the expression of varying attitudes toward the mentally ill, and improved rates of mental illness recognition, can be "cued" by situational factors that inform the respondent what answers would be considered most "enlightened" or socially desirable.

Old beliefs die hard and slowly. Taken together, these studies provide a warning to those who harbor enthusiasm over the wholesale success of the mental health education campaign. There are strong indications that the public knows more about mental illness, and feels more positively inclined toward the mentally ill. Still, words change more easily than feelings, and there yet remains a gap between saying and believing.

From Attitudes to Action

Perhaps the largest problem in the research on attitudes remains virtually untouched: If people *say* they like and accept the mentally ill, what implication does this have for what they will *do*? Ellsworth (1965) reports a rare attempt to bridge the gap between attitudes and behavior.

Ellsworth chose the psychiatric ward of a Veterans Administration hospital as a setting to measure the congruence between the attitudes and behavior of 65 nurses and aids on the ward staff. Two standard attitude scales were used, *Opinions about Mental Illness* (Cohen & Streunig, 1962) and *Staff Opinion Survey* (Berger, 1962). Staff behaviors toward mental patients were also measured. Hospitalized patients, who had been carefully screened for their ability to recognize ward personnel (N=188), rated the staff on 55 behavior items. These items included such statements as "reserved and cool," "gives freely of himself," "treats me like a child," and "trusts patients."

Ellsworth factor-analyzed the ward staff's responses to the attitude scales, finding three separate attitude dimensions that related to staff behavior. One dimension, *restrictive control*, reflects a punitive, controlling, and rigid attitude toward the mentally ill. Staff scoring high on restrictive control would agree with such statements as, "If a patient in a mental hospital attacks someone, s/he should be punished so s/he doesn't do it again." Not unexpectedly, patients viewed the ward staff who endorsed such attitudes as "hard-boiled and critical," "bossy and domineering," and never "treats me as an equal" or "finds time to listen to me." In general, the ward staff scoring high on restrictive control were seen as "inconsiderate, impatient, rigid, domineering, (and) skeptical" (Ellsworth, 1965).

In striking contrast to the restrictive control staff are those Ellsworth called *nontraditional*. These staff members tended to disagree with such common conceptions of mental illness as, "People who are mentally ill let their emotions control them; normal people think things out." They were most highly regarded by their patients. Their behaviors were seen as a constellation of positive acts, i.e., "dependable and reliable," "friendly and approachable," "sensitive and understanding." The nontraditional staff member "gives advice freely," "keeps his promises," and "looks out for my welfare," and never "avoids patients."

The most puzzling of the attitude dimensions that emerged was named *protective benevolence* by Ellsworth. Ostensibly, staff holding this view expressed quite favorable attitudes toward the mentally ill. They argued that "the staff should be as friendly with patients as they are with one another." This attitude toward patients seemed to be one of kindliness and tolerance, yet their behaviors present an entirely different picture. Patients said that this staff member "stays by himself," is "reserved and cool," and gave him low ratings on "lets patients get to know him," "patients turn to him for advice and help," and "keep his promises to me." In short, these staff expressed friendly attitudes, but their behaviors indicated their discomfort when dealing with the mentally ill. Ellsworth hypothesized that this seeming incongruence between attitudes and behaviors is due to the wish of the protectively benevolent staff not to hurt the patient's feelings. He supposes that "what the protectively benevolent person may really be saying is that he finds it preferable to indulge, placate, generally go along with, and accept the patient as he is" (p. 197). The first priority is to maintain a comfortable relationship. The staff member holding protective benevolent attitudes seems to accomplish this goal by presenting an outwardly agreeable face but avoiding interaction when discomfort threatens (Ellsworth, 1965).

This conflict between expressed attitudinal humanism toward the mentally ill and behavioral rejection can serve as one of the much-sought-after links between increasingly positive attitudes and continuing reports of stigmatization. The general public, as well as psychiatric personnel, may find it easy to placate the former mental patient, but difficult to deal with his constant, uncomfortable presence. Attitudes can appear favorable, but the long-term aloofness that springs from discomfort at confrontation and the overly cautious care not to "upset" the patient only lead the patient to feel that others treat him with dishonesty and avoidance. It is impossible to say what portion of the current surveys of attitudes toward the mentally ill has tapped the superficial, positive feelings of "self-protective benevolence" and what portion has tapped a truly humanistic acceptance. Ellsworth's seminal study serves only to hint at the complicated processes that transform attitudes toward the mentally ill into action.

On Sickness and Acceptance

In attempting to change community attitudes, mental health reformers chose a strategy with interesting consequences. The essential message was that the mentally ill are sick, that like other sick people, they should be absolved of blame for their problems and helped to get well. There is evidence, however, that while the public may be increasingly willing to see insanity as "an illness like any other," this view has not led to a corresponding acceptance of the mentally ill. In fact, Kirk (1975) has proposed that just the opposite may be true; people who see the mentally ill as "sick" may reject them more strongly. In an ingenious study using versions of Star's vignettes, Kirk measured the social distance his college respondents indicated they would prefer to keep between themselves and the men described. In addition, he obtained an index, based on some theorizing by Parsons (1951), of the degree to which the men described were seen as legitimate occupants of the *sick role*. According to Kirk, the sick role is defined by the following factors: (1) the sick person is exempt from some normal social responsibilities, (2) he is not expected to get well without help; (3) the illness is seen by both the patient and others as undesirable; (4) the person should want to get well; (5) the sick person is obligated to seek professional help.

Kirk reasoned that if seeing the mentally ill as sick is associated with increased positive feelings toward them, then the more a disturbed person is seen as sick, the more he should be accepted and liked. His results indicated just the opposite. Respondents who were most willing to extend the sick role to Kirk's mentally ill stimulus persons were also significantly more likely to reject them. Kirk also found that social rejection of the mentally ill was not lessened by relieving them of responsibility for their own sickness. Even respondents who were willing to see the mentally ill as sick sometimes held them responsible for their own problems. Respondents who agreed that the person was sick, and who did not expect him to get well by himself, showed the highest rates of rejection in the study.

Kirk summarized the results of his investigations with a warning that should be taken seriously by all who aim to change public attitudes on mental illness: "The public is increasingly willing to grant the sick role to those they define as mentally ill, only instead of the sick role serving to neutralize rejection, it may serve as a justification or rationalization for rejection. Thus, defining the person as sick may facilitate segregation of the mentally ill, rather than paving the way for social reintegration" (Kirk, 1975, p. 324).

Expectations of the Public Regarding Ex-patients

In 1966, the U. S. Supreme Court ordered 946 inmates of Dannemore and Matteawan state hospitals released to community hospitals (*Baxtrom* v. *Herold*, 1966). These were supposedly the most dangerous inmates in New York State: convicted criminals who had become insane while serving their sentences, persons civilly committed but too potentially violent to remain in less restrictive settings, defendants judged not guilty by reason of insanity, or persons incompetent to stand trial. Understandably, mental health professionals were upset and the recipient hospitals took precautions to prevent a catastrophe. Ward staffing was increased and a crash program in karate was instituted. The atmosphere was one of fear and expected disaster. Such apprehension was unjustified, however. When some of these patients were subsequently released to the community, their criminal activity was no more frequent than one would expect from a normal sample (Steadman, 1973; Steadman & Cocozza, 1974; Steadman & Kevels, 1972).

The idea of mental illness creates a climate of fear and uncertainty. In the absence of any other data, knowledge that a person is mentally ill sets one to expect the unexpected, to fear unpredictable, extreme, or dangerous behavior, even when there is no basis whatsoever for believing that such actions might occur. Thus, communities, fearing increases in crime, may use zoning ordinances to prohibit locally based mental health centers or halfway houses, on the barest chance that something might happen. Or a woman who is an ex-mental patient may be denied the adoption of a child, even though there is no specific reason to think she would be an inadequate mother. The label of mental illness seems to add an unacceptable element of risk for many people. Statistics may show that nothing is likely to happen, since ex-mental patients as a class are not particularly criminal, nor inadequately parental, nor viciously violent. Prior psychological treatment establishes a presumption of danger; that initial element of fear can lead to increased isolation of a person who may be particularly sensitive to rejection, and who is especially in need of support.

The concern and anticipation associated with the return of the mentally ill to the community is no better exemplified than in the reaction to the community mental health movement. Nationwide, the current policy has transferred the focus of mental health care from central institutions specializing in long-term treatment, to new community centers delivering short-term and emergency care. Both professional and lay observers have protested the "dumping" of marginally adjusted individuals into an unprepared community (Doll, 1975).

Fears and Expectations: The Family

If the public is subject to some apprehensions about the mentally ill, by far the most apprehensive are those who are closest to the problem—the mental patient's family. Rachlin et al. (1975), in speaking of experiences with a locked psychiatric ward in New York City, point out that the principal job of the hospital administrator in charge of public relations is to soothe and reassure families who protest a mental patient's release. Rarely, if ever, do families complain of an unjust detention of a disturbed relative. Leavitt (1975) found that "at the termination of hospitalization, they [the families] remained as they were at the beginning—confused and frightened custodians of the mentally ill" (p. 39). Clausen and Yarrow (1955), found a "predominant expectation" of stigma among family members of patients. Almost all displayed signs of uncertainty and discomfort. They indicated an unwillingness to reveal the hospitalization to outsiders, but admitted a need to talk about it with someone.

Nevertheless, despite some preliminary worrying about potential negative reactions by others in the community, families seem to adapt fairly well to the presence of a former mental patient, and few families avoid their friends or unduly restrict their lives (Freeman & Simmons, 1961). Interestingly, the higher the education of the informant, the greater the reports of restricted behaviors. Freeman and Simmons hypothesize that the more educated informant, by virtue of his higher class status and aspirations, is often more concerned with a derogatory evaluation of the family by his community associates.

These expectations of negative evaluations are the result of what could be termed *extended stigma*, since the anticipated mistreatment is not directed to the mental patient himself, but extended to family members by virtue of their association with him. Some families continue to feel ashamed by the ex-patient's presence, even though they try to hide this feeling. When Doll (1975) surveyed the families of 125 ex-patients in the Cleveland area, 70% of the families whose kin were still disturbed felt "humiliated," and 65% agreed that it was best to avoid them. These negative feelings occurred despite the families' generally positive attitudes toward the mentally ill.

Family shame possibly reflects not so much extended stigma, but rather a reaction to the disruptive behavior of the formerly hospitalized relative. Doll reports data on humiliation and avoidance only for families with relatives who remain disturbed. Additionally, Schwartz, Myers, and Astrachan (1974) have reported a connection between disruptive behavior and fear of the mentally ill. These researchers found a significant relationship between disturbed behaviors of former mental patients and their families' negative reactions to others who are mentally ill. Rejection was more pronounced among whites, persons of lower social class, and those with a relative displaying symptoms of anxiety, depression, and somatic concerns. Surprisingly, neither repeated rehospitalizations nor the more bizarre and disturbing psychotic symptoms were strongly associated with rejection by family members. The authors theorize that it is not the strangeness nor severity of behavior *per se* that leads to avoidance, but the disruption of normal social interaction following from neurotic symptoms.

In summary, the family of the returning mental patient fears that possibly both the anticipated extended stigma and the patient's disturbed behavior will lead to restricted and disruptive social interactions. Nevertheless, research has shown that, after a short time, the family makes a good adjustment to the former patient's return. It appears that with appropriate guidance the *family* can work through its initial concerns and provide a less tense and more supportive milieu for the returning ex-patient.

Fears and Expectations: The Former Patient

Upon first entering the community after discharge, the ex-patient may still be troubled and uncertain about returning to a life that has changed. Overwhelming fears of rejection from friends and community may cause him to restrict his living in many ways.

An investigation of the social activities of 159 first-admission mental patients one year after their return to the community revealed a "closing in" when compared to their activities in the pre-hospitalization year (White, McAdoo, & Phillips, 1974). All had significantly decreased their involvement with community organizations and increased their inward orientation in the posthospitalization year. Males decreased their general activity level, too. These trends seem surprising since the year just prior to the first hospitalization was doubtless the time of greatest personal disturbance for both the patient and the family; yet upon returning to the community, the patient retreated still further. The researchers contend that these data indicate patient fear of social rejection.

Possibly, former mental patients' fears of community rejection are becoming unjustified. Given favorable shifts in attitudes, community members might be induced by their own enlightenment to respond with sympathy and understanding, if given an opportunity to do so. However, the fears of ex-patients can lead them to restrict their contacts with society, to shut themselves in, and thereby to deny themselves the support of others.

Fear of Seeking Help

The expectation that receiving mental health treatment has negative consequences may occur prior to seeking help as well as after. A small but important percentage of people continue to report unwillingness to seek psychological treatment because of the associated stigma, as shown in a Brooklyn College survey (Perlman, 1966) and in a national survey (Veroff & Douvan, cited in Herbert, 1978). Respondents in a British study also cited the stigma of treatment as the reason for failure to follow through on referrals to a psychiatric outpatient clinic (Skuse, 1975).

The Basis of Fear

Is there any justification for the anticipation of stigma associated with mental illness? Phillips (1966), Farina and Ring (1965), and Farina, Holland, and Ring (1966) have all demonstrated that in the absence of any behavioral evidence of disturbance, the mere knowledge that a man had been in a mental hospital led people to reject him. Loman and Larkin (1976), using standardized videotaped interviews, found that the label of "psychiatric problem" strongly decreased the stimulus person's rated social acceptance and social competence; the severity of behavior had little to no effect on the ratings.

Similar studies in more realistic situations generally document the labeling effects (Termerlin, 1968; Sushinsky & Werner, 1975; Caetano, 1974; Foster, Ysseldyke, & Reese, 1975; Gillung & Rucker, 1977), although the researchers were more interested in ratings of psychopathology than of social rejection.

Recent studies have demonstrated that when people attend strictly to behavior, the stigmatizing effects of a label seems to disappear (Pollack, Huntley, Allen, & Schwartz, 1976; Langer & Abelson, 1974). With increasing contact between patient and public, an emphasis on what a person *does* rather than what s/he *is* can result in a lessening of fears.

REACTIONS TO THE EX-PATIENT

"I'll tell you what the root of the problem is. I think farm animals have more dignity. You wonder after coming out if people can simply look into your face and see where you have been. Does it show?"

These are the words of a former mental patient from Massachusetts, written in a letter to Rosalynn Carter (1978). They express succinctly the newly released mental patient's fears of contact with others, the terrible dread that everyone will *know*, and that this knowledge will change others. The fears and expectations of the ex-mental patient can cause him to behave in a way that effects others' behavior toward him. Friends greeting the mental patient after his release may be overly considerate, cautious not to do or say anything that might cause upset; the latter, reacting with increasing tenseness and confusion, thus confirms the original need for delicate treatment in their view.

The Self-fulfilling Prophecy

Snyder, Tanke, and Berscheid (1977) have ingeniously demonstrated how a stereotype may lead to biased expectations and self-fulfilling behaviors, using a stereotype other than mental illness—that of "beautiful people are good people." In their experiment, men were given photos of attractive or unattractive women. Then they talked with different female "targets" (also subjects) over the telephone. The men were told that the target was the female in the photo. Both sides of the conversation were taped separately and later rated by naive judges. Those men who thought they were speaking to attractive women were rated by the judges as more sociable, interesting, humorous, and socially adept in their conversations than were those who thought their targets were unattractive. Not only did the behaviors of the men change when they thought they were speaking with attractive women, but the behaviors of their "target" females also changed to confirm the men's expectations. Namely, the conversations of the women "targets" who were assumed to be attractive manifested greater confidence, animation, and liking for their partners than did the conversations of women thought to be unattractive. Apparently this behavior pattern occurred simply as a result of the men's altered expectations; the targets had no idea that they were involved in a test of the stereotype.

Employment and Housing

Current and former mental patients are likely to encounter resistance when seeking employment. Weinstock and Haft (1974) obtained questionnaire data from approximately 35 industrial physicians about their firms' policies on hiring people with a variety of physical and psychiatric illnesses for managerial, clerical, or maintenance positions. Hypothetical patients, who were currently being treated with either medication or psychotherapy, were considered to be nonemployable for these various positions by 49% to 63% of the respondents. Prospective employees with previous psychiatric hospitalization for a nonpsychotic illness were judged by an average of 28% of the physicians to be not employable.

Ex-patients often face the practical problem of obtaining living accomodations. Page (1977) telephoned Ontario landlords who had advertised apartments or rooms in a local newspaper. When the caller identified herself as soon-to-be released mental patient, she was denied accommodation significantly more often than when no mention of mental illness was made.

The Extra Break

It would be a mistake to assume that *all* behaviors directed toward those who are mentally ill invariably lead to uncomfortable interactions and ultimate rejection. Quite the contrary ṣeems often true; increasingly positive attitudes toward the mental health system may induce people to make a particular effort at friendliness toward the labeled person. In effect, people may compensate for the negative stereotype by giving the former mental patient an "extra break" in initial interactions, a chance to prove the stereotype wrong. Two reports by Farina and his colleagues (1973, 1975) find just this extra break in a series of four experimental field studies.

In the first study (Farina, Felner, & Bondreau, 1973), 48 female department store workers were requested to interview a woman supposedly under consideration for a job at the store. The workers were told that the woman was part of a group of soon-to-be-discharged mental patients whom the store was considering for jobs, or they were told that she was a normal applicant included for comparison with the patient group. Additionally, when playing the part of the job applicant, the female confederate behaved in the appropriate manner (tense or relaxed) during the interview.

The researchers expected that prospective coworkers would view the mental patient applicant more negatively than her normal counterpart; but, surprisingly, this was not the case. The department store workers discriminated between the tense and relaxed applicants, but the mental patient applicant was not rated as being any different on adjustment, predictability, reliability, value, or trustworthiness; and the two "applicants" received equally high recommendations for hiring. In fact, the female subjects predicted that they themselves would get along *better* with the mental patient than with the normal applicant.

In an attempt to explain the divergence of this "extra break" from the stigma found to be associated in other studies with mental illness, the investigators pointed out one crucial difference: Prior studies had always used males rather than females as subjects. A series of three studies were directed at clarifying the hypothesized sex difference in interactions with the mentally ill (Farina et al., 1973; Farina & Hagelauer, 1975). It is possible to conclude from these studies that, at least when the perceiver is female, contact with the former mental patient does not necessarily lead to an endless cycle of expected disturbance and consequent rejection. Farina and Hagelauer (1975) propose that females may be more attentive than males to the actual behavioral content of the interaction, and thus are less susceptible to the biasing influence of a mental illness label. While this hypothesis has yet to be tested, it is in line with other research (Pollack et al., 1976; Langer & Abelson, 1974), which indicates that increased attention to the behavioral content of interactions may erase the stigma engendered by a history of mental illness.

SELF-PERCEPTION

A large part of the experience of mental hospitalization and, indeed, of many less drastic treatment approaches is the change it induces in the self-conceptions of the patient. The power of situations to change an individual's perception of himself is explained by *societal reaction theory*, or *labeling theory*. Society shapes and maintains behaviors associated with mental illness (Price & Denner, 1973; Weinberg, 1967). In essence, mental illness is not viewed as a series of observable behaviors that lead to community recognition and response. Rather, the community reponse itself perpetuates originally *transient* behavior patterns via the imputation of mental illness (see Scheff, 1966).

If one asks, "What regulates abnormal behavior?" then societal reaction factors are of major importance, especially if eliminating a label has the *effect* of reducing further deviant behavior. For example, most people would see witchcraft or possession by demons as incorrect causes of mental illness. Yet in Ceylon, such a belief has exceptionally beneficial effects. Immediately after the exorcism rituals, the mental illness label is removed and the person is expected to return quickly to normal life (Waxler, 1974). As a result, episodes of mental illness in Ceylon are typically brief and nonrecurring. In fact, the recovery rate was higher than in a comparable group in England treated under the medical model, which included extended labeling and elaborate aftercare. It was possible to rule out other factors, such as level of industrialization and life stress as alternative explanations, thus permitting the conclusion that it was the social reactions to mental illness that determined the differences.

Societal reaction theory has one distinct advantage. It offers a prescription for what the therapist and family can do, locally, to ease the confusion, guilt, and disturbance of an already troubled former mental patient. Namely, they can communicate the conviction that the illness is gone and that the former patient can function normally. On the preventive side, the mental health system can insure against exacerbation of deviant behaviors and feelings by changing society's expectations and assumptions about mental illness. Such changes would serve to head off the self-fulfilling prophecy and the "conversion" of the individual before a career of deviance begins.

In further support of the differential effects of societal expectations on the outcome of mental illness, Waxler (1974) cites two long-term follow-up studies of first-admission schizophrenics in England (Brown, Bone, Dalison, & Wing, 1966) and in Mauritius (Murphy & Raman, 1971), two cultures that vary in their beliefs about the mental illness "sick role." At the time of first admission, samples from both cultures were similar. However, at follow-up, the Mauritian sample, who received far inferior hospital treatment, had fared much better than the British sample once back in the community. Even within the British sample, there were outcome differences that Waxler attributed to differential societal labeling. Waxler suggested that the length of time a patient remains under aftercare treatment is correlated with the community's identification of the person as mentally ill. After five years, patients discharged from the hospital that provided the most complete and extensive aftercare services were either not significantly different or were significantly worse than the other British patients in the sample. These and other data lead Waxler to conclude: "Any or many casual factors . . . genetic, biochemical, familial . . . can cause the original symptoms, but it is the society's response that sustains the illness" (Waxler, 1974, p. 391).

Mordecai Rotenberg (1974) has suggested that the societal perpetuation of mental illness may operate primarily through the individual's self-labeling of deviance. He points out that Russian political prisoners in mental institutions are subjected to societal labels and treatment for insanity, but never come to identify themselves as mentally ill. Such people have alternative explanations for their deviant behaviors, explanations that can be maintained despite pressures to convince them they are "sick."

BELIEVING OTHERS BELIEVE

Regardless of whether current and former mental patients believe themselves to be mentally ill, other people may believe it. The changes in behavior and self-perception that arise when a person feels that his condition is public knowledge are multiple. Normal citizens in interaction with the mentally ill alter their cognitions and behaviors toward avoidance or placation, but their contributions are only half of the interaction. The mentally ill themselves, out of fear of mistreatment, may unintentionally contribute to their own stigmatization. In essence, the belief that one is publicly labeled as mentally ill may have an impact totally divorced from what others actually believe and do.

Apparently, the fear of stigmatization can lead the former mental patient to change his social behavior in a negative way and thus perpetuate his problem. There are, however other possible reactions with positive consequences. Instead of reacting with discomfort in the presence of others who "know," the person labeled as mentally ill may attempt to compensate for the anticipated negative reactions with increases in constructive, adjusted behavior.

It seems that the mental patient himself can initiate a self-fulfilling prophecy. Whether he performs poorly or well, he communicates something during his interaction with others. The question of what exactly it is he communicates, and how he does so, remains unanswered.

When a person believes he is mentally ill, when others believe he is mentally ill, and even when he merely *thinks* that others believe he is mentally ill, behaviors change. Usually these changes are in the direction of greater isolation, rejection, or maladjustment. In considering all the negative aspects associated with the label of mental illness, one is led to an interesting theoretical question regarding treatment. What would happen if disturbed individuals were simply told they were perfectly normal and confronted with demands to behave normally?

Though this notion bears a superficial resemblance to "throwing out the baby with the bath water," it is not totally without foundation. Increased demands on former patients for normal behavior do seem to be correlated with better levels of adjustment. In an excellent and thorough review of variables affecting the ex-mental patient's prognosis, Clum (1975) finds that any number of factors that place on the ex-patient greater demands for normal behavior (i.e., low toleration of deviance by family, more family responsibility, high social status) also lead to better social performance and improved symptomatology. When taken together with Waxler's (1974) cross-cultural comparisons and Doherty's (1975) work indicating better outcomes for persons who end up denying mental illness, these findings make the idea of this *normality therapy* less absurd.

In fact, two brave researchers (Chesno & Kilman, 1975) attempted just this therapy strategy with a number of patients newly committed to a state mental hospital. Experimental and control groups were matched for age, education, number of previous psychiatric admissions, and ratio of psychotic to nonpsychotic patients. After all subjects were given psychological tests, the control group patients returned to their wards. The experimental group was told that regulations required them to remain in the hospital for 30 days, although their test results indicated no mental illness. They were invited to join a group of patients who met daily "in order to allow healthy friendships in a place filled with so many sick people." In this session the experimenter reiterated his beliefs about the patients' normality and allowed discussion of the "sick" behavior seen in *other* patients.

Initially, the experimental group seemed confused by the denial of their mental illness; later, "bewilderment haltingly changed to expressions of relief and agreement" (Chesno & Kilman, 1975, p. 51). The critical dependent variable was, however, the number of patients in the experimental and control groups who were retained in the hospital after the 30-day observation period. Decisions to release made by staff members unaware of the patients' status in the study were as follows: Patients in the experimental normality therapy were released significantly more often than were controls; over 94% of the experimental group was discharged, compared to about 57% of the controls.

Thus, in some sense, normality therapy worked. It is unclear whether the efficacy of the therapy might have been because of a Hawthorne effect, since the experimental group was given special attention in their daily group meeting. Also, whether the normality therapy gains can be maintained when the former patient returns to family and society is unknown. Because of recent changes in guidelines for research on human subjects, these issues may remain unresolved. Even so, the question, "Why not treat the mental patient as perfectly normal?" seems less outrageous than it did at first glance.

IMPLICATIONS FOR MENTAL HEALTH PROFESSIONALS AND THE COURTS

Numerous research studies have been cited demonstrating that professionals are susceptible to the biases resulting from the mental illness label. Termerlin (1968), for example, reported that psychiatrists rated a healthy interviewee as psychotic after the interviewee was so labeled by a prestigious figure. Caetano (1974) replicated these findings, while Sushinsky and Wener (1975) found the label biasing effect in various types of mental health workers. These reports show that mental health professionals can be induced to base their diagnoses on irrelevant characteristics of an individual, such as the mental illness label. On the other hand, Langer and Abelson (1974) have shown that behaviorally oriented therapists are less susceptible to label biasing than are traditionally oriented analytic therapists. It appears that a therapist's belief system may have a greater effect on assessment than do the client's behaviors. This study and others, such as that of Pollack et al. (1976), demonstrate that it is important for professionals to concentrate on a client's current behavior rather than on a previously applied labels.

The attitudes of mental health workers toward mental illness are an important determinant of therapeutic success and, therefore, worthy of investigation. Rabkin (1975) has suggested that the medical model is being replaced by a psychosocial or public health model only among the more highly trained professionals and is rarely found among lower ranking personnel in psychiatric institutions. The literature indicates that psychiatrists, psychologists, and social workers differ from nurses, aides, and nonpsychiatric physicians in their opinions about mental illness. Cohen and Struening (1962) have observed that personnel with lower status are more restrictive and authoritarian in their attitudes, while those with advanced training are more aware of patients' strengths, more liberal and tolerant in their attitudes, and are more optimistic about prognosis. The implications of Ellsworth's (1965) investigation of the various attitudes and behaviors of hospital workers should give important direction to the training of mental health professionals and paraprofessionals. It appears that staff attitudes toward mental illness are largely shaped by such variables as age, education, and social class, rather than by occupational role, since job category is highly correlated with demographic characteristics (Rabkin, 1975).

The perpetuation of symptomatology, as outlined by societal reaction theory, can also be the result of our modern comprehensive and bureaucratic treatment system, a system the patient may be powerless to resist. Waxler (1974) outlines the "negotiation process" a potential patient undergoes with his family and mental health professionals. The usual outcome of this process is that the potential patient accepts the expected sick role and is reinforced for appropriate "patient behavior" by the treatment professional. The danger of this was demonstrated by Doherty (1975), who found that individuals who denied their mental illness had a better prognosis than did those with an accepting reaction. In this regard, treatment professionals should seriously consider the implications of the normality therapy proposed by Chesno and Kilman (1975) in their effort to eliminate the long-term negative effects of treatment or hospitalization. In addition, professionals should resist "trapping" the patient in the bureacracy of the treatment system, especially by extensive aftercare services; the patient should be given the opportunity to shed the sick role (Rosen & Holmes, 1978; Waxler, 1974).

The work by Goffman (1961) and Scheff (1966) has encouraged mental health personnel to examine the social dimensions of their professional activity and their role as agents of social control. This role is especially salient when mental health professionals are functioning as an arm of the judicial system. Every individual is supposed, legally, to be sane and mentally sound and to continue so until the contrary is shown. The state is then legally empowered, after due process, to segregate and isolate those whom psychiatrists find to be commitable because of mental illness. Once the court has decided that an individual is insane or "incompetent," then he or she is presumed legally to remain in that condition until the court determines that s/he has regained his/her sanity. Moreover, it is the individual's task to prove that he or she is again competent and sane.

Since mental hospital commitment and release are civil, not criminal, procedures, the same safeguards afforded criminals are not present in competency hearings. Courts, attorneys, and even mental health professionals operate under the assumption that people are committed in order to be treated, not punished. As a result, it is often impossible for the individual to assert his rights in court, and, as a patient, he loses virtually all of his rights to the hospital staff (Haeberle, 1978).

Although there are variations between states, the usual commitment procedure includes detention in a general hospital, observation and diagnosis by court-appointed psychiatrists, and the court commitment hearing (Caetano, 1974). Scheff (1966) has provided data that show that these procedures do not perform their intended screening function properly. For example, diagnostic interviews are often rapid, impersonal, and perfunctory for a variety of financial, ideological, and political reasons. In addition, a high proportion of individuals are in fact committed, leading Scheff to conclude that the presumption of illness, not health, is present. This raises the possibility that the commitment procedure itself labels the individual as mentally ill, and, as the data reviewed in this chapter suggest, such labeling can exert powerful influences on diagnostic outcome. The court-appointed mental health professional should therefore guard against the presumption of illness and attend to the individual's current behaviors rather than to past labeling or hospitalization.

REFERENCES

Baxtrom v. Herold, *United States Reports.* 1966, *383*, 107.

Bentz, W. K., & Edgerton, J. W. Consensus on attitudes toward mental illness. *Archives of General Psychiatry,* 1970, *22*, 468–473.

Berger, D. Staff opinion survey. An unpublished factor analyzed attitude scale arising out of the Medical Audit Research. Perry Point, Maryland: Veterans Administration Hospital, 1962.

Brown, G., Bone, M., Dalison, B., & Wing, J. *Schizophrenia and social care.* London: Oxford University Press, 1966.

Caetano, D. F. Labeling theory and the presumption of mental illness in diagnosis: An experimental design. *Journal of Health and Social Behavior,* 1974, *15*, 253–260.

Carter, R. We have to stop running away. *McCall's,* 1978 (June), *105*, 121, 198, 200, 202.

Chesno, F. A., & Kilman, P. R. Societal labeling and mental illness. *Journal of Community Psychology,* 1975 *3*, 49–52.

Clausen, J., & Yarrow, M. R. (Eds.) The impact of mental illness on the family. *Journal of Social Issues,* 1955, *11*.

Clum, G. A. Intrapsychic variables and the patient's environment as factors in prognosis. *Psychological Bulletin*, 1973, *82*, 413–431.

Cohen, J., & Struening, E. L. Opinions about mental illness in the personnel of two large mental hospitals. *Journal of Abnormal and Social Psychology*, 1962, *64*, 349–360.

Crocetti, G. M., Spiro, H. E., & Siassi, I. Are the ranks closed? Attitudinal social distance and mental illness. *American Journal of Psychiatry*, 1971, *127*, 41–47.

Cumming, J., & Cumming, E. *Closed ranks*. Cambridge: Harvard University Press, 1957.

D'Arcy, C., & Brockman, J. Changing public recognition of symptoms: Blackfoot revisited. *Journal of Health and Social Behavior*, 1976, *17*, 302–310.

Doherty, E. G. Labeling effects in psychiatric hospitalization: A study of diverging patterns of inpatient self-labeling processes. *Archives of General Psychiatry*, 1975, *32*, 562–568.

Doll, W. Home is not sweet anymore. *MH (Mental Hygiene)*, 1975, *59*, 22–24.

Elinson, J., Padella, E., & Perkins, M. *Public image of mental health services*. New York: Mental Health Materials Center, 1967.

Ellsworth, R. B. A behavioral study of staff attitudes toward mental illness. *Journal of Abnormal Psychology*, 1965, *70*, 194–200.

Ennis, B. *Prisoners of psychiatry*. New York: Harcourt Brace Jovanovich, 1972.

Farina, A., Felner, R. D., & Bondreau, L. A. Reactions of workers to male and female mental patient job applicants. *Journal of Consulting and Clinical Psychology*, 1973, *41*, 363–372.

Farina, A., & Hagelauer, H. D. Sex and mental illness. The generosity of females. *Journal of Consulting and Clinical Psychology*, 1975, *43*, 122.

Farina, A., Holland, C. H., & Ring, K. Role of stigma and set in interpersonal interaction. *Journal of Abnormal Psychology*, 1966, *71*, 421–428.

Farina, A., & Ring, K. The influence of perceived mental illness on interpersonal relations. Journal of Abnormal Psychology, 1965, *70*, 47–51.

Foster, G. G., Ysseldyke, J. E., & Reese, J. H. I wouldn't have seen it if I hadn't believed it. *Exceptional Children*, 1975, *41*, 469–473.

Freeman, H., & Simmons, O. Feelings of stigma among relatives of former mental patients. *Social Problems*, 1961, *8*, 312–321.

Gillung, T. B., & Rucker, C. N. Labels and teacher expectations. *Exceptional Children*, 1977, *43*, 464–465.

Goffman, E. *Asylums: Essays on the social situation of mental patients and other inmates*. Chicago: Aldine, 1961.

Goldstein, K. M., & Blackman, S. Generalizations regarding deviant groups. *Psychological Reports*, 1975, *37*, 278.

Grandison, R. J. *College students' attitudes toward stigmatized work partners*. Unpublished manuscript, University of Georgia, 1978.

Haeberle, E. J. *The sex atlas*. New York: The Seabury Press, 1978.

Herbert, W. Stigma, she said . . . but some aren't so sure. *APA Monitor, 9* (1), 4, 22.

Kirk, S. A. The psychiatric sick role and rejection. *Journal of Nervous and Mental Disease,* 1975, *161,* 318–325.

Langer, E. J., & Abelson, R. P. A patient by any other name . . . : Clinician group difference in labeling bias. *Journal of Consulting and Clinical Psychology,* 1974, *42* 4–9.

Leavitt, M. The discharge crisis: The experience of families of psychiatric patients. *Nursing Research,* 1975, *24,* 33–40.

Loman, L. A., & Larkin, W. E. Rejection of the mentally ill: An experiment in labeling. *Sociological Quarterly,* 1976, *17,* 555–560.

Murphy, H. B. M., & Raman, A. C. The chronicity of schizophrenia in indigenous tropical peoples: Results of 12-year follow-up survey in Mauritius. *British Journal of Psychiatry,* 1971, *118,* 489–497.

Nunnally, J. C. *Popular conceptions of mental health: Their development and change.* New York: Holt, Rinehart, & Winston, 1961.

Olmstead, D. W., & Durham, K. Stability of mental health attitudes: A semantic differential study. *Journal of Health and Social Behavior,* 1976, *17,* 35–44.

Page, S. Effects of the mental illness label in attempts to obtain accomodation. *Canadian Journal of Behavioral Science,* 1977, *9,* 85–90.

Page, S., & Yates, E. Effects of situational role demands on measurement of attitudes about mental illness. *Journal of Consulting and Clinical Psychology,* 1975, *43,* 115.

Parsons, T. *The social system.* New York: Free Press of Glencoe (MacMillan), 1951.

Perlman, S. The college student views his mental health experience. *Journal of American College Health Association,* 1966, *14* (4), 277–283.

Phillips, D. L. Public identification and acceptance of the mentally ill. *American Journal of Public Health, 1966, 56,* 755–763.

Pollack, S., Huntley, D. Allen, J. G., & Schwartz, S. The dimensions of stigma: The social situation of the mentally ill person and the male homosexual. *Journal of Abnormal Psychology,* 1976, *85,* 105–112.

Price, R. H., & Denner, B. *The making of a mental patient.* New York: Holt, Reinhart and Winston, Inc., 1973.

Rabkin, J. G. The role of attitudes toward mental illness in evaluation of mental health programs. In M. Guttentag & E. L. Struening (Eds.), *Handbook of evaluation research* (Vol. 2). Beverly Hills, CA: Sage Publications, Inc., 1975.

Rachlin, S., Pam, A., & Milton, J. Civil liberties versus involuntary hospitalization. *American Journal of Psychiatry,* 1975, *132,* 189–191.

Rosen, C. E., & Holmes, S. Pharmacist's impact on chronic psychiatric outpatients in community mental health. *American Journal of Hospital Pharmacy,* 1978, *35,* 704–708.

Rotenberg, M. Self-labeling: A missing link in the societal reaction theory of deviance. *Sociological Review,* 1974, *22,* 335–354.

Sarbin, T. R. & Mancuso, J. C. Paradigms and moral judgment: Improper conduct is not disease. *Journal of Consulting and Clinical Psychology,* 1972, *39,* 1–5.

Scheff, T. J. *Being mentally ill: A sociological theory.* Chicago: Aldine, 1966.

Schwartz, C. C., Meyers, J. K., & Astrachan, B. M. Psychiatric labeling and the rehabilitation of the mental patient. *Archives of General Psychiatry,* 1974, *31,* 329–334.

Skuse, D. H. Attitudes to the psychiatric outpatient clinic *British Medical Journal,* 1975, *3,* 469–471.

Snyder, M., Tanke, E. D., & Berscheid, E. Social perception and interpersonal behavior: On the self-fulfilling nature of social stereotypes. *Journal of Personality and Social Psychology,* 1977, *35,* 656–666.

Spiro, H. R., Siassi, I., & Crocetti, G. The issue of contact with the mentally ill. *American Journal of Public Health,* 1974, *64,* 876–879.

Star, S. A. *The public's idea about mental illness.* Chicago: National Opinion Research Center, University of Chicago, 1955.

Steadman, H. Follow-up on Baxtrom patients returned to hospital for the criminally insane. *American Journal of Psychiatry,* 1973, *130,* 317.

Steadman, H., & Cocozza, J. *Careers of the clinically insane: Excessive social controls of deviance.* Lexington, Mass.: Lexington Books Co., 1974.

Steadman, H., & Kevels, M. A. The community adjustment of the Baxtrom patients: 1966–1970. *American Journal of Psychiatry,* 1972, *129,* 80.

Sushinsky, L. W., & Wener, R. Distorting judgments of mental health: Generality of the labeling bias effect. *Journal of Nervous and Mental Disease,* 1975, *161,* 82–89.

Termerlin, M. K. Suggestion effects in psychiatric diagnosis. *Journal of Nervous and Mental Disease,* 1968, *147,* 349–353.

Tringo, J. L. The hierarchy of preference toward disability groups. *The Journal of Special Education,* 1970, *4,* 295–306.

Waxler, N. E. Culture and mental illness: A social labeling perspective. *Journal of Nervous and Mental Disease,* 1974, *159,* 379–395.

Weinberg, S. K. *The sociology of mental disorder: Analyses and readings in psychiatric sociology.* Chicago: Aldine Publishing Company, 1967.

Weinstock, M., & Haft, J. I. The effect of illness on employment opportunities. *Archives Environmental Health,* 1974, *29,* 79–83.

Whatley, C. Social attitudes toward discharged mental patients. *Social Problems,* 1958-1959, *6,* 313–320.

White, W. C., McAdoo, W. G., & Phillips, L. Social competence and outcome of hospitalization: A preliminary report. *Journal of Health and Social Behavior,* 1974, *15,* 261–266.

Wilkins, J. E. *A semantic differential investigation of children's attitudes towards three stigmatized groups.* Paper presented at the meeting of Eastern Psychological Association, Washington, D. C., Spring 1978.

Chapter 3

THE INVOLUNTARY PATIENT:
Empirical Literature from
a Clinical Viewpoint

James Spensley, M.D.
Paul H. Werme, M.A.

Involuntary psychiatric treatment, until recently synonymous with commitment to state psychiatric hospitals, originated in English common law that empowered the king to act as guardian of "idiots and lunatics." The mentally ill at that time were frequently neglected, confined in poor houses and jails, beaten, ridiculed, robbed, and excluded from their communities. A benign hospital setting (asylum) for these individuals was viewed as a progressive and humane alternative to the neglect and degradation from which they were generally suffering.

In the early 1800s in the United States, Dorothea Dix headed a reform movement that campaigned for "moral treatment" to be made available to all citizens. This movement culminated in the development of a state system of public psychiatric hospitals. *In re Oakes* (1845) found civil commitment applicable to the mentally ill for their own benefit. Unfortunately, over a century has now passed without substantial empirical support for the premise that commitment is beneficial. Together with current social concerns about civil rights in general, this situation has increased professional and public objections to the commitment process and its underlying assumptions. A consequence has been new legislation and major legal precedents altering the legal process of commitment. Most recently, the U.S. Supreme Court (*Addington* v. *Texas,* 1979) set a new standard for involuntary commitment in rejecting the standard of evidence used for criminal cases, but requiring more certainty than a simple preponderence of evidence for commitment. In this ruling, the Court for the first time distinguished between the therapeutic intent of hospitalization and the punitive intent of imprisonment.

Four major observations are often made concerning involuntary treatment: (1) Involuntary treatment may be essential to provide for effective medical and psychiatric care of serious mental illness. Advocates of this position cite instances of neglect particularly of severely depressed or psychotic individuals because of legal restrictions on commitment. (2) Involuntary treatment may be ineffective; the effects may not be positive and, on occasion, may even be detrimental. Evidence cited for this latter concern comes from reports of destructive effects of prolonged institutionalization and serious, possibly even irreversible, side effects of some psychotropic drugs. (3) Involuntary treatment may be overutilized. Criteria for distinguishing among mental illness, criminality, social deviance, and normality are weak or nonexistent. Psychiatric diagnosis has had poor reliability and validity and so is suspect. Also, criteria for beginning and ending involuntary treatment are vague and subjective. The charge of inappropriate social control is a part of this concern. (4) Involuntary treatment often ignores due process and violates basic civil rights. This review will examine empirical literature relating to these four issues.

INVOLUNTARY TREATMENT ESSENTIAL

Numerous opinion papers repeat the general assumption made by most physicians that involuntary treatment is necessary to care properly for serious mental illness. The only data supporting the necessity of involuntary treatment are case reports documenting a variety of disasterous outcomes when individual patients were able to refuse treatment recommendations (Chodoff, 1976; Kirstein & Weissman, 1976; Treffert, 1975). Even the value of hospital treatment for the voluntary psychiatric patient remains unestablished despite extensive attempts (Erickson, 1975). Erickson carefully documents how large-scale studies involving several hospital units have proved costly, impractical, and inapplicable to small, acute treatment settings. The difficulty in controlling for nonspecific factors, such as program expectations and staff energy and enthusiasm (attention-placebo effects), and an overemphasis on form rather than content of treatment further complicate studies of hospital treatment. Treatment outcome may also be profoundly influenced by who is included in the treatment sample. Leon and Micklin (1978) found that interpersonal factors exert a significant influence on the process of assigning cases to alternate types of care (hospital, outpatient, and no treatment).

It is striking that no major research has defined with any precision when and where involuntary treatment is essential. No study has compared involuntary treatment with no treatment. Erickson's (1975) recommendation that hospital outcome studies define small subgroups and apply differential treatments could be fruitfully applied to involuntary treatment. Carrying out this recommendation requires a careful separation of different mental illnesses and subsequent use of specific treatment methods for specific types of involuntary patients.

One form of treatment (often thought to require hospitalization) shows considerable promise. Many reviewers of literature on psychopharmacolgy (American Psychiatric Association, 1975; Bielski & Friedel, 1976; Zovodmick, 1976) concur that major psychoactive drugs are superior to placebo in the treatment of major affective illness and schizophrenia. No other form of treatment has been so carefully researched. What is needed now are longitudinal studies of specific conditions where specific types of psychoactive drugs are used followed by various outcome measures for patients who are initially involuntary.

INVOLUNTARY TREATMENT INEFFECTIVE

Perhaps the most complete review of scientific evidence inimical to involuntary treatment is presented by Ennis and Litwack (1974), who cite numerous studies from the psychiatric literature. They concluded that the empirical data reveal a complete lack of reliability and validity of psychiatric judgments about diagnosis, need for hospitalization, and treatment and effects of hospitalization and treatment.

Lack of data to support reliability and validity of psychiatric judgment does not define when and where involuntary treatment is ineffective. Most studies of therapy in general have been inconclusive because of inadequate methodology. Even in the area of diagnostic reliability and validity, new data prevents sweeping conclusions.

Recent research provides new evidence for valid and reliable psychiatric judgment in some circumstances. Validity and reliability require new diagnostic criteria that employ careful definition of terms, observable symptoms, signs, duration of course of illness, and levels of severity of impairment. Feighner, Robins, Guze, Woodruff, Winokur, and Munoz (1972) described a group of diagnostic criteria of high statistical reliability for use in psychiatric research. Robins, Gentry, Munoz, and Marten (1977) utilized these criteria in an outcome study and reported these diagnoses were 84% accurate and 88% reliable.

Spitzer, Endicott, and Robins (1978) reported high reliability of diagnostic judgments using criteria somewhat different from those described by Feighner et al. (1972). Spitzer, Forman, and Nee (1979) reported fairly high interrater reliability in field trials of a new diagnostic manual based on this research. Reliable and valid diagnoses may be the first step in separating patients who benefit from involuntary treatment from patients for whom involuntary treatment is ineffective.

There is little doubt that involuntary treatment has the potential for harmful effects. There is much current concern about *tardive dyskinesia,* a delayed neurologic side effect of neuroleptic drugs, which may be irreversible (Casey, 1978; Tarsy, Granacker, & Bralower, 1977). All medication carries the risk of mild and serious toxic side effects. An *institutionalization syndrome* has been postulated as a harmful effect of prolonged hospitalization, but persistent methodological problems in studying this syndrome make firm conclusions impossible (Erickson, 1975; Honigfield & Gillis, 1966). Other possible harmful effects include those described by Hadley and Strupp (1976), who reviewed the many undesired outcomes associated with various psychological therapies.

INVOLUNTARY TREATMENT OVERUTILIZED

Most empirical studies of involuntary treatment fall under this category. Particular points include criteria for involuntary treatment, the proportion of mentally ill patients who can be treated voluntarily, and details of the process of treatment itself.

There is considerable debate and uncertainty about the criteria for involuntary treatment. Historically, Isaac Ray in the 18th century proposed three purposes for the confinement of the insane. These are: (1) restoration of health, (2) comfort and well-being, and (3) security of society (summarized by Derschowitz, 1971). These broad purposes are still the goals that are defended by most supporters of commitment, yet not one of these three outcomes has substantial empirical support.

Restoration of health is receiving increased emphasis in the current medical literature. This purpose offers the most hope for empircial study, given the use of valid and reliable diagnoses, specific treatment methods, and outcome measures. Chodoff (1976) succinctly described criteria for involuntary treatment: (1) the presence of mental illness, (2) a serious disruption of functioning together with an impairment of judgment to such a degree that the individual is incapable of considering his condition and making decisions about it in his own interest, and (3) the need for care and treatment. Stone (1975) emphasized that psychiatry has the ability to concern itself with the presence of clinical states and to describe those that require drastic intervention for appropriate treatment to occur. He observed that this does not involve prediction of future events, but rather rests on the observation of the usual course of these clinical states and the effects of clinical intervention.

Major barriers to effective research on involuntary treatment arise when one considers Ray's latter purposes: comfort and well-being of the insane and security of society. Comfort and well-being are subjective and probably impossible to operationalize as a criterion. The evaluation of the security of society purpose is a task beyond the competence of mental health professionals and hospitals.

Stone (1975) believes that hospitalization in the case of suicidal or homicidal behavior is not for the purpose of preventing that behavior, but rather for the purpose of treating the underlying disorder. Clarifying the purpose of hospitalization is especially important, because research studies have concluded that predictions of suicide or violence have very low validity and treatment interventions for the prevention of these behaviors are generally unsuccessful.

Greenberg (1974) concluded in a comprehensive review that empirical studies reveal suicide to be an infrequent event prone to overprediction. He recommended limitations on the duration and extent of involuntary intervention in the treatment of suicide, since data are lacking to support the belief that civil commitment can in fact prevent suicide except during the first few days following an attempt. Light (1973) reported the lack of demonstrated effectiveness of suicide prevention centers and concluded that professionals have no demonstrable expertise in the area. Light contrasted professional efforts with the nonprofessional suicide prevention effort in England (the Samaritans), where preliminary studies noted reduction in suicide rates in association with the presence of these centers. But a more recent study (Jennings, Barraclough, & Moss, 1978) found Samaritan centers had no effect on the suicide rate in Britain. Nonetheless, the effect of suicidal behavior on medical decision-making does not seem to be influenced by the empirical data. Most striking is a report by Kristein and Weissman (1976) of suicidal patients who were not hospitalized. They described a recurrent dilemma for psychiatric residents between medical responsibility, on one hand, and social control on the other hand, when a suicidal individual refuses voluntary admission. Lacking legal license to treat all suicidal patients, the residents were confused as to who to treat. The authors imply that this produces a situation in which some seriously disturbed patients did not receive appropriate treatment.

Steadman has reviewed the evidence on prediction of dangerousness in this volume. Despite these data, physician preoccupation with dangerousness is widespread. Kumasaka, Stokes, and Gupta (1972) described a controlled clinical evaluation of involuntary hospitalization at Bellevue in New York City, which revealed that protection of the patient and dangerousness to self or others were the two major working criteria for involuntary hospitalization. Yet, Albers, Pasewark, and Smith (1976) found that, in most cases of involuntary treatment in a Western state hospital, the breaking of residual rules was used by psychiatrists as the basis for the determination of dangerousness. Albers et al. (1976) suggested that psychiatrists label patients as dangerous because they act as agents of social control. This viewpoint is consistent with a public opinion survey (Bentz & Edgerton, 1970), where 70% of the respondents believed the primary purpose of the psychiatric hospital was social control. It is clear that the benefits of involuntary treatment cannot be demonstrated as long as unknown numbers of patients are included in involuntary treatment samples where the prime purpose for their inclusion is care and comfort or security of society rather than treatment.

There are sparse data to support the alternative position, namely, that most mentally ill individuals can be voluntarily admitted. The attitude of staff appears to be a key factor in this process. Schwartz and Dumpman (1972) reported 81% of 1,357 mental health center patients in Pennsylvania were voluntary admissions when staff attempted to persuade all patients to enter the hospital on a voluntary basis. Other public hospital reports include Sata and Goldenberg (1977) where 70% of county hospital patients in Seattle were voluntary, and Spensley, Barter, Werme, and Langsley (1974) where 80% of mental health center patients in Sacramento were voluntary. In addition, according to a recent news item (Involuntary hospitalization, May, 1978, p. 1), 83% of 501 private patients in Springfield, Illinois were voluntary. Despite these data and a position paper by the American Psychiatric Association (1973, p. 392) supporting voluntary admission, it is common to find both state and local psychiatric hospitals where a striking percentage, even a majority, of admissions are involuntary. One report (Teknekron, 1978) documents marked differences in the involuntary admission rates of county mental health programs in California.

One study directly suggests some staff prefer restrictive admission procedures. Gilboy (1977) described the process of informal admission: no written application is required and individuals may leave on demand. In contrast, formal voluntary admission requires some notification of intent to leave and provides staff with legal methods to prevent voluntary patients from leaving the hospital against advice. Gilboy discovered that in six states where both procedures were available, staff were more likely to use formal rather than informal voluntary admission. He described how staff justified this behavior by expressing concern that a large percentage of voluntary patients may leave precipitously, and concluded that these fears appeared unfounded on the basis of the limited data he had available. Albers et al. (1976, p. 132) have proposed that ". . . psychiatrists, as a group, experience considerable difficulty in managing their own aggressive feelings." Unfortunately, this observation is seriously limited by the lack of relevant data. A number of authors (Dickes, Simons, & Weisfogel, 1970; Grasz & Grossman, 1964; Raines & Rohrer, 1960) have identified how, in general, personal bias or unconscious conflict of the psychiatrist may result in observations and judgments that are more consistent with the psychiatrist's personality than with the patient's problems.

Multiple variables besides staff attitudes, such as available beds, financial incentives, local criteria for admission, other resources, legal restrictions, percentage of minorities, and local public policy, complicate the question of what constitutes an appropriate amount of involuntary treatment.

The Treatment Process

Research on the involuntary treatment process will be discussed with regard to three distinct though overlapping categories: diagnostic and emergency treatment (48–72 hours), acute treatment (2–6 weeks), and prolonged involuntary treatment (1 year). This division permits a degree of task analysis and provides for the need to recognize associated differences in the degree of loss of freedom and the concomitant requirement for differing degrees of protection of civil rights. Much of the literature assumes that involuntary treatment is a single phenomenon, and this assumption inhibits both precise discussion and careful research.

Diagnostic and Emergency Treatment Period (48–72 hours).   An initial period of involuntary assessment and treatment may serve several purposes: (1) It provides for a period of observation and evaluation leading to a diagnosis; (2) it permits emergency life-saving treatment to be initiated; and (3) it provides time to establish rapport and form a therapeutic alliance that can lead to further voluntary treatment. No empirical study has examined these purposes directly. Indirect evidence supporting these purposes can be found in rapid discharge or agreement to voluntary treatment in a large proportion of involuntary admissions. Spensley et al. (1974) found that 81%, and a recent report to the California legislature (Teknekron, 1978) found that 61%, of involuntary admissions were discharged or became voluntary within three days.

Acute Treatment Period (2–6 weeks). Following the diagnostic and emergency treatment period, patients should be classified into four categories. A majority of involuntary patients will either be, firstly, competent and enter into voluntary treatment or, secondly, found to be not mentally ill. A small number may be categorized as incompetent and unlikely to respond to treatment (e.g., chronic organic brain syndrome). These individuals need some form of guardianship. Finally, individuals with serious mental illness and a likelihood of significant improvement as a result of treatment may require a trial of treatment.

During the acute treatment period, a majority of involuntary patients would be expected to improve sufficiently to make an informed judgment about refusing further treatment or contintuing on a voluntary basis. This is supported by 1976 data for the entire state of California, where 22,562 patients were treated involuntarily for more than 3 days, and 75% of these became voluntary patients or were discharged within 17 days (Teknekron, 1978).

Other studies comparing involuntary and voluntary patients provide data in support of the appropriateness of ready access to an acute treatment setting for patients whose mental state impairs their decision-making process. Spensley et al. (1974) reported on all involuntary patients discharged from a county hospital during 1971. The involuntary stay was short (average 3 days), and a majority (68%) of involuntary patients recommended for ongoing treatment voluntarily accepted outpatient treatment. Lengthy involuntary treatment was rarely needed (8%). Sata and Goldenberg (1977) reported on a group of involuntary patients where more than half were discharged in 10 days, and the treatment of the involuntary patients was judged to be equal to or better than that of voluntary counterparts. A recent satisfaction survey (Spensley, Edwards, & White, 1980) found no significant differences between voluntary and involuntary patients: 92% of the total believed clinical staff were helpful, and 79% were highly or moderately satisfied with the treatment they received. The small number of dissatisfied patients were, however, almost all involuntary.

Clinical Psychiatry News ("Involuntary hospitalization said to protect patient" May, 1978, p. 1) reported a study of involuntary patients in a private general hospital where a significant percentage eventually shifted to voluntary status. This study by Bornstein found that involuntary patients (N=85) tended to be from lower socioeconomic levels more often than voluntary counterparts (N=416) and that the involuntary patients had less familial support, a greater degree of socially disruptive behavior, and a longer stay in the hospital. Higher rates of involuntary treatment in California were associated with counties having larger percentages of blacks, but not with larger poverty populations (Teknekron, 1978).

Two other studies compare voluntary and involuntary patients in a state hospital setting. Zwerling, Karasu, Plutchik, and Kellerman (1975) studied 78 involuntary patients and compared them with 47 voluntary patients. Involuntary patients were commonly never married, had antisocial attitudes and behaviors, and were frequently brought to the hospital by police. Their symptoms commonly included: belligerence, negativism, anger, agitation, hyperactivity, and assaultiveness. Voluntary couterparts tended to be more often depressed and preoccupied with somatic concerns. Gove and Fain (1977) found committed patients had fewer social and economic resources and more serious impairments. The type of hospitalization (voluntary or involuntary) seemed to be primarily a consequence of the nature and severity of the individual disorder. Both voluntary and involuntary groups received comparable treatment and both experienced some improvement in instrumental roles, but not in interpersonal roles. The slight improvement differences favored the committed patients. Gove and Fain concluded that the commitment process had no long-term detrimental effects.

In summary, studies of short-term involuntary treatment of patients in community settings and longer treatment of involuntary patients in state hospital settings reveal that a significant number of involuntary patients will quickly accept voluntary treatment when given the opportunity, and involuntary patients tend to improve at about the same rate as their voluntary counterparts. All studies indicate that involuntary patients tend to have few social supports. Severity or types of symptoms (i.e., belligerence, anger, agitation) seem to be key factors in differentiating involuntary from voluntary patients.

A frequent warning in the medical literature about limiting involuntary treatment is that large numbers of disturbed mentally ill patients will not have access to appropriate medical care. Urmer (1975) described the effects of the implementation of California's 1969 Mental Health Law limiting involuntary treatment, and he concluded that a new service delivery system developed in response to the new legislation resulted in a greater emphasis on crisis intervention, improved availability of direct services, and increased community awareness and concern regarding mental health. Thus, in this study of one state, limiting of involuntary treatment was not found to be associated with adverse consequences.

Prolonged Treatment/Rehabilitation (1 year).   The research literature provides less evidence about the effects of prolonged involuntary treatment. The studies that are available generally examine narrow aspects of long-term involuntary treatment and are not applicable to the general question of benefits.

Recent studies of committed patients suggest that most individuals do return to the community. Tomellerri, Lakshiminarayanan, and Herjanic (1977) reported on a community mental health population in Missouri (N=2404). Only 4% were legally committed (N=93). In this population, blacks and individuals over 70 were overrepresented. Schizophrenia was the most frequent diagnosis, and one-third of the patients were hospitalized for more than 3 months. A majority of those committed were eventually able to return to the community, one-fifth being placed in boarding or nursing homes. Previous and subsequent admissions for a large percentage of committed patients who had multiple hospitalizations were predominately voluntary. Peele, Chodoff, and Taub (1974) described individuals involuntarily hospitalized in the District of Columbia. Three-fourths of the involuntary patients improved in their ability to live in the community as a result of their hospital experience.

Other studies emphasize a high rate of inappropriate commitment. Using the case study method, Perr (1974) described nine cases where involuntary hospitalization was imposed; he found three did not merit involuntary intervention. Steadman (1972) described a state mental hospital where a group of criminally insane patients was transferred against medical advice. This group was compared with an otherwise similar group of patients transferred with medical recommendations. The group transferred against medical advice faired better than expected and was released at a rate higher than the approved transfer group, and had only slightly higher criminal activity following release. The success of both groups led Steadman to raise serious questions about the ability of psychiatrists to predict need for involuntary hospitalization. Allen (1977) participated in a court ordered review of 600 patients held in a maximum security facility for the criminally insane in Ohio. He personally evaluated 111 of these patients and found that 80% did not meet criteria for involuntary hospitalization in a maximum security facility. He concluded that many patients are incarcerated inappropriately in state hospitals, particularly hospitals for the criminally insane.

An opposing conclusion was reached by Zwerling, Conte, Plutchik, and Karasu (1979) who reported an attempt to reduce commitments through the use of a "no commitment week." Based on the failure of their procedures to alter the commitment rate at one hospital, the authors concluded that inappropriate commitment was not a significant problem. The methodology in this study is open to serious question, however, since a few simple procedures are unlikely to alter a complex social system, particularly when applied in such a brief time-period.

One study reported outstanding success with prolonged involuntary treatment. Rappenport (1974) described a group of offenders who were referred to a special program in a psychiatric treatment facility. The recidivism rate of patients who completed the entire program and were released with staff recommendation was found to be only 7%, a figure that compared very favorably with a national recidivism rate of 65% and an initial recidivism rate of 81% for patients recommended for commitment at this facility but not committed. This careful study deserves replication in the area of involuntary treatment of nonoffenders. It does provide some support for the position that prolonged enforced treatment can be beneficial.

Involuntary treatment also occurs in nonhospital settings. Spensley and Werme (1979) reported a preliminary study of over 1,000 conservatees (*conservatorship* is a one-year renewable form of guardianship utilized in California and some other Western states). While only 10% of subjects were living in state hospitals, there was a steady overall increase in the incidence of conservatorships each year, indicating increasing community reliance on this form of legal control. About half of the individuals completed their conservatorship in one year or less, but no data could be found that characterized the treatment of conservatees. Lamb and Goertzel (1977) described a study of chronic mentally disordered patients where 64% had not had a recent hospitalization. Most of these patients were able to live in nonsegregated, noninstitutional settings. This finding suggests that most chronic mental patients function better than professionals believe possible. The U.S. Supreme Court application of the principle of the least restrictive alternative for the care of the mentally ill in *Donaldson* v. *O'Conner* (1975) is likely to give increasing importance to involuntary treatment in outpatient settings.

Naturally, application of the least restrictive alternative is severely limited by whether or not alternatives to hospitalization actually exist in the community. For example, Deasy and Steele (1976) studied 369 Florida state hospital patients facing release under a new community mental health act. Eighty percent of these patients were over 45 and 55% were black. Twenty-five per cent were incontinent, 20% required nursing assistance eating, and 40% required nursing care facilities, yet no nursing beds were available within the community. The authors emphasized that changing the law did not provide for adequate treatment alternatives for patients who might be discharged.

Current data are insufficient to confirm any benefits from prolonged involuntary treatment. The data simply define the patient population by certain characteristics, such as single, black, poor, regressed, angry, and prone to antisocial behaviors. Prolonged involuntary treatment seems to be overutilized and community alternatives are often severely limited.

INVOLUNTARY TREATMENT AND NEGLECT OF CIVIL RIGHTS

The act of committing an individual to treatment should be understood first and foremost as a legal process. Care and/or treatment are processes in and of themselves that may follow the act of commitment and that vary extensively according to the individual involved, the available resources and statutes relating to civil commitment. Excellent reviews of the subject by the American Bar Foundation (1974) and the Mental Health Law Project (1977) are the most thorough and comprehensive yet available for the interested reader. The legal issues reviewed here are those where empirical data are available; defining incapacity, the effect of the presence of counsel, and studies of the hearing process itself.

Defining *incapacity* is often complex and difficult even with voluntary treatment. Owens (1977) described how cognitive disorientation may limit an individual's capacity to make choices. He pointed out that many voluntary patients are in fact not capable of giving fully informed voluntary consent for psychiatric treatment and hospitalization. Fluctuating cognitive and emotional impairment are the rule rather than the exception in most serious mental disorders. Therefore, assessment of objective behaviors (such as the California standard, gravely disabled) represent a more useful guide to incapacity since its serious effects can be identified (Teknekron, 1978). Thus, a more objective basis for expert testimony can be provided. Wilbert, Jorstad, Loren, and Wirrer (1976) described a method to determine grave disability based on occupational therapy tasks, and tested this method with patients in several diagnostic categories. This method indicated that grave disability was predictable using a mental status examination for patients with organic brain syndrome, but not for patients with chronic schizophrenia, and even less so with other diagnostic categories.

The presence of counsel may significantly alter the hearing process. Hiday (1977) and Wenger and Fletcher (1968) found a significant relationship between absence of counsel and the likelihood of commitment. Other studies, however, show that counsel may adopt a perfunctory role (Maisel, 1970; Shah, 1974).

One study evaluated the importance of legal counsel following commitment. Epstein and Lowinger (1975) studied 50 patients newly admitted to a state hospital, questioning them about their felt need for legal aid. In the opinion of the authors, nearly all patients responded in a meaningful manner, and half indicated the need for legal aid.

These individuals were generally older, involuntary, previously hospitalized, and classified as paranoid. A bit more than 2/5 of the involuntary patients wanted legal aid in assisting them to get out of the
hospital. Legal assistance was also requested in order to insure proper
management of some individuals' assets and for assistance to resolve
problems of divorce, tenant relations, and custody of children.

Empirical data about the hearing process were reported by Albers
and Pasewark (1974), who studied 300 consecutive involuntary hospital petitions. In 98% of the cases, the court concurred with psychiatric
recommendations. Mean and median time for such proceedings were
9.2 and 8.0 minutes respectively. These results point to: (1) presumption of illness on the part of the court; (2) an overreliance on psychiatric findings; and (3) a deprivation of rights of potential patients. In
many states, the individual may even be excused from the hearing
process based upon some notion of traumatizing effects of the hearing.
There is no empirical evidence to support this belief, and the presence
of the individual might be beneficial (American Bar Foundation,
1974). Despite sparse data, the evidence suggests neglect of civil rights
in several areas where research studies have examined specific issues.

SUMMARY AND POLICY IMPLICATIONS

A constructive beginning toward reconciliation of the diverse
viewpoints of physicians, lawyers, and legislators in the area of involuntary treatment could occur if all parties would attend more to the
empirical literature. Each profession has its own area of expertise. The
legal profession has as its concern the preservation of human rights,
the medical profession focuses on diagnosis, treatment, and rehabilitation, and legislators carefully attempt to enact laws to facilitate both
human rights and treatment.

Physicians must work for more precision in their diagnostic and
treatment methods. Vague and overly inclusive diagnoses have ham-
pered outcome research. New research diagnostic criteria represent a
good beginning, but more outcome studies are needed to establish
validity, especially when applied to the involuntary patient. Modest
evidence supports a continuation of involuntary treatment when diagnoses are based on observable symptoms, signs, and severity of impairment, and when time limits are carefully set to limit the loss of liberties.
In many states, this limitation would result in drastic reductions in the
number of patients committed. Extensive research is needed to separate more precisely conditions highly responsive to involuntary treatment from conditions less likely to improve. A major infringement on
individual liberties can only be justified, if then, by significant benefits.

More physician emphasis is needed, especially in the public sector, on developing a cooperative therapeutic alliance with initially uncooperative patients. Preliminary evidence suggests this is possible with the majority of initially uncooperative patients. Legal limitations on psychoactive drugs in these circumstances seem unwarranted considering other safeguards (especially legal advocacy and time limits on treatment) and the large body of data documenting their benefits.

Incapacity is a key area that is relatively unstudied. A large number of psychiatric patients manifest diminished competence, such as perceptual disturbances, impaired ability to reason, impaired memory and concentration, and impaired emotional integration. In a legal sense, incapacity is either present or absent, but when dealing with serious psychiatric problems, cognition and emotion are highly variable and may change rapidly in response to the environment or a treatment intervention. The additional problem of ambivalent wishes, such as the patient who comes to the hospital requesting help and then equivocates or refuses it, is an area not taken into account by most lawyers. Research is needed to produce a body of empirical evidence to support one or perhaps several levels of incapacity. Another related area untouched by research involves defining carefully the specific diagnoses where incapacity may characteristically occur. Incapacity, severity of symptoms, and likely benefits following a specified treatment form the best current bases for recommending involuntary treatment. More constructs, such as that of gravely disabled, are needed to incorporate aspects of both severity and incapacity in a form that can be tested.

Effective involuntary treatment can best occur under *parens patriae,* the legal doctrine that orphans, dependent children, and incompetent persons require special protection and control by the state. For this to occur, physicians and lawyers must work cooperatively to influence the legislative process in states with vague or overly inclusive commitment laws and in states where dangerousness is the sole standard for commitment. Brief involuntary diagnostic and emergency treatment should be possible without a hearing. Time limits for acute treatment (6 weeks or less) provide the patient some protection. An informal hearing with active legal counsel could ensure that serious mental illness and incapacity were proved by a preponderance of evidence. For prolonged involuntary treatment, further safeguards such as a formal hearing and degree of likely benefits could be introduced. Where incapacity and possible dangerousness coexist, treatment should be tried under *parens patriae.* If treatment fails, police power procedures could then be utilized.

When prevention of violent or self-destructive behavior is the principal purpose, police power necessitates different medical and legal procedures. For the physician, diagnosis and treatment must outweigh prevention of violence or social control since these latter are not areas of demonstrated medical competence. Two time periods may be necessary, one for gathering diagnostic and predictive evidence, the other for preventive detention. Research is needed to establish conditions where treatment may be of major benefit. Until empirical evidence more strongly supports predictive accuracy or therapeutic benefits, involuntary treatment for violent or self-destructive behavior will continue to be highly controversial. Lawyers and physicians would do well to more clearly separate hospitalization where behavioral control is the principal purpose. Separate institutions for these individuals may be necessary in light of the different procedures, purposes, and possible benefits of treatment.

Lawyers and legislators need to be more mindful that the law can guard against injustice and the abuse of power, but law cannot cure illness or improve the quality of medical treatment. Laws should facilitate the implementation of effective medical treatment while simultaneoulsy guarding against abuses of power; such laws would recognize the concerns of both professions. For example, a law limiting involuntary treatment must also provide funds and mechanisms for the development of alternate services. Correcting the abuses of the past, while promoting effective treatment for the most serious mental illnesses, requires a careful balancing of priorities in a rapidly changing and complex area.

REFERENCES

Addington v. Texas, 99 U.S. Supreme Court Reporter, 1979, 1804.

Albers, D. A., & Pasewark, R. A. Involuntary hospitalization: Surrender at the courthouse. *American Journal of Community Psychology*, 1974, *2*, 287–289.

Albers, D. A., Pasewark, R. A., & Smith, T. C. Involuntary hospitalization: The social construction of danger. *American Journal of Community Psychology*, 1976, *4*, 129–132.

Allen, A. A review of criminally insane patients in Ohio: A personal narrative. *Hospital & Community Psychiatry*, 1977, *28*, 837–840.

American Bar Foundation: Civil commitment of the mentally ill. *Harvard Law Review*, 1974, *87*, 1190–1399.

American Psychiatric Associaton. Position statement of involuntary hospitalization of the mentally ill (revised). *American Journal of Psychiatry*, 1973, *130*, 392.

American Psychiatric Assoication. The current status of lithium therapy: Report of the APA task force. *American Journal of Psychiatry*, 1975, *132*, 997–1001.

Bielski, R. J., & Friedel, R. O. Prediction of tricyclic antidepressant response. *Archives of General Psychiatry,* 1976, *33,* 1479–1489.

Bentz, W. K., & Edgerton, J. W. Concensus on attitudes toward mental illness. *Archives of General Psychiatry,* 1970, *22,* 468–473.

Casey, D. W. Managing tardive dyskinesia. *Journal of Clinical Psychiatry,* 1978, *39,* 748–752.

Chodoff, P. The case for involuntary hospitalization of the mentally ill. *American Journal of Psychiatry,* 1976, *133,* 496–501.

Deasy, L. C., & Steele, C. I. An analysis of a state hospital population subject to release under Florida law. *Hospital & Community Psychiatry,* 1976, *27,* 42–44.

Derschowitz, A. M. Two models of commitment: The medical and the legal. *The Humanist,* 1971, *31,* 19–23.

Dickes, R., Simons, R. C., & Weisfogel, J. Difficulties in diagnosis introduced by unconscious factors present in the interview. *Psychiatric Quarterly,* 1970, *44,* 55.

Donaldson v. O'Conner, 422 U.S. Supreme Court Reporter, 1975, 563–575.

Ennis, E. J., & Litwack, T. R. Psychiatry and the presumption of expertise: Flipping coins in the courtroom. *California Law Review,* 1974, *62,* 693–752.

Epstein, L., & Lowinger, P. Do mental patients want legal counsel? *American Journal of Orthopsychiatry,* 1975, *45,* 88–92.

Erickson, R. C. Outcome studies in mental hospitals: A review. *Psychological Bulletin,* 1975, *82,* 519–540.

Feighner, J. P., Robins, E., Guze, S. B., Woodruff, R. A., Winokur, G., & Munoz, R. Diagnostic criteria for use in psychiatric research. *Archives of General Psychiatry,* 1972, *26,* 57–63.

Gilboy, J. A. Informal admission of patients to state psychiatric institutions. *American Journal of Orthopsychiatry,* 1977, *47,* 321–330.

Gove, W. R., & Fain, T. A comparison of voluntary and committed psychiatric patients. *Archives of General Psychiatry,* 1977, *34,* 669–676.

Greenberg, D. F. Involuntary psychiatric commitments to prevent suicide. *New York University Law Review,* 1974, *49,* 227–263.

Grosz, H. J., & Grossman, K. G. Sources of observer variation and bias in clinical judgments: 1. The item of psychiatric history. *Journal of Nervous and Mental Disease,* 1964, *138,* 105–111.

Hadley, S. W., & Strupp, H. H. Contemporary views of negative effects in psychotherapy. *Archives of General Psychiatry,* 1976, *33,* 1291–1302.

Hiday, V. A. The role of counsel in civil commitment: Changes, effects, and determinants. *Journal of Psychiatry & Law,* 1977, *5,* 551–569.

Honigfield, G., & Gillis, R. The role of institutionalization in the natural history of schizophrenia (Report No. 64). Perry Point, Md.: Central Neuropsychiatric Research Laboratory, 1966.

Involuntary hospitalization said to protect patient. *Clinical Psychiatry News,* May, 1978, p. 1.

Jennings, C., Barraclough, B. M., & Moss, J. R. Have the Samaritans lowered the suicide rate? A controlled study. *Psychological Medicine,* 1978, *8,* 413–422.

Kirstein, L., & Weissman, M. N. Utilization review, attempted suicide, and involuntary hospitalization. *Journal of Nervous and Mental Disease,* 1976, *163,* 102–197.

Kumasaka, Y., Stokes, J., & Gupta, R. K. Criteria for involuntary hospitalization. *Archives of General Psychiatry,* 1972, *26,* 399–404.

Lamb, H. R., & Goertzel, V. The long-term patient in the era of community treatment. *Archives of General Psychiatry,* 1977, *34,* 679–682.

Leon, C. A., & Micklin, M. Who shall be hospitalized? Some social and psychological correlates of alternative dispositions of the mentally ill. *Acta Psychiatriae Scandanavica,* 1978, *58,* 97–111.

Light, D. W. Treating suicide: The illusions of a professional movement. *International Social Sciences Journal,* 1973, *25,* 475–488.

Maisel, R. Decision making in a commitment court. *Psychiatry,* 1970, *33,* 352–361.

Mental Health Law Project: Civil commitment. *Mental Disability Law Reporter,* 1977, *2,* 77–126.

In re Oakes, 8 Law Rep. 122 (Mass. 1845).

Owens, H. When is voluntary commitment really voluntary? *American Journal of Orthopsychiatry,* 1977, *47,* 104–110.

Peele, R., Chodoff, P., & Taub, N. Involuntary hospitalization and treatability: Observations from the District of Columbia experience. *Catholic University Law Review,* 1974, *23,* 744–753.

Perr, I. N. Independent examination of patients hospitalized against their will. *American Journal of Psychiatry,* 1974, *131,* 765–768.

Raines, G. N., & Rohrer, J. H. The operational matrix of psychiatric practice, II: Variations in psychiatric impression and the projection hypothesis. *American Journal of Psychiatry,* 1960, *117,* 133.

Rappenport, J. R. Enforced treatment—is it treatment? *Bulletin of the American Academy of Psychiatry & the Law,* 1974, *2,* 148–158.

Robins, E., Gentry, K. A., Munoz, R. A., Marten, S. A contrast of the three more common illnesses with the ten less common in a study and 18-month follow-up of 314 psychiatric emergency room patients. *Archives of General Psychiatry,* 1977, *34,* 285–291.

Sata, L. S., & Goldenberg, E. E. A study of involuntary patients in Seattle. *Hospital & Community Psychiatry,* 1977, *28,* 835–836.

Schwartz, W. C., & Dumpman, S. Voluntary commitment by persuasion. *Hospital & Community Psychiatry,* 1972, *23,* 128–129.

Shah, S. A. Some interactions of law and mental health in the handling of social deviance. *Catholic University Law Review,* 1974, *23,* 674–719.

Spensley, J., Barter, J. T., Werme, P. H., & Langsley, D. G. Involuntary hospitalization: What for and how long? *American Journal of Psychiatry*, 1974, *131*, 219–223.

Spensley, J., Edwards, D. W., & White, E. Patient satisfaction and involuntary treatment. *American Journal of Orthopsychiatry*, 1980, *50*, 725–727.

Spensley, J., & Werme, P. H. Conservatorship: An involuntary legal status for "gravely disabled" mentally disordered persons. *Western Journal of Medicine*, 1979, *132*, 476–484.

Spitzer, R. L., Endicott, J., & Robins, E. Research diagnostic criteria. *Archives of General Psychiatry*, 1978, *35*, 773–782.

Spitzer, R. L., Forman, J. B. W., & Nee J. DSM-III field trials: 1. Initial interrater diagnostic reliability. *American Journal of Psychiatry*, 1979, *136*, 815–817.

Steadman, H. J. The psychiatrist as a conservative agent of social control. *Social Problems*, 1972, *20*, 263–271.

Stone, A. A. Comment. *American Journal of Psychiatry*, 1975, *132*, 829–831.

Tarsy, D., Granacher, R., & Bralower, M. Tardive dyskinesia in young adults. *American Journal of Psychiatry*, 1977, *134*, 1032–1034.

Teknekron. Improving California's mental health system: Policy making and management in the invisible system. Berkeley, Calif.: Teknekron, Inc., 1978.

Tomelleri, C. J., Lakshminarayanan, N., & Herjanic, M. Who are the "committed"? *Journal of Nervous and Mental Disease*, 1977, *165*, 288–293.

Treffert, B. A. The practical limits of patients' rights. *Psychiatric Annals*, 1975, *5*, 158–161.

Urmer, A. H. Implications of California's new mental health law. *American Journal of Psychiatry*, 1975, *132*, 251–254.

Wenger, D. L., & Fletcher, C. R. The effect of legal counsel on admissions to a state mental hospital: A confrontation of professions. *Journal of Health & Social Behavior*, 1968, *9*, 215–221.

Wilbert, D. E., Jorstad, V., Loren, J. D. & Wirrer, B. Determination of grave disability. *Journal of Nervous and Mental Disease*, 1976, *162*, 35–39.

Zwerling, I., Karasu, T., Plutchik, R., & Kellerman, S. A comparison of voluntary and involuntary patients in a state hospital. *American Journal of Orthopsychiatry*, 1975, *45*, 81–87.

Zwerling, I. M., Conte, H. R., Plutchik, R., & Karasu, T. B. "No-commitment week": A feasibility study. *American Journal of Psychiatry*, 1978, *135*, 1198–1201.

Zovodnick, S. Suggestions for a rational approach to the chemotherapy of schizophrenia. *Diseases of the Nervous System*, 1976, *12*, 671–675.

Chapter 4

THE INSANITY PLEA:
Much Ado About Little

Richard A. Pasewark
Mark D. Pasewark

Historically, persons making the insanity plea have comprised but an insignificant proportion of those entering the criminal justice system. Disproportionate to this impact upon the criminal justice system, the plea has evoked continued and widespread interest, comment, dissatisfaction, and criticism; and, periodically, endeavors are made to alter statutes governing the defense. Uniquely observed in this domain of the law is a continual striving for perfection in conceptualization and application. There is a constant demand by legislators, the public, and some members of the mental health system that laws enacted lead to the almost utopian result of acquitting only those deserving acquittal, convicting those meriting conviction, and developing a "fail-safe" procedure whereby those adjudicated *not guilty by reason of insanity (NGRI)* are either "cured" or restrained in such manner so that they pose no immediate or future threat to society. This attitude stands in pronounced relief to a general acceptance among these groups that, in other spheres, the law functions as an imperfect instrument. The guilty are not always convicted, the innocent are not invariably exonerated, and, persons committing criminal acts do not always refrain from future antisocial behavior.

In this perfectionist striving, critics of contemporary NGRI statutes seem also to seek a precise definition of "insane" to achieve the results they demand. *Insane* must have a precise definition, and, application of this definition must result in the incarceration of those meriting punishment, and hospitalization of those deserving treatment. In marked contrast, relatively little concern is expressed in defining the hypothetical "reasonable" man, about whose extrapolated actions revolve determination as to whether an act is to be judged as either criminal or as self-defense. Determination of the reasonable-man standard is typically left to juries or the judge. There is a reluctance to impart that same responsibility to these agents in determining the nature of the "insane" man, despite the fact that legal and psychiatric definitions have probably not improved greatly upon the common-sense conceptualization held by the lay juror.

On the contemporary American scene, there is again observed a new wave of interest in the operation of the NGRI plea and its supposed imperfections. Basically, this concern seems characterized by a desire to make more stringent the law that governs the plea, and thereby eliminate, if not the availability of the plea to criminal defendants, the number of defendants for whom the plea proves successful. In New York (Kolb, Steadman, Carnahan, & Wright, 1978) and Illinois (Chicago Tribune, 1977; Pasewark & Pasewark, 1979) this cry is more intense and the proposal is made to eliminate the NGRI completely. Underlying this stance appears to be a belief that the NGRI defense is used too frequently; its success rate is too high; it serves to exculpate criminals of the consequences of their antisocial behavior; and, it permits the return of individuals to society who will present a threat to the safety of others.

Perhaps partially responsible for the renewed interest in revising the insanity plea in various states might be such factors as: (1) A steadily rising nationwide crime rate that increases the absolute, if not the proportionate, number of defendants entering the plea. (2) The decrease in the general psychiatric patient population of mental hospitals, with a corresponding increase in the proportion of those patients not guilty or not triable by reason of insanity. Intensifying this trend, also, have been court decisions, such as *Baxstrom* v. *Herold,* (1966) requiring placement of such individuals in civil rather than correctional facilities. Resultingly, persons hospitalized under various criminal procedures have probably come to form a larger segment of the management responsibilities of mental hospital administrators than was previously true. (3) A gradual shift in the theoretical stance of mental health professionals from a psychodynamic to an existential philosophy and a concomitant emphasis upon the explanatory concept of "free will" as a determinant in behavior. This trend has most probably been accentuated by the cogent stance of Szasz (1963, 1965) and his adherents proposing individual responsibility for actions as an alternative to exercise of the state's *parens patriae* doctrine in which the state assumes parental-like rights for the case of disabled individuals. (4) Extensive press coverage provided for a few notorious cases of deranged individuals who commit numerous homicides, such as the "Son of Sam" (*The New York Times,* 1977) and Speck cases (*The New York Times,* 1966).

In reviewing the NGRI literature, one is impressed by the dearth of data-based investigations concerning operation of the plea. This situation is in marked contrast to the plethora of philosophical discourse in the legal and psychiatric literature. Despite this lack of empirical data, members of the judiciary, the legal and psychiatric professions, and legislative bodies argue vociferously on behalf of altering the plea or the disposition made of persons adjudicated NGRI following trial for a criminal act. The authors do not argue the right or duty of concerned citizenry, including judges, lawyers, and psychiatrists, to advocate altering the legal fabric, or of legislative bodies to institute these changes. Properly, this is both a function and responsibility of these groups. Considering the limited and inadequate scope of data in this sphere, however, we do decry the fact that their arguments must, of necessity, be based upon subjective impressions as to the manner in which the plea operates, rather than upon objective knowledge of the system and its procedures. In decision making, rhetoric based upon subjective impression does not seem a reasonable substitute for an organized data base from which reasonable decisions can be made. Unfortunately, relative to the insanity plea, this stance appears analogous to that of an *Alice in Wonderland* character: We do not wish to know the facts bacause they might confuse us.

Within the general framework of patient rights adopted by this text, we shall attempt to present the findings of the very limited data-based investigations relative to the insanity plea and then discuss the implications of the insanity plea within the context of patient rights.

FREQUENCY AND SUCCESS OF THE NGRI PLEA

Probably the most extensive data available on the NGRI plea are those reported by Walker (1968) and Walker and McCabe (1973). The work of these authors is important in that it provides data of both a historical and somewhat contemporary nature regarding the insanity plea in England from the 1700s to 1964. Somewhat surprising, in selected periods from 1740–1930, and except for the interval 1909–13, the frequency with which the plea was made on behalf of all defendants tried at Old Bailey remained relatively comparable, ranging from 2.9 to 7.9 for each 1,000 accused persons.

While the success rate varied between 28% to 56%, it demonstrated no particular temporal ordering despite rather significant court decisions during this period (Walker, 1968, p. 67). Similarly, of all persons indicted for murder from 1894 through 1956, the year in which England adopted the diminished responsiblity test in murder trials, the percentage of defendants found NGRI varied between 23% and 31% (Walker, 1968, p. 86).

For the United States, there exist no data comparable to that compiled by Walker and McCabe in England. Two studies, by Scheidemandel and Kanno (1969) and by Matthews (1970), provide some nationwide information. Both investigations are beset by serious methodological shortcomings, however, that preclude definitive conclusions and generalization to the national scene.

In a nationwide survey of treatment provided to disturbed offenders, including those adjudicated NGRI, Scheidemandel and Kanno (1969) report that 409 (4%) offenders admitted to institutions providing treatment facilities were NGRI patients. This figure is obviously a gross underestimation of the NGRI population, because, in this segment of their analysis, data were used from only 58 of the 90 facilities identified as providing treatment for the mentally ill criminal offender. Addtionally, despite efforts of the authors to identify all institutions providing such treatment, this goal was not realized fully. Data from two states are not reported; and, in some states, facilities known to have disturbed offenders and NGRI cases are not included (e.g., Colorado and Hawaii). Additionally, some states allow for dispositions other than institutionalization for acquitted NGRI defendants.

The Matthews study, sponsored by the American Bar Association, provides a sporadic and inconsistent sampling of the NGRI plea in various judicial jurisdictions. The survey suffers seriously, though, from failure to specify the reasons for the geographical regions included and excluded from the study. Other limitations of this study are the variable time-periods employed, an almost complete exclusion of all but metropolitan areas, and failure to identify the means by which defendants were making, and/or were successful in making, the plea. Specification of this identification process is extremely crucial to NGRI research because of the varied procedures among the states as to when the plea is actually entered following arraignment. In some states, for example, the plea is entered upon arraignment. In others, it may be made at any point in a criminal trial, and identification of NGRI defendants in these locales entails the actual physical examination of all criminal trial transcripts.

Generally, the observations of Matthews (1970) suggest that the plea is rarely made, at least in those jurisdictions examined. For example, during a four-month period in both Chicago and San Francisco in 1963, there was but one NGRI plea in each jurisdiction. Each plea was to a charge of murder, and each proved successfui. In a three-month period in the city of New York, one unsuccessful plea was made to a homicide charge. In two- and three-month periods in Detroit and Miami, respectively, no insanity plea was entered; and, during a two-month period in Michigan, but one such plea was recorded. According to Matthews, the insanity plea was used but 464 times (1.3%) in 34,643 felony dispositions made by California courts during 1965. In 213 of these 464 cases, the plea was subsequently withdrawn. Another 56 cases were dismissed or withdrawn from the court calendar. Thus, the 195 NGRI pleas remaining represented .53% of all felony dispositions. Of these, 109 were acquitted and 86 convicted. Unfortunately, because of California's bifurcated trial system, in which guilt is first established, then responsibility considered at a secondary trial, Matthews was unable to determine the number of persons actually acquitted by reason of insanity, and those adjudicated not guilty.

Lacking adequate national statistics, estimates concerning the frequency and success of the NGRI plea are dependent upon data derived from individual states. These data are also sparse. As will be discussed later, the wide variation observed among states, and even among judicial districts within a given state, makes it apparent that these data cannot be utilized to generate national rates with any accuracy.

In Massachusetts, during the fiscal year 1970, although there were 2,101 pretrial hospitalizations of defendants, there were no reported posttrial commitments of persons adjudicated NGRI (Laboratory of Community Psychiatry, 1974).

For Wyoming, during the period July 1, 1970 to June 30, 1972, Pasewark and Lanthorn (1977) found that of 22,012 felony indictments, only 102 (.46%) defendants entered the NGRI plea. Only one of these defendants was adjudicated NGRI. These statistics probably seriously underestimate the power of the plea, since the combined dismissal and acquittal rate among persons making the plea was approximately double (22%) that of persons who did not enter the plea (9%). At the time of this study, Wyoming law was governed by the McNaughton Rule, with an appended irresistible impulse clause[1]. Cooke and Pogany (1975) report upon a similar finding

[1]Until recently, the McNaughton rule governed the insanity plea in most judicial jurisdictions within the United States. Strictly applied, it required the destruction of cognitive and reasoning capacities to render an NGRI verdict. In some jurisdictions, the "irrestible impulse" clause was appended to McNaughton to allow for those instances in which the defendant, although able to recognize the wrongful nature of the criminal act, was unable to contain this action because of an impairment of will or conscious control induced by mental disorder. Representative of the McNaughton-irresistible impulse rule is the statute of Colorado:

wherein referral of defendants for psychiatric evaluation was found to influence eventual disposition.

In a subsequent Wyoming study coverning the period 1975–77 (Pasewark & Bunting, 1979), in which the American Law Institute (ALI)[2] rule and a bifurcated trial procedure were operative, the insanity plea was made by 117 felony defendants. An NGRI adjudication resulted in 5 of these cases. These figures do not differ markedly from those found in the 1970–72 investigation (Pasewark & Lanthorn, 1977), when the state functioned under the McNaughton irresistible-impulse rule and a single-phased trial procedure.

In Maryland, Sauer (1975) reports that, during the 1973 fiscal year, 380 males, charged with felonies, were admitted to the Perkins Hospital Center for pretrial mental examination. The center reported to the court that 73 (19%) were insane. Due to the somewhat confusing manner in which data of this study are reported, it is not possible to determine accurately: (1) whether the 380 cases represent all defendants referred by courts for pretrial examination; (2) the number of these cases that actually made the NGRI plea; and, (3) the number who were subsequently adjudicated insane.

The applicable test of insanity shall be, and the jury shall be so instructed: "A person who is so diseased or defective in mind at the time of the commission of the act as to be incapable of distinguishing right from wrong with respect to that act, or being able so to distinguish, has suffered such an impairment of mind by disease or defect as to destroy the willpower and render him incapable of choosing the right and refraining from doing the wrong is not accountable; and this is so howsoever such insanity may be manifested, by irresistible impulse or otherwise. But care should be taken not to confuse such mental disease or defect with moral obliquity, mental depravity, or passion growing out of anger, revenge, hatred, or other motives, and kindred evil conditions, for when the act is induced by any of these causes the person is accountable to the law." (*Colorado Revised Statutes,* 1973).

[2]The ALI rule represents the most recent effort to evolve a legal standard for insanity in criminal cases. Promulgated by the American Law Institute (1962), it has since been adopted by a number of jurisdictions, including Wyoming, where that state's law reads:

(a) A person is not responsible for criminal conduct if at the time of the criminal conduct, as a result of mental illness or deficiency, he lacked substantial capacity either to appreciate the wrongfulness of his conduct or to conform his conduct to the requirements of law.

(b)As used in this section, the terms "mental illness or deficiency" do not include an abnormality manifested only by repeated criminal or otherwise antisocial conduct. (*Wyoming Statutes,* 1977).

In New York State, there were 278 successful NGRI cases from March 1, 1965 to July 30, 1976 (Pasewark, Pantle, & Steadman, 1979a; 1979b). During this period, New York was governed by the ALI rule with the "inability to conform" segment of that principle deleted. In New York, the issue of insanity may be raised at any point in a trail. Thus, it was not possible to determine the frequency with which the defense was actually made and, thereby, its rate of success. Similarly, because of the format in which New York criminal statistics are compiled, the relationship of the plea to arrest and indictment rates could not be established. Suggested by the New York data, however, is the possibility that there is a greater likelihood for use of the plea if the NGRI acquittal entails compulsory hospitalization at a civil mental hospital, with prospect of treatment, rather than confinement at a facility exclusively housing the criminally insane. Thus, during the period in which an NGRI determination resulted in commitment to a hospital for the criminally insane, there was an average of 8.04 persons found NGRI each year. In the period following an alteration in New York's Code of Criminal Procedure that required commitment to a civil mental hospital, NGRI acquittals averaged 44.16 per year. Of course, this hypothesis is highly speculative in nature. It would be negated if, for example, it were determined that the increased frequency of successful NGRI pleas was not related to an increasing rate of use but, instead, reflected a burgeoning crime, arrest, and indictment rate in that state.

Simon's (1967) data reporting upon the insanity plea before and after the Durham ruling[3] by the District of Columbia Court of Appeals has aroused considerable interest. Aside from Walker's English study and the later Wyoming studies, it is the only investigation that provides information before and after a fairly significant statutory change.

Essentially, Simon found that approximately .24% of criminal defendants were found NGRI in the four years preceding Durham, while 2.29% were found NGRI in the six years following its adoption. Because of trial procedures employed in the district, Simon was unable to report the number of defendants who actually entered the plea, and, thus, its success rate.

[3]The Durham ruling was an attempt on the part of the District of Columbia Court of Appeals to "modernize" the insanity plea and allow for greater use of psychiatric testimony. It stated simply: "(A)n accused is not criminally responsible if his unlawful act was the product of a mental disease or mental defect" (*Durham* v. *United States,* 1954). Despite widespread publicity given to the Durham ruling, it was adopted by only a few jurisdictions and has, in fact, since been abandoned by the District of Columbia (*United States* v. *Brawner,* 1972; *McDonald* v. *United States,* 1962).

In Hawaii, during the years 1969–76, Fukunaga (1977) determined that 458 defendants pled NGRI. Of these, 86 were acquitted as
insane and 31 had the criminal charges against them dismissed because of insanity, an option available under Hawaiian law. In the study
period examined, Hawaii was governed by the ALI rule.

CHARACTERISTICS OF PERSONS MAKING AND SUCCEEDING IN THE NGRI PLEA

Criminal Charge

A persistent myth surrounding the insanity plea is that it is employed almost exclusively in cases involving serious crimes against the
person and, conversely, it is rarely used as a defense in property
crimes. Available data suggest that this is not the true situation. Although it is probable that the defense is raised proportionately more
in cases of serious crimes against the person, such as murder, assault,
or rape, it also seems to be frequently entered in property crimes and
even, at times, in misdemeanors. This phenomena, observed by
Walker in his historical analysis of the plea in England, is substantiated
by the few American studies providing information on this issue.

The Wyoming studies (Pasewark & Lanthorn, 1977; Pasewark &
Bunting, 1979) indicate that defendants making the NGRI plea have
been indicted on a wide variety of charges ranging from check passing
to homicide (Table 4–1). In New York State (Pasewark et al., 1979a),
defendants determined NGRI by the courts were also charged with a
gamut of criminal acts that varied from a motor vehicle violation to
murder (Table 4–2). In Hawaii, a comparable situation prevails, with
persons entering the plea, as well as those found NGRI, representing
a host of criminal offenses varying from misdemeanors to serious
felonies (Fukunaga, 1977).

Generally similar findings are reported for the District of Columbia (Arens, 1976), California (Matthews, 1970); and Michigan (Cooke
& Sikorski, 1974).

Victims

Another persistent myth surrounding the insanity plea is that the
victim tends to be random and that multiple crimes of violence are
committed by the offender. The only known investigation providing
information on this matter is that by Pasewark et al. (1979a) for New
York State. This erroneous impression is probably the result of widespread publicity afforded dramatic episodes in which an apparently

Table 4-1   Alleged Most Serious Offense of Persons
Pleading Insanity in Wyoming, 1970-72

	N	%
Against Property		
Larceny-theft	16	15.69
Check	16	15.69
Burglary—Breaking and entering	13	12.75
Forgery	4	3.92
Arson	3	2.94
Fraud	1	0.98
Against Person		
Rape	13	12.75
Criminal homicide	9	8.82
Assault, aggravated	8	7.84
Sex, excluding rape	5	4.90
Robbery	4	3.92
Family, children	2	1.96
Kidnapping	1	0.98
Hit-run	1	0.98
Drugs	5	4.90
Other		
Jailbreak	1	0.98

deranged individual kills numerous victims who are unknown to him. Such, for example, was the case in the "Son of Sam" episode (*New York Times*, 1977). Contrary to these notorious cases, the New York data suggest that the victim, in what later will become an NGRI case, tends to have the same relationship to the NGRI offender as does the victim in comparable nonNGRI cases. For offenses involving violence, the victim most often is someone well known to the offender and usually a member of the perpetrator's family (Table 4-3).

Prior Psychiatric Hospitalizations

Probably at odds with the view of mental health workers concerning individuals who enter the NGRI plea is the information available concerning prior psychiatric hospitalizations. Essentially, a rather large proportion of individuals found to be NGRI are characterized by no previous psychiatric hospitalizations. Thus, in New York, during the period 1965-76, 56% of the males and 85% of the females found insane had no prior psychiatric hospitalization. In Wyoming, for the years 1975-77, 52% of males and 67% of females entering the plea had no known previous hospitalizations. Cooke and Sikorski (1974)

Table 4–2   Most Serious Offense of Persons Acquitted for
Insanity in New York, 1965–76

	Male		Female		Total	
	N	Percent	N	Percent	N	Percent
Against person						
Murder	118	49.3	30	76.9	148	53.2
Manslaughter	12	5.0	4	10.3	16	5.8
Robbery	17	7.1	2	5.1	19	6.8
Assault	42	17.6	0	0.0	42	15.1
Kiddnapping	1	0.4	0	0.0	1	0.4
Rape	6	2.5	0	0.0	6	2.2
Sexual, other	5	2.1	0	0.0	5	1.8
Reckless endangerment	4	1.7	0	0.0	4	1.4
Menacing	1	0.4	0	0.0	1	0.4
Endanger, child welfare	1	0.4	0	0.0	1	0.4
Resisting arrest	1	0.4	0	0.0	1	0.4
(Subtotal)	(208)	(86.9)	(36)	(92.3)	(244)	(87.9)
Against property						
Burglary	7	2.9	0	0.0	7	2.5
Possession burglary tools	0	0.0	1	2.6	1	0.4
Forgery	1	0.4	0	0.0	1	0.4
Possession forged instrument	1	0.4	0	0.0	1	0.4
Arson	13	5.4	2	5.1	15	5.4
(Subtotal)	(22)	(9.1)	(3)	(7.7)	(25)	(9.1)
Drugs						
Selling controlled substance	3	1.3	0	0.0	3	1.1
Other						
Possession weapon	1	0.4	0	0.0	1	0.4
Escape, absconding	3	1.3	0	0.0	3	1.1
Criminal mischief	1	0.4	0	0.0	1	0.4
Motor vehicle violation	1	0.4	0	0.0	1	0.4
(Subtotal)	(6)	(2.5)	(0)	(0.0)	(6)	(2.2)
TOTAL	239	100.0	39	100.0	278	100.0

indicate that 43% of their Michigan NGRIs had a previous psychiatric hospitalization. From their data, however, it in not possible to determine whether or not any of these hospitalizations were associated with the criminal charge leading to the NGRI verdict (e.g., evaluations for competency or insanity, restoration of competency) or whether the hospitalizations were civil in nature and incurred prior to commission of the criminal act of concern.

Prior Arrests and Incarcerations

Again, and probably at variance with the conceptualization held by many, defendants in NGRI cases and those adjudicated NGRI tend to have a previous arrest history. Thus, in Wyoming, of the 102 defendants using the NGRI plea, 63 (62%) had at least one previous arrest. Frequency of arrest varied from 20 defendants with one arrest to one individual with 24 arrests. Unfortunately, the Wyoming investigation does not present the reasons for the arrest of these defendants (Pasewark & Lanthron, 1977), nor is it possible to compare the arrest records of this group with that of the general population because of a lack of relevant statistics.

Concordant with the Wyoming data are those of New York for the period 1965–76 for persons found insane. Of the 278 individuals adjudicated NGRI by New York courts, 119 had a least one previous arrest preceding the crime of concern. Frequency of arrests ranged from 27 individuals with one arrest to one individual with 21 prior apprehensions. Arrest reasons varied from minor misdemeanors, such as criminal trespass, to major felonies, such as rape, aggravated assault, and murder. In all, 537 arrests were accumulated by these 119 subjects. Of these arrests, 31% were crimes against the person of varying severity, 32% were property crimes, 23% were victimless offenses, 8% com-

Table 4–3   Relationship of Victim in Target Cases Where
Victim-Patient Relationship Was Known,
New York, 1965–76 (N = 210)

	Male		*Female*		*Total*	
	N	*Percent*	*N*	*Percent*	*N*	*Percent*
Spouse	17	9.9	4	10.5	21	10.0
Child or children	7	4.1	20	52.6	27	12.9
Parent or parents	22	12.8	3	7.9	25	11.9
Other relative	5	2.9	0	0.0	5	2.4
In-law	6	3.5	0	0.0	6	2.9
Boy- or girlfriend	7	4.1	2	5.3	9	4.3
Relative of girlfriend	1	0.6	0	0.0	1	0.5
Employer	2	1.2	0	0.0	2	0.9
Coworker	3	1.7	0	0.0	3	1.4
Acquaintance, well-known	25	14.5	2	5.3	27	12.9
Acquaintance, casual	9	5.2	0	0.0	9	4.3
Stranger	36	20.9	4	10.5	40	19.1
Police officer	14	8.1	0	0.0	14	6.7
No victim	18	10.5	3	7.9	21	10.0
TOTAL	172	99.9	38	99.9	210	100.0

prised drug violations, and 6% were other offenses, such as possession
of a weapon or burglar tools, and unspecified offenses. Of these 278
subjects, 21 males had prior imprisonments in the New York penal
system. Incarceration reasons varied from petty larceny to assault.
For their Michigan group, Cooke and Sikorski (1974) report that 26%
had a previous criminal conviction, but the authors do not provide
arrest or imprisonment data, while Morrow and Peterson (1966) report that 66% of a Missouri NGRI group had previous criminal
offenses.

NGRI Hospitalization

There are but three studies known to the authors containing information about hospitalization periods of NGRI patients. Data derived
from New York are presented in Table 4–4 and suggest that hospitalization time is quite variable and bears little relationship to the severity
of the criminal act leading to the NGRI verdict. This finding should not
prove surprising. In states mandating commitment following an NGRI
acquittal, as in New York, the individual is supposedly hospitalized
until such time as he is sane and no longer poses a danger to others.
The New York data are at odds with that reported by Cooke and
Sikorski (1974) who determined that, in Michigan, hospitalization time
was related to the severity of the crime. In this study, for example,
discharged murderers averaged 34.68 months of hospitalization, while
assault and rape cases averaged 7.75 and 11.00 months; respectively.
Females, married and widowed persons, urban residents, the more
educated, and those not previously hospitalized were found to spend
less time in the hospital. The Canadian study of Quinsey, Preusse, and
Fernley (1975) indicates a much longer period of hospitalization following NGRI acquittal than do the previously cited investigations,
averaging eight years.

Subsequent Careers of NGRI Cases

Unfortunately, there are but few studies providing follow-up information on the course of NGRI cases subsequent to acquittal.

At the time of termination of the New York study, 139 (50%) of
the 278 NGRI patients remained hospitalized and 10 were known to
be deceased (Table 4–5). Of the 107 discharged, 24 (22%) experienced a subsequent hospitalization. Hospitalizations for the group
totaled 49, of which 42 were civil and seven associated with additional
criminal charges.

Following release from the NGRI commitment, none of the 19
discharged New York females incurred an arrest. Of the 88 discharged

Table 4-4   In-hospital Days and Total Days Under
Jurisdiction of the New York Department of
Mental Hygiene, 1965–76

		In-hospital days		Total days	
	Number	Range	Mean	Range	Mean
For discharged males (N = 88)					
Murder	34	1–2326	488.26	1–2326	602.26
Manslaughter	3	143–446	249.67	143–446	332.67
Robbery	5	6–262	116.40	7–560	203.60
Assault	21	33–1033	361.00	68–1958	486.38
Reckless endangerment	2	78–91	84.50	78–92	85.00
Burglary	5	20–549	220.80	154–794	369.80
Rape	1	—	1042.00	—	1045.00
Sexual abuse	3	36–614	256.33	56–614	263.00
Arson	5	45–1434	390.60	45–1444	498.20
Possession weapon	1	—	863.00	—	1541.00
Forgery	1	—	152.00	—	181.00
Driving intoxicated	1	—	7.00	—	7.00
Endanger, child welfare	1	—	322.00	—	753.00
Criminal mischief	1	—	71.00	—	71.00
Selling drugs	1	—	58.00	—	58.00
Resist arrest	1	—	76.00	—	77.00
Escape	1	—	39.00	—	699.00
Absconding	1	—	94.00	—	95.00
For discharged females (N = 19)					
Murder	14	28–1698	494.29	28–1704	531.57
Manslaughter	1	—	92.00	—	92.00
Criminally negligent homicide	1	—	61.00	—	61.00
Robbery	2	62–110	86.00	62–114	88.00
Possession burglary tools	1	—	191.00	—	523.00

males, 21 (23%) were apprehended by the police following discharge.
Arrests for this group totaled 66, an average of 3.14 per person. The
frequency of arrests ranged from seven persons with one apprehension to one individual with nine posthospitalization arrests. Reasons
for these arrests varied, from a subject charged with murder and subse-

quently convicted in another state to 15 apprehensions for misdemeanors. Crimes against the person comprised 26% of the 66 arrests: murder (1), assualt (6), rape (1), sodomy (2), robbery (3), endangering a child's welfare (2), and resisting arrest (2). Property crimes contributed 36% of the posthospitalization apprehensions: burglary (14), grand larcency (5), and possession of stolen property (5). Drug charges accounted for 14% of the postarrests: possession (8) and selling (1). Other felonies contributed 2%, and other misdemeanors 23% of the arrests.

Of the 21 males arrested, 13 also had been arrested prior to apprehension for the target crime, totaling 57 arrests. Of additional interest is the observation that seven of those subsequently arrested were apprehended for the same crime for which they were acquitted by reason of insanity.

Subsequent to their NGRI commitment, six New York subjects, all males on discharge status, were incarcerated in the state's prison system. Of these, one had two incarcerations, both for burglary. The crimes leading to imprisonment in the five other cases were assault, robbery, burglary, arson, and criminal possession of a weapon. For one of these individuals the posthospitalization incarceration was for the same type of crime (robbery) as that for which he was found NGRI. Prior to their NGRI adjudication, three of the six subjects had accumulated eight arrests, although none had been previously imprisoned.

In many ways, the follow-up results of Morrow and Peterson

Table 4-5   Status of New York NGRI Subjects
On June 30, 1976

	Male		Female		Total	
	N	Percent	N	Percent	N	Percent
Hospitalized	122	51.05	17	43.59	139	50.00
Complete discharge	74	30.96	17	43.59	91	32.73
Discharged from conditional release	4	1.67	2	5.13	6	2.16
Discharged from unauthorized leave	4	1.67	0	0.00	4	1.44
Discharged from escape	6	2.51	0	0.00	6	2.16
Conditional release	12	5.02	1	2.56	13	4.68
Family care	2	0.84	0	0.00	2	0.72
Unauthorized leave	2	0.84	0	0.00	2	0.72
Escape	4	1.67	0	0.00	4	1.44
Leave, over 60 days	1	0.42	0	0.00	1	0.36
Deceased	8	3.35	2	5.13	10	3.60
Total	239	100.00	39	100.00	278	100.01

(1966), subsequent to hospital discharge of 44 Missouri NGRI cases, parallel that of the New York investigation. By the end of the three-year period, 37% had committed new felonies.

The arrest rates of the New York sample differed markedly from that of the Canadian NGRI, and "unfit to stand trial" patients of Quinsey et al. (1975). In the latter study, only three arrests of the 28 persons discharged are reported. One obvious explanation for the differential rate observed in the New York and Canadian studies is the much longer period of hospitalizaiton for Canadian subjects, which averaged eight years. Therefore, upon discharge, they were in an older age-bracket, beyond the age associated with highest frequency of criminal behavior.

Basically, the New York study, if substantiated by future investigation, suggests that criminal recidivism of the NGRI group, as indicated by official arrest reports, tends to be relatively high. This raises the possibility that within the NGRI group is contained a group of crime-prone individuals who have had their criminal careers interrupted by the NGRI hospitalization.

BELIEFS ABOUT THE INSANITY PLEA

Although previous research does not provide consistent data that permit a well-founded conclusion relative to the frequency and success rate of the NGRI plea, data do seem to permit the general, tentative statement that the plea probably represents but a very small proportion of criminal defenses and that, once entered, it is not highly successful.

Given the fact that even in some of our more populated states, such as California (Matthews, 1970) and New York (Pasewark et al., 1979a), as well as in the rural state of Wyoming (Pasewark & Lanthorn, 1977; Pasewark & Bunting, 1979), a miniscule proportion of defendants are acquitted by reason of insanity, there are realistically but few people who possibly "escape" culpability for a criminal act in the court system.

If comparable rates are established in other states, the insanity plea, whatever its shortcomings, if any, should be regarded as an extremely low problem priority area. Yet, this is not the case. Commissions and legislative committees struggle unendingly with the problem, debate continuously the wording of a phrase or the placement of a comma or period, and argue interminably about the meaning of such terms as "know" and "conform." Considering the number of persons involved, it seems reasonable that society's limited resources might be husbanded or expended in other areas harboring problems of greater magnitude. In other spheres of the legal system, society accepts laws that do not lead to accurate dispositions. This is particularly true of the criminal system where the "beyond a reasonable doubt" standard is generally condoned. All who commit crimes are not found guilty; all convicted are not incarcerated.

Preliminary results of a series of studies being conducted by Pasewark and associates suggest that a factor contributing to the intense concern and criticism of the insanity plea might be the misconceptions held by various segments of the public concerning the plea. Thus, for example, during the period 1971–73 in Wyoming, 22,102 persons were indicted for felonies; 102 persons made the NGRI plea; and one defendant was so adjudicated by the court. Yet, a relatively well-educated college group estimated that the plea was made in more than 8,000 cases and was successful in about 3,600 cases (Pasewark & Seidenzahl, 1979). A similar gross overestimation was made by legislators, who opined that the plea was made in nearly 4,500 cases and was successful in nearly 3,000 of these trials (Pasewark & Pantle, 1979). Although not yet fully analyzed, cursory examination of responses made in sampling citizens of two communities, law enforcement officers, and mental health workers also suggests their overestimation of both the frequency and success of the plea. From these estimates, we are led to suspect that sensationalized news stories of crimes committed by the mentally ill do have a profound effect upon citizenry's attitude toward the NGRI plea.

INFLUENCE OF STATUTORY LANGUAGE

In a classic study of the influence of statutory language and various rules on cases involving the insanity plea, Simon (1967) simulated the trial of the same defendant utilizing wording of the McNaughton and Durham rules. In a mock incest case it was found that jurors had a higher acquittal rate under Durham than McNaughton.

Sauer and Mullens (1976) examined results of psychiatric evaluations at a Maryland institution performed under the McNaughton rule in 1965–66, and under the ALI rule during 1972–73. In 1965–66, 8% of the defendants were evaluated as insane, while in 1972–73 19% were so evaluated. Unfortunately, the final court decisions in these cases are not reported. Although, on their face, results indicate that statutory changes did increase the proportion of cases evaluated as insane, it is possible, as Rappeport (1976) suggests in his accompanying commentary to the study, that other factors might have been responsible. Among these are changing attitudes of staff and the greater availability of public defenders during the later years.

Simon's 1967 pre- and post-Durham data derived from the District of Columbia, at first glance, also suggest that different statutory provisions do, in fact, affect trial outcome. Despite these findings, it is believed that considerable further research is necessary to substantiate this position, particularly in light of the Walker (1968) and Pasewark studies (Pasewark & Lanthorn, 1977; Pasewark & Bunting, 1979) suggesting no such pronounced changes followed significant court decisions and statutory changes. Thus, one might reasonably argue that the mock trial situation does not accurately reflect that which occurs when an individual's fate is determined in the real courtroom situation. Similarly, alternative explanations to that presented by Simon concerning the effect of statutory change in Washington, D. C. must be examined. For example, it can be argued that the increase in NGRI acquittals that followed introduction of the Durham rule was, in large part, accountable for by the acquittal of persons who ordinarily would be found unfit to proceed with criminal proceedings (Goldstein, 1967, p. 84). Alternately it might be argued that the Durham rule itself was not the primary determinant in increasing the number of post-Durham NGRI acquittals. Instead, judges, and juries in the few cases in which they were employed, were faced upon appeal with a court sympathetic to the notion of a dynamic interpretation of behavior and a shunting of defendants from the criminal system into the mental health system for treatment and "cure."

In this matter, there also appears some evidence to support the position of Clyne (1973) and Arens, Granfield, and Susman (1965) who argue that jurors do not understand the fine legal distinctions in the various rules governing insanity. Or, if they do, these distinctions are ignored. Instead, jurors utilize a commonsense definition of insanity and base their decision upon their sympathy toward the defendant and the perceived reprehensibility of a given crime. Somewhat supporting Clyne's notion are the findings by Pasewark and associates who report a marked variation among counties of a given state in the frequency of the plea and its success rate that is not related to county population. In addition, relatively comparable counties evidence markedly discrepant rates. Although they offer no data to substantiate their speculations, the authors suggest that factors other than statutory language, such as the receptivity of a particular court to a psychodynamic approach of behavior, might be a determining factor in whether or not a defendant enters the NGRI plea or is so adjudicated. In the New York study, other factors also appeared to be operative in the NGRI adjudication. Particular groups tended to be overrepresented in the NGRI population. Among these were Caucasians, females, both the more poorly and better educated, mothers who committed infanticide, and law enforcement officials. In a sense, these findings suggest that there are particular individuals who are more likely to be found NGRI, and tend to negate the importance played by statute language.

Also bearing upon the influence of statutory language are the results of Arens and Susman (1966) of a content analysis of charges provided juries considering the issue of insanity during the years 1960–62 in Washington, D. C. while the Durham rule was operative. Results suggested that judges continued to instruct juries in terms of the McNaughton criteria, requiring a dramatic breakdown of the defendant's reasoning capacity and an inability to distinguish right and wrong, despite the fact that Durham was the operative law. Similar conceptualizations of insanity were also held by jury members in the district (Arens et al. 1965).

PATIENT RIGHTS AND THE INSANITY PLEA

In this chapter, we are dealing with a specific subgroup of the mentally ill. These are persons accused of crimes and subsequently determined NGRI by the courts. As such, they represent but a small proportion of the mentally ill, but their limited number should not preclude an active consideration and protection of their rights. In our minds, within the past 10 years, much has been accomplished by the courts toward this purpose. Rulings have been promulgated suggesting that criminal charges against defendants incompetent to stand trial must be dismissed after a reasonable period (United States ex rel. *Wolfersdorf* v. *Johnson,* 1970); that the adjudicated NGRI defendant has either a statutory (*Rouse* v. *Cameron,* 1966, 1967) or constitutional (*Bell* v. *Wayne County General Hospital,* 1974; *Wyatt* v. *Aderholt,* 1974; *Nason* v. *Superintendent,* 1968) right to treatment and that he/she must be housed in the least restrictive treatment facility (*Baxstrom* v. *Herold,* 1966; United States ex rel. *Wolfersdorf* v. *Johnson,* 1970; *People* v. *Feagley,* 1975; *Covington* v. *Harris,* 1969). Despite these advances, however, other problems or potential problems concerned with rights of this category of patient or prospective patient remain to be resolved.

Abolishing the Plea

Currently, it is probable that the most crucial issue involving this class of individuals is whether they have a right to the insanity defense at all. As remarked upon before, there is an apparent ground wave of feeling that the NGRI plea is abused, and strong suggestions have been made for its elimination. It is regrettable, we believe, that among proponents advancing this notion can be counted mental health administrators—a group from whom greater sympathy toward the mentally ill might be hoped.

While there is evidence to suggest that the insanity plea is entered in but a small proportion of criminal cases and seems to be not overly successful once it is entered, there exist, to the authors' knowledge, no data to either support or refute the argument of proponents for elimination of the plea that a substantial number of those adjudicated NGRI are, in fact, not insane and perhaps not even mentally ill. We can only assume, until other facts are presented, that the courts responsible for these decisions have done an adequate task in determining these defendants as insane, despite the fact that preliminary data of the New York studies by Pasewark and associates suggest the possibility that variables other than the individual's mental state might enter into the insanity decision. Essentially, conclusions relative to this particular argument must await the generation of appropriate data.

Depite the preceding remarks, we should seriously question the constitutionality of any move to abolish the insanity plea, even should it be demonstrated that a substantial segment of those defendants found NGRI are not, in fact, legally insane or mentally disturbed. The notion of nonculpability for criminal acts because of lack of reason is historically founded in English common law to exculpate particular classes of individuals, such as children, the severely retarded, and the mentally ill from responsibility and guilt for a criminal act. Two classic court decisions deal with efforts of states to eliminate or restrict use of the plea. The Washington Supreme Court in *State* v. *Strasburg* (1910) declared unconstitutional a statute eliminating the defense of "insanity, idiocy, or imbecility" in criminal trials. A similar ruling was made by the Supreme Court of Mississippi on a statute seeking to eliminate the defense for first degree murder (*Sinclair* v. *State,* 1931). In both cases, the respective courts opined that intent was an element necessary for guilt and that elimination of consideration of an element bearing upon intent, such as insanity, deprived the individual of a constitutional right.

Mandatory Commitment

The practice and procedures whereby a defendant is committed to a mental hospital following a successful NGRI plea are deserving of particular scrutiny. In some states, involuntary commitment to a mental institution automatically follows the NGRI adjudication. In other jurisdictions, some type of formalized hearing is conducted to determine the acquittee's mental state and his/her need for hospitalization.

In Missouri, for example, the adjudicated NGRI defendant is subjected to automatic commitment. Following commitment, the burden reposes with the patient to request a hearing challenging his continued hospitalization (Missouri Annotated Statutes, 1979; *State* v. *Kee,* 1974). In the District of Columbia, *Bolton* v. *Harris* (1968) originally demanded that a procedure similar to an involuntary civil commitment proceeding be instituted to determine the necessity for hospitalization. However, in the later case of *United States* v. *Ecker* (1977), the District of Columbia Court of Appeals decided that equating the *procedures* to commit an NGRI and a civil committee does not necessarily mean that the *standards* are identical for the acquitted NGRI individual and the person civilly committed. *Ecker* decided that, following a successful NGRI defense, the burden of proving the impropriety of commitment was upon the patient, rather than the state.

The presumption of continuing insanity created by placing the burden on the committee seems questionable for two reasons. Firstly, in addition to being found insane at the time of the crime, the defendant has also been found competent to stand trial. Temporally, the latter finding relates more closely to the defendant's status at the time of acquittal. Despite the fact that standards for competency and insanity differ markedly, and many severe psychotics, such as paranoids, are able to effectively participate in their own defense, it appears reasonable to the authors that the competency finding should control on the question of mental illness. Present freedom from mental illness affecting one sphere of activity has been established. In contrast to the rules of many states, this would mean that, once found competent to stand trial, the acquittee would be presumed sane. Deprivation of liberty following acquittal could be grounded only in the civil commitment procedures and standards; and, in fact, some jurisdictions, such as Indiana, have required that the state justify commitment subsequent to an NGRI commitment with reference to the standards for civil commitment (*Wilson* v. *State,* 1972).

Secondly, where the state places the burden on the individual, this burden may extend well beyond negating the grounds of the original NGRI adjudication. The committee must show that either mental illness is absent or that the individual's present mental state will not cause him to be dangerous in any way. In other words, although the state may only be able to present evidence of mental illness entirely different from that which led to the NGRI verdict and a totally different danger, the NGRI is still forced to negate the state's claim (*Lee* v. *Kolb,* 1978). Thus, a paranoid individual killing his mother in response to a delusional and hallucinatory system is placed in a rather anomalous position. It would be necessary for him to demonstrate that, not only is he devoid of the paranoic symptomology that led to the homicidal offense, but also that he does not possess the propensity to commit another "dangerous" act, such as child molestation, that might be completely unrelated to the original paranoid condition.

Indeterminant Length of Commitment

A problem related to mandatory hospitalization following a NGRI verdict is that created by the indeterminant length of the commitment of the NGRI. Typically no statutory provision is made for regular review of these patients, despite the fact that it may be available to civil committees. In *Dorsey* v. *Solomon* (1977), the court specifically refused to require such periodic review. The holding of *Dorsey* purports to be based upon *Suzuki* v. *Quisenberry* (1976), which dealt with the rights of civil committees to periodic review. Far from holding that there was no entitlement of periodic review, *Suzuki* held that the Hawaii statute, requiring a reevalutation of the patient at six-month intervals, "does not seem unreasonable" (p. 1134). In some jurisdictions, like the District of Columbia, the NGRI acquittee is entitled to the standards and procedures for the civil committee after the maximum sentence for his underlying crime has elapsed. In practice, however, this provision is relatively meaningless. There is a broad range of sentences for a particular crime, and the maximum tends to be quite long. Thus, in the District of Columbia, the sentence for robbery can range from 2 to 10 years. (D. C. Code, 1973). Additionally, the NGRI patient is typically tried upon the most serious criminal charge that can be culled from his act. The NGRI defendant who commits homicide is usually tried for some degree of murder. Plea bargaining does not typically transpire to reduce the charge to manslaughter. Similarly, the NGRI defendant is almost invariably tried for rape rather than a reduced sexual molestation or assault charge.

In *United States* v. *Ecker* (1977) the district of Columbia Court of Appeals decided that, because the acquittee's maximum possible sentence had not yet elapsed, he was ineligible for the standards and procedures used by civil comittees. Ecker had served seven years for murder; the maximum sentence was life. This despite *United States* v. *Brown* (1973), which indicated that the standards for a civil committee are to be applied after a five-year period when the presumption of insanity would vanish.

Differential Treatment During Hospitalization

The differential treatment accorded NGRI patients following hospitalization also merits examination. Typically, after admission, the patient is housed in a separate area and subject to special security measures. This occurs despite the fact that he has been convicted of no crime.

Use of NGRI to Hospitalize

Ironically, there is the possibility of another emerging threat to civil rights posed by an apparent interplay between the NGRI and involuntary hospitalization procedures. Thus, as civil commitment laws become more stringent and make it more difficult to hospitalize persons, there is the possibility that increasing recourse will be made to the NGRI procedure. Arens (1974) remarks upon this phenomenon in citing *Overholser* v. *Lynch* (*Overholser* v. *Lynch,* 1961; *Lynch* v. *Overholser,* 1962) in the District of Columbia, where both the prosecution and judge may raise the issue of insanity despite the defendant's plea of guilty, in this instance, to a misdemeanor. This phenomenon has also been observed in Hawaii, following *Suzuki* v. *Quisenberry* (1976), which established dangerousness as an essential element necessary for nonconsensual hospitalization. Thus, where previously a middle-aged female disrobing in Honolulu would have been hospitalized under emergency or involuntary commitment procedures, she might now be arrested for indecent exposure, found NGRI in trial, and thence committed to a mental health facility.

Differential Hospitalization Periods

The differential hospitalization periods subsequent to the NGRI decision reported in Michigan by Cooke and Sikorski (1974) raise some measure of concern for the rights of NGRI patients. The Cooke and Sikorski study indicates that, in that state, length of hospitalization is associated strongly with the severity of the criminal act for which the NGRI patient was tried. For example, if it cannot be demonstrated that persons acquitted of the more serious crimes, such as murder, are in fact, not less amenable to treatment, or more immediately dangerous, the suspicion must be held that criteria other than recovery of sanity and dangerousness are involved in discharge decisions; and, despite provisions of law, those persons charged with more serious crimes are hospitalized for longer periods, despite their contemporary mental state. These facts may also support the hypothesis that a strong punitive element might be involved in some sites in determining length of hospitalization for the NGRI patient.

Expert Witnesses

As is true in other criminal cases, the type and quality of expert witnesses available to the defense pose problems for the person entering the insanity plea. As a result of the strong relationship between social class and criminal behavior, most efendants can be classified as legally indigent and are thus dependent upon public resources in the construction of a defense. In the area of the insanity plea, this invariably means that expert witnesses are provided through the particular mechanism financed by a state to garner psychiatric evaluations as to whether the defendant is competent to stand trial or was insane at the time of the alleged crime. In some states, like Hawaii, evaluations are conducted by a sanity commission established by the court from persons willing to serve in this capactiy. Although this procedure ensures that expert witnesses are drawn from both the public and private sectors, question might be raised as to the competency of those volunteering. While the defendant may also utilize additional experts to those comprising the commission, these must be financed by the defendant. In practice, use of other experts is probably rare, although no data exist concerning this matter. Further, to the authors' knowledge, there is no available study that critically compares the qualifications of persons volunteering for this function with those who do not volunteer.

In states with laws similar to those of Wyoming, this issue assumes greater significance. In Wyoming, upon entering the plea "not guilty by reason of insanity," evaluation of the defendant's mental state is made at either the state hospital or another facility deemed appropriate by the court. In practice, NGRI defendants are uniformly evaluated at the state hospital. At the defendant's expense, additional psychiatric evaluations can be secured. However, because of the indigent status of most defendants, this seems rarely done. In practice, therefore, psychiatric testimony is provided by only a limited number of state hospital personnel, with whatever bias this small group of experts might harbor. In this regard, for example, Arens (1974) raises the question of the possibly greater punitive orientation of public psychiatrists as compared to private psychiatrists, athough he reports no substantial data to support this contention.

In addition to the problem created by a few institutionally employed psychiatrists presenting the only psychiatric testimony heard in trial, one may legitimately question the appropriateness of one branch of state government prosecuting a defendant while another arm provides the basic information relative to culpability based upon insanity. In this vein, Arens (1974) implies that a more-or-less accepted alliance prevails between mental hospitals and the prosecution. According to Arens, representatives of the prosecution have easier access to hospital records than do representatives of the defense who are regarded somewhat hostilely by hospital personnel. Unfortunately, no systematic data exist to support or refute Arens' claim.

The use of psychiatrists, particularly those employed in the public sector, as expert witnesses in NGRI cases creates other possible problems. For example, it is possible that psychiatrists, whose primary mission is treatment, might be biased by this orientation in the evaluation of a defendant's insanity. Being the ultimate recipient of those adjudicated NGRI, their treatment orientation might predispose them to prescreen from the NGRI ranks those defendants whom they regard as "nontreatable" so as not to inundate treatment facilities with this type of potential patient. Preliminary results of interviews with Wyoming defense attorneys who have represented NGRI cases (Pasewark & Craig, in press) suggest that a substantial proportion believe this to be the case. Whether their opinion is an accurate reflection of the fact is currently unknown. While meriting future investigation, on its face, this view is somewhat inconsistent with the previously expressed argument implying a punitive orientation of psychiatrists as responsible for the more lengthy hospitalization of persons found NGRI to the more serious felonies. If such a situation does prevail, it harbors inherent danger for the NGRI defendant. For example, Albers and Pasewark (1974) determined that psychiatric opinion was apparently quite influential in court decisions relative to involutary hospitalization. In their study, a 98% concordance rate was found between psychiatric recommendations and judicial dispositions. Results of a study being conducted by Fukunaga also suggest a high concordance rate between psychiatric judgment concerning insanity and ultimate court disposition when the NGRI plea is entered in Hawaii.

Other Concerns

The present gray legal area of adjudicated NGRI patients appears to be one demanding test cases to determine the rights of these patients. Under the laws of many states, they are alternately treated as civil and noncivil patients. For example, like involuntarily committed civil patients, they do not generally have the right to refuse mental health treatment as do convicted felons. Yet, as previously mentioned, they do not have the right to automatic periodic review, for discharge purposes, as does the civilly committed patient.

Another emerging sphere of concern relates to the present thrust in some states to include the NGRI patient within the criminal justice system, despite the fact that such patients have been convicted of no crime. Reference to this trend was made in regard to the efforts in the states of New York and Illinois to alter the insanity plea. In other states, such as Hawaii, a more insipid manifestation of this trend is observed. There, courts have placed some NGRI cases who have not been hospitalized under custody of probation officers. Considerable question remains as to the legality of this practice. For example, various judicial districts have ruled that those not triable by reason of insanity (United States ex rel. *Wolfersdorf* v. *Johnson,* 1970) or persons civilly committed

(*Craig* v. *Hocker,* 1975; *Kesselbrenner* v. *Anonymous,* 1973; In re Anonymous, 1972) cannot be confined in correctional institutions without consideration of the degree of dangerousness posed by the patient. Transfers of civil patients from an institution giving care and treatment, a hospital, to an institution with no duty to treat, a prison, have also been prohibited even though the patient is dangerous (In re Anonymous, 1972). Similarly, other courts have ruled that felons confined in a correctional institution cannot be transferred administratively to a mental hospital without compliance with a procedure comparable to that provided to persons subject to involuntary hospitalization proceedings, because of the additional deprivaitons accruing to those prisoners by being labeled mentally ill. (United States ex rel. *Schuster* v. *Herold,* 1969). Although the Hawaii procedure represents a reverse type of transfer, the principle of double stigmatization appears to apply.

SUMMARY

A review of the literature concerning the NGRI plea suggests the following: (1) There currently exist but few empirical studies dealing with the insanity plea. Because of the lack of a substantial body of data relating to the plea, it seems obvious that statements made about and changes suggested for the plea are based upon subjective impressions and/or emotional reactions to that which is believed to occur in the operation of the plea, rather than to that which actually transpires. To correct this gross deficiency, it is apparent that manifold studies on the operation of the plea are required. (2) Although there have been many court decisions concerned with the rights of NGRI patients, these have been restricted almost exclusively to those bearing upon the rights of these patients to treatment and to the least restrictive treatment alternative. Many other problems concerning the rights of these patients remain to be resolved. These include such matters as the exclusive use of public psychiatrists as expert witnesses in some states; the treatment of hospitalized NGRI patients as both criminal and civil; and the increasing tendency of some states to include the NGRI patient in the criminal justice rather than in the mental health system.

REFERENCES

Albers, D. A., & Pasewark, R. A. Involuntary hospitalization: Surrender at the courthouse. *American Journal of Community Psychology,* 1974, *2,* 287–289.
American Law Institute Model Penal Code, proposed official draft § 4.01, (1962).

Arens, R. *Insanity defense.* New York: Philosophical Library, 1974.

Arens, R., Granfield, D. D., & Susman, J. Jurors, jury charges, and insanity. *Catholic University of America Law Review,* 1965, *14,* 1–29.

Arens, R., & Susman, J. Judges, jury charges, and insanity. *Howard Law Journal,* 1966, *12,* 1–34.

Baxstrom v. Herold, 383 U.S. 107 (1966).

Bell v. Wayne County General Hospital, 384 F. Supp. 1085 (E.D. Mich. 1974).

Bolton v. Harris, 395 F. 2d 642 (D.C. Cir. 1968).

Clyne, P. *Guilty but insane.* London: McDonald, 1961.

Colorado Revised Statutes § 16–8–101 (1973).

Cooke, G., & Sikorski, C. Factors affecting length of hospitalization in persons adjudicated not guilty by reason of insanity. *Bulletin of the American Academy of Psychiatry and the Law,* 1974, *2,* 251–261.

Covington v. Harris, 419 F.2d 617 (D.C. Cir. 1969).

Craig v. Hocker, 405 F. Supp. 656 (D. Nev. 1975).

District of Columbia Code, § 22–2901 (1973).

Dorsey v. Solomon, 435 F. Supp. 725 (D. Md. 1977).

Durham v. United States, 214 F. 2d 862, 874–75 (D.C. Cir. 1954).

Fukunaga, K. *The criminally insane.* Honolulu: Hawaii State Department of Health, 1977.

Fukunaga, K., Pasewark, R. A., Hawkins, M., & Gudeman, H. Insanity plea: Inter-examiner agreement and concordance of psychiatric opinion and court verdict. *Law and Human Behavior,* in press.

Goldstein, A. *The insanity defense.* New Haven, Connecticut: Yale University Press, 1967.

In re Anonymous, 69 Misc. 2d 181, 329 N.Y.S.2d 542 (Sup. Ct. 1972).

Kesselbrenner v. Anonymous, 33 N.Y. 2d 161, 305 N.E. 2d 903, 350 N.Y.S. 2d 889 (1973).

Kolb, L. C., Steadman, H. J., Carnahan, W. A., & Wright, J. B. *The insanity defense in New York: A report to Governor Hugh L. Carey.* Albany, N.Y.: State of New York, Department of Mental Hygiene, February 17, 1978.

Laboratory of Community Psychiatry, Harvard Medical School, *Competency to stand trial and mental illness.* New York: Jason Aronson, 1974.

Lee v. Kolb, 449 F. Supp. 1368 (W.D.N.Y. 1978).

Lynch v. Overholser, 369 U.S. 705 (1962).

Matthews, A. R., Jr. *Mental disability and the criminal law: A field study.* Chicago: American Bar Association, 1970.

McDonald v. United States, 312 F.2d 847 (D.C. Cir. 1962).

Missouri Annotated Statutes, § 202.010(11), § 202.123 (2) (Vernon Supp. 1979).

Morrow, W. R., & Peterson, D. B. Follow-up on discharged offenders—"not guilty by reason of insanity" and "criminal sexual psychopaths." *Journal of Criminal Law, Criminology, and Police Science,* 1966, *57,* 31–34.

Nason v. Superintendent, 353 Mass. 604, 233 N.E. 2d 908 (1968).

The New York Times, August 17, 1977, 2:1.

The New York Times, July 21, 1966, 17:1, 6.

Overholser v. Lynch, 288 F.2d 388 (D.C. Cir. 1961). *rev'd.,* 369 U.S. 705 (1962).

Pasewark, R. A. & Bunting, B. *Characteristics and disposition of defendants making the insanity plea under bifurcated trial procedure.* Research in progress, 1979.

Pasewark, R. A., & Craig, P. L. *Insanity plea: Defense attorneys' view. Journal of Psychiatry and Law,* in press.

Pasewark, R. A., & Lanthorn, B. W. Disposition of persons utilizing the insanity plea in a rural state. *Journal of Humanics,* 1977, *5,* 87–98.

Pasewark, R. A., & Pantle, M. L. Insanity plea: Legislator's view. *American Journal of Psychiatry,* 1979, *136,* 22–223.

Pasewark, R. A., Pantle, M. L., & Steadman, H. J. Characteristics and disposition of persons found not guilty by reason of insanity in New York State, 1971–76. *American Journal of Psychiatry,* 1979, *136,* 655–660. (a)

Pasewark, R. A., Pantle, M. L., & Steadman, H. J. The insanity plea in New York State, 1965–76. *New York State Bar Journal,* 1979, *51,* 186–189, 217–225. (b)

Pasewark, R. A., & Pasewark, M. D. Insanity revised: Once more over the cuckoo's nest. *Journal of Psychiatry and Law,* 1978, *6,* 481–498.

Pasewark, R. A., & Seidenzahl, D. Opinions concerning the insanity plea and criminality among mental patients. *Bulletin of the American Academy of Psychiatry and the Law,* 1980, *7,* 199-202.

People v. Feagley, 14 Cal. 3d 338, 535 P. 2d 373, 121 Cal. Rptr. 509 (1975).

Quinsey, V. L., Pruesse, M., & Fernley, R. A follow-up of patients found "unfit to stand trial" or "not guilty by reason of insanity." *Canadian Psychiatric Association Journal,* 1975, *20,* 461–467.

Rappeport, J. R. Editorial comment upon "The Insanity Defense." *Bulletin of the American Academy of Psychiatry and the Law,* 1976, *4,* 75.

Rouse v. Cameron, 373 F.2d 451 (D.C. Cir. 1967).

Sauer, R. H. The insanity defense in Maryland. *Maryland State Medical Journal,* 1975, *24,* 51–52.

Sauer, R. H., & Mullens, P. M. The insanity defense: M'Naughton vs. ALI. *Bulletin of the American Academy of Psychiatry and the Law,* 1976, *4,* 73–75.

Scheidemandel, P. L., & Kanno, C. L. *The mentally ill offender: A survey of treatment programs.* Washington, D.C.: Joint Information Service, 1965.

Simon, R. J. *The jury and the defense of insanity.* Boston: Little, Brown, & Co., 1967.

Sinclair v. State, 161 Miss. 142, 132 So. 581 (1931).

State v. Kee, 510 S.W. 2d 477 (Mo. 1974).

State v. Strasburg, 60 Wash, 106, 110 P. 1020 (1910).

Suzuki v. Quisenberry, 411 F. Supp. 1113 (D. Hawaii 1976).

Szasz, T. S. *Law, liberty, and psychiatry.* New York: MacMillan Publishing Co., 1963.

Szasz, T. S. *Psychiatric justice.* New York: MacMillan Publishing Co., 1965.

United States v. Brawner, 471 F.2d 969 (D.C. Cir. 1972).

United States v. Brown, 478, F.2d 606 (D.C. Cir 1973).

United States v. Ecker, 543 F.2d 178 (D.C. Cir. 1976), *cert. denied* 429 U.S. 1063 (1977).

United States ex rel. Schuster v. Herold 410 F.2d 1071 (2d Cir.), *cert. denied,* 396 U.S. 847 (1969).

United States ex rel. Wolfersdorf v. Johnson 317 F. Supp. 66 (S.D.N.Y. 1970).

Walker, N. *Crime and insanity in England.* Vol. 1, Edinburgh, Scotland: University Press, 1968.

Walker, N., & McCabe, S. *Crime and insanity in England.* Vol. 2, Edinburgh, Scotland: University Press, 1973.

Wilson v. State, 259 Ind. 375, 287 N.E. 2d 875 (1972).

Wyatt v. Aderholt, 503 F.2d 1305 (5th Cir. 1974).

Wyoming Statutes, § 7-11-304 (1977).

Chapter 5

THE RIGHT NOT TO BE A FALSE POSITIVE:
Problems in the Application of the Dangerousness Standard*

Henry J. Steadman, Ph.D.

Among the rights of mental patients that have been affirmed in the past decade of mental health law activism, the right not to be a false positive is missing. This potential right has been overlooked, despite its close association with one of the major issues of this era—the definition and application of the dangerousness standard for involuntary commitment. That a right not to be a false positive was reasonable corollary to other protections surrounding the dangerousness standard was raised by Wilkins (1974) in a rarely cited, but seminal, article. Wilkins analyzed the moral trade-offs that society might be willing to make in its decisions for involuntary commitment or differential treatment because of assessments of a person's violence potential. Just how significant Wilkins' observation is becomes evident when the uses of the dangerousness standard for involuntary treatment and differential treatment are reviewed.

Shah (1978) has cited at least 15 different points in the criminal justice and mental health systems where questions of an individual's dangerousness may be addressed. These range from decisions of

*The research reported herein was partially supported by PHS Grant MH28850 from the National Institute of Mental Health Center for Studies in Crime and Delinquency.

emergency civil commitment in mental hospitals through release decisions from such facilities to the use of the death sentence in capital
crime, as is the case currently in Texas. Fagin (1976) noted that 38 of
the 45 U.S. jurisdictions with emergency commitment statutes limit
commitment to individuals who appear dangerous to themselves or
others. The number of individuals retained under the dangerousness
standard in state mental hospitals has been estimated by Scheidemandel and Kanno (1969) to be about 50,000 people per year. An additional 30,000 persons per year are evaluated within the criminal justice
system for dangerousness to decide either to which type of secure
facility they will be sent or whether or not they will be released. Thus,
estimations of a person's dangerousness are widespread in the U.S. in
terms of both the numbers of persons and the range of situations to
which they apply, from child custody cases to release of defendants
who have been acquitted by reason of insanity.

One of the basic difficulties in addressing the empirical evidence
on predictions of dangerousness is imprecison as to what the concept
of danger to self or others means conceptually and operationally.
Megargee has pointed out that: "*dangerousness* is an unfortunate term,
for it implies there is a trait of 'dangerousness' which, like intelligence,
is a relatively constant characteristic of the person being assessed. . . .
It is better to eschew the term 'dangerousness' in favor of discussing
the problems involved in 'predicting dangerous behavior' " (1976; p.
5). This distinction highlights two core characteristics of the concept
of *dangerousness*. The first is that as a prediction, dangerousness is an
estimation of the potential that a person will do something that is
defined as dangerous. As such, dangerousness is a perception of the
evaluator and not a characteristic, constant or otherwise, of the evalu-
atee. Second, dangerousness is by its nature a prediction. It means that
because of certain characteristics or behaviors, a person is seen to have
a high probability of performing certain acts in the future. Thus, the
essence of dangerousness is that it is a perception and a prediction.

Because of its definition, one of the key questions in assessing the
empirical data on predictions of dangerous behavior becomes specify-
ing what behavior is dangerous. Clearly, dangerous behavior includes
murder and assault and probably rape. However, the courts have included other behaviors such as writing "rubber" checks (*United States
v. Charnizon* 232 A. 2d 586). Monahan's (1975) review of the relevant
research notes that the behaviors most often used to test predictive
accuracy are arrests for violent crimes or physical assaults. In reviewing the empirical literature here, both definitions will be employed,
although it is more useful in mental health settings to limit dangerous
behavior to any assaultive behavior (Steadman & Cocozza, 1974).

Before proceeding to review the empirical evidence on the accuracy of predicting dangerous behavior, it remains to be clarified why Wilkins' discussion of the right not to be a false positive is so important. The dangerousness standard required predictions by professionals within both the mental health and criminal justice systems, with psychiatrists the most frequent predictors. As Scheff (1966) has observed, for all types of medical interventions, medical ideology favors consistently erring towards overtreatment, i.e., treating a healthy person rather than not treating the sick person. When this ideology is combined with infrequent behaviors, such as those included under the rubric of dangerous behavior, consistent overidentification of people as dangerous occurs. That is, in a group of 100 persons about, say, five might be expected to engage in an assaultive act in the next 12 months. In order to pick even three or four of these five who will be assaultive, with current levels of technology, probably 25 or 30 will be incorrectly identified. Public pressure and medical ideology both encourage the 25 or 30 to be incorrectly included in the assaultive group to control the three or four who will be. Thus, a false positive rate of 8 or 10 to 1 occurs. The alternative to reduce this false positive rate is to not identify any, or at best a few, of those who will actually be assaultive. Thus, what rights a mental patient or offender may have not to be so identified are important policy questions, and are a productive framework in which to examine the empirical evidence on the accuracy of predictions of future dangerous behavior.

EVIDENCE ON THE ACCURACY OF PREDICTIONS OF DANGEROUS BEHAVIOR

The reports dealing with the prediction of dangerous behavior fall into three general categories: (1) essays without data or with irrelevant data; (2) reviews of the primary research, occasionally with some secondary analysis; and (3) a few research studies with relevant primary data. The first category of articles predominate in law reviews and psychiatric journals. Most articles cited in the law journals and legal briefs have marginal data bases to them (Ennis & Litwack, 1974; Stone, 1975) or offer little more than anecdotes (Treffert, 1974; Peele, Chadoff & Taub, 1974). Many of these articles are seen as weighty contributions to the field, and their legal views are no doubt important. If carefully examined, however, there is often more ideology than empiricism at the core of their arguments. The other type of article in this first category contains those that relate to the arrest rate of ex-mental patients. The inappropriate entry of these studies into assessments of predictive accuracy we have discussed elsewhere (Cocozza & Steadman, 1976). Since the majority of persons released from state mental hospitals are voluntary patients whose release in no way relates to psychiatric or legal assessments of their dangerousness, these arrest-rate studies are at best tangentially related to questions of the validity of estimations of future assaultive behavior.

The second category of published work on dangerousness includes many valuable pieces. Among these works are Shah (1977, 1978), Monahan (1978) Laves (1975), Mesnikoff and Lauterbach (1975), and Rubin (1972). In many ways, each of these reviews covers the same literature up to its publication date, and then draws some empirically grounded policy implications. In many ways, these surveys are so comprehensive that they raise the question as to why this chapter was written. The answer to this question is twofold. Firstly, there have been some significant developments in the evidence in this field, even in the last year or two, that warrant inclusion. Secondly, and perhaps more importantly, none of the prior reviews groups the research studies in a manner that highlights their key trends.

Of particular interest in this chapter is the distinction between the clinical and statistical predictions of dangerous behavior and the evidence on the various groups of professionals who are legally empowered to make such assessments in civil and criminal courts. It will become quite clear that, while this research literature is unusually consistent in its findings on both clinical and statistical prediction, there is considerably less evidence than there is generally assumed to be.

It is the third category of studies mentioned earlier that will be the focus here, i.e., those with primary data. Since many of these studies have been included in the review articles already cited, the earlier research will be skimmed with a greater concentration on four studies of more recent vintage together with the research and policy implications that are suggested by all the existing evidence.

Clinical Prediction of Dangerous Behavior

Most of the data related to the accuracy of clinical predictions of dangerous behavior come from research that followed mental patients released, contrary to psychiatric advice, from maximum security facilities by court decisions. The first study was that of Kozol and colleagues (1972) that reported a follow-up of offenders released from the Bridgewater State Hospital program for dangerous sex offenders. One group (N=49) was released by the committing courts against the evaluation team's advice, and another group (N=82) was released with psychiatric approval after diagnosis and treatment. The criterion for failure was arrest for a violent crime during the follow-up period. Of those released against psychiatric advice, 35% were arrested for violent crime, compared to 6% of those released after treatment with the approval of the psychiatric staff. One of the very serious problems with Kozol's work is that the length of time at risk of rearrest was not controlled (Cocozza, 1973). Because those fully treated remained in Bridgewater, the group released against psychiatric advice could have been at risk as much as four years longer. Therefore, there are serious questions as to whether the two groups may be directly compared. What is clear is that, even among the high recidivating group, the false positive rate was about 2:1, with 35% accurately identified by the psychiatrists, but with 65% of those so identified not violently recidivating.

A second study that is often included in assessments of clinical accuracy in predicting dangerous behavior (e.g. Monahan, 1978) is the 1973 report from Patuxent Institute in Maryland (State of Maryland, 1973). This report should not be included because of the widely differing treatment that the "comparison groups" received. As we have noted elsewhere (Steadman, 1977), and as will be discussed below in more detail, all of the reports on the clinical successes of the Patuxent program published prior to 1977 compared "fully treated" individuals who had been in very effective supervised parole for up to three years with those released against the clinicians' advice whose recidivism rates began being calculated at the moment they first returned to the community. This meant that one group's recidivism was assessed only after they had been in the community for three years and all failures during this time were not counted. In contrast, the comparison group's failures in the same time period were counted. Thus, the methodological unsoundnesses preclude the inclusion of these Patuxent studies in the literature relevant to the questions under review here.

The next study relevant to clinical estimations of future dangerous behavior was our follow-up of the Baxstrom patients (Steadman & Cocozza 1974). This study followed 967 patients who had been inmates in maximum security correctional mental hospitals prior to the 1966 *Baxstrom v. Herold* decision of the United States Supreme Court. Following this ruling that appropriate due process protections had not been extended in the retention of this group, all 967 inmates were transferred en masse during a four-month period to regular security mental hospitals, despite having been retained for an average of 14 years because of their mental illness and dangerousness. During the four years that they were followed through mental hospitals and the community, 20% were assaultive at some time. Thus, the false positive rate was approximately 4:1. Our contention that these transfers provide documentation for psychiatric inabilities to predict dangerous behavior accurately has been argued by others (Halpern, 1975). Given the information contained in the court decision, however, and the legal statutes under which they were detained, it seems that, indeed, the Baxstrom patient transfers were a naturalistic study of clinical predictions of dangerous behavior. Further discussion of the research and its critics can be found in Steadman and Cocozza (1980).

In an amazingly similar study, Thornberry and Jacoby (1974) arrived at similar conclusions in Pennsylvania. Their study was strikingly similar in that they followed a group of 596 patients who were mass transfers after a Pennsylvania decision (*Dixon* v. *Attorney General of the Commonwealth of Pennsylvania,* 323, F. Supp. 966 (1971)), ruling that proper review had not occurred in decision of their retention in a hospital for the criminally insane. The study is also similar in its findings. It was found that 14% of the 438 subjects at risk displayed some type of assaultive behavior in the community during a four-year follow-up period. Thus, the false positive rate for an older, long-term institutionalized group was about 6:1.

The next study in the chronology of research on clinical predictions of dangerous behavior did not involve judicial intervention. In this work (Cocozza & Steadman, 1976), the legal action precipitating the research was a statutory revision requiring two psychiatrists to assess whether indicted felony defendants who were incompetent to stand trial were dangerous. This determination by the court resulted in placement in either a mental hygiene facility, if not dangerous, or correctional facility, if dangerous. During the first year of this statute, there were 257 males for whom a determination was made by psychiatrists. In 154 of these cases, the defendants were evaluated as dangerous, and in 113 cases, they were evaluated as not dangerous. As reported in detail elsewhere (Steadman & Cocozza, 1978a) 51% of the dangerous were assaultive while hospitalized, and 39% of the not dangerous were. After release, 16% of those evaluated as dangerous were assaultive, resulting in either rehospitalization or arrest, and 23% of the not-dangerous group were assaultive. Overall, there was no difference in the frequency of assaultive behavior between the two groups beyond that obtainable by chance. Further, while the clinical false positive rate for in-hospital assaultiveness was only 1:1, for community assaultiveness it was 5.4:1 (81 classified as dangerous who were not assaultive to 15 so classified who were assaultive).

Adding to the research on judicial interventions into psychiatric and administrative practices that produced clinical follow-up opportunities was the recently completed work reassessing the efficacy of Patuxent Instutute for Defective Delinquents in Maryland (Steadman, 1977). In this work, the comparison groups were reconceptualized from the inhouse reports that had previously been reported. In our work, five groups were designated. They reflected all possible pathways into and through Patuxent. Four groups are of particular interest:

the three evaluated as dangerous by the staff, which include (1) a "fully treated" group, (2) a partially treated group released by the courts against staff recommendation, and (3) a group disapproved for admissions despite staff estimations of their dangerousness, and, finally (4) the group evaluated by the staff as not dangerous. Of the fully treated group, 31% were arrested for violent crimes. Of the partially treated group, 33% were arrested, and of the group not admitted at all despite the staff's evaluations as dangerous, 41% were arrested. Thus, the mean percentage arrested for violent crimes among the three study groups clinically evaluated as dangerous was 33.8%. However, in the fourth study group, those evaluated as not dangerous, 33.3% were arrested for violent offenses. There was no indication from these data of any ability on the part of the staff to identify accurately those who would be dangerous.

A study currently in progress in Texas directly addresses clinical accuracy in predicting dangerous behavior, and is closely linked to judicial action. This study (Sheldon, 1977) involves the sequelae of a class action suit, *Renolds* v. *Neil*, that required the review of 188 inmates at Rusk State Hospital for the Criminally Insane for possible placement in less restrictive alternatives. To perform these evaluations, the staff developed an instrument that was used in the assessments of all 188 inmates. Based on these instruments and other clinical information, 34 were defined as "very dangerous" and retained at Rusk, 87 were defined as "dangerous," thus requiring civil commitment, and 67 were discharged outright. Currently, all three groups are being followed to determine the utility of the assessment instrument. Sheldon states that, "To date, there has been no report of any serious criminal offense by any of the patients who were discharged with or without follow-up care." However, since the data are so incomplete at this time, any conclusions are premature.

The final study of clinical predictions involves no judicial action at all. It is also the only study of clinical predictions reviewed here in which the evaluations were not performed by psychiatrists. This research by Levinson and Ramsey (1979) assessed the accuracy of predictions of dangerous behavior by paraprofessionals called *mental health associates* (MHAs). Studying clients of a county emergency mental health unit, the files were checked to locate the routine estimates of danger to self or others that had been made during the work-ups. It was felt that since the MHAs were not as bound to the hospital and psychiatric ideology by training and job definition as were psychiatrists, and because their backgrounds were closer to those of the clients than is typically the case with psychiatrists, they would have certain advantages in making such estimates. The data did not support this hypothesis. Considering only violent behavior, the MHAs were wrong

in 71% of the cases in which they predicted the person to be dangerous. However, the researchers found that there were substantial differences in the accuracy of the predictions based on perceptions of the
level of stress in the clients' living situations. Where the environments
were perceived as being low stress, predictions were wrong in only
seven of 26 cases (27%). Where the environments were seen as being
high stress, predictions were wrong in 15 of 23 cases (65%). Nevertheless, the false positive rates did not vary. Instead, the increase in
accuracy grew from the successful identification of the not-dangerous
group in the low stress settings. This means that the MHAs in this
limited sample did have a false positive rate of 2.4:1 overall, which was
better than most other clinical studies.

These, then, as summarized in the upper portion of Table 5–1 are
the studies of clinical predictions of dangerous behavior. They are
most consistent in that, even among what are generally considered
extremely high risk groups, clinical estimations rarely exceeded that
which was obtainable simply by chance. Phrased another way, the
predictive accuracy rarely exceeded the base rate of the behaviors
predicted, i.e., where 40% accuracy is attained, about 40% of the total
group for whom predictions were made exhibited the criterion behaviors. Thus clinical prediction attaining 40% accuracy would have been
obtainable strictly by chance.

Even in those studies where the false positive rate was low, little
special clinical acumen was apparent. Rather, it simply was that the
base of the behavior in both the dangerous and not-dangerous groups
was so high that regardless of which group any individuals were placed
clinically, there was, for example, a 2:1, or in some cases an even
chance that an individual would exhibit assaultive behavior. Thus, a
low false positive rate reflects high base-rate behavior, rather than
accurate clinical discriminations. Greater accuracy in each case was
obtainable by predicting that no one would be dangerous. All other
types of predictions increased the error rate, usually by identifying
many persons as dangerous who were not on the indicators used. An
excellent example of this phenomenon is the work of Bloom, Lang,
and Goldberg (1970) looking at clinical predictions of rehospitalization for mental patients. Of the 563 staff judgments for 92 released
patients, 60% were correct in predicting no rehospitalizations within
one year. However, of the 92 patients, 58% (53) remained out of
hospital. Thus the predictions, while 60% accurate, were obtainable
strictly by chance given the frequency of the criterion event. Thus, as
we have noted elsewhere (Cocozza & Steadman, 1976), if any of the
evidentiary standards employed in criminal courts were applied to
clinical predictions of dangerous behavior, none would be met, even
the weakest of "more likely than not," which is a probability of .51.

Table 5-1   False Positive Rates in Clinical and Statistical
Studies of the Prediction of Dangerous Behavior

Study	Clinical predictions			
	N predicted dangerous	Not assaultive	Assaultive	False positive rate
Kozol, Boucher, and Garolfalo (1972)	49	32	17	1.9-1
Steadman and Cocozza (1974)	199	164	35	4.7-1
Thornberry and Jacoby (1975)	438	377	61	6.2-1
Steadman-Patuxent (1977)	257	170	87	2.0-1
Sheldon (1977)	121	—	—	—
Levinson and Ramsey (1977)	17	12	5	2.4-1
Steadman and Cocozza (1978)	154	75	79	.95-1
	96	81	15	5.4-1
	Statistical predictions			
Wenk (1972a) (1972b) (1972c)	1,400			6.1-1
Hedland (1973)	138	83	55	1.5-1
Steadman and Cocozza (1974)	36	25	11	2.3-1
Jacoby (1975)	173	133	40	3.3-1
Koppin (1977)	60	31	29	1.1-1
Steadman and Cocozza (1978)	80	37	43	.86-1
	51	36	15	2.4-1
	48	33	15	2.2-1

There is simply no empirical evidence that psychiatrists or any other clinicians can clinically identify who will be dangerous beyond the accuracy anyone could attain simply by the probabilities of chance.

Statistical Predictions of Dangerous Behavior

Given the inabilities of clinical predictions to show the level of accuracy needed to justify their expanding uses, as summarized in the lower section of Table I, there have been a number of statistical forays into such predictions. A number of these have been linked to the research on clinical accuracy. The first set of very important studies by Wenk and coworkers (1972 a, b, c) have been comprehensively and concisely reviewed by Monahan (1978) and do not require further iteration here. It is sufficient to note that, using sophisticated multivariate statistical procedures, Wenk was able to reduce his false positive rate among slightly over 4,000 California Youth Authority wards to no less than 8:1. While his ratio was better than any that he felt were obtainable from the informal criteria employed by parole boards, which generally depended simply upon a history of prior violence, the high statistical false positive rate precluded any direct application.

A second statistical prediction study that also was not linked to specific clinical predictions focused on 2,762 mental patients in mental hospitals in Missouri (Hedlund, Sletten, Altman, & Evenson, 1973). Using a very wide variety of sociodemographic, mental status, and admissions information, stepwise discriminant function analysis was used in an attempt to identify those patients who were assaultive while hospitalized. On three criteria of assaultiveness, the statistical "hits" were 90%, 90%, and 94%. However, the authors concluded that "they [including the prospective user of the predictive information] are faced with the inevitable dilemma of being wrong more often than right when a false positive prediction is made, even if we use the best predictive information available" (1973, p. 446). This results from the low base rate of the respective behaviors, which were 8%, 4%, and 10%. Thus, predictive accuracy could better be improved by always making negative predictions.

A third piece of statistical prediction was one segment of the Baxstrom research, discussed earlier (Steadman & Cocozza, 1974). After determining a 4:1 false positive rate for the clinical predictions, we attempted to determine to what extent statistical prediction could have reduced this error rate. Of the various sociodemographic and criminal history variables available, the two that together best discriminated between those with assaults and those patients without assaults were age and the *Legal Dangerousness Scale* (LDS), a summary scale of prior criminal history. The high-risk group among the Baxstrom patients included those under 50 years of age and with an LDS score of 5 or more. This group included 80% of those who displayed assaultiveness in the community. Nevertheless, the false positive ratio still was 2:1, with two persons incorrectly identified as dangerous for everyone accurately designated.

The LDS scale was further tested at Colorado State Hospital on a group of released criminally insane patients. Koppin (1977) employed a wide variety of psychiatric and social history indicators in conjunction with the LDS and obtained some statistically significant differentiations of those subsequently arrested for violence and those not. However, she concluded, "Almost all accuracy rates computed were remarkably close to the base rate of 30% dangerous disruption among the patients in the sample" (1977, p. 19). Similarly, when the LDS was employed in our study of incompetent felony defendants, it was not as powerful an identifier, together with age, as had been the case among the Baxstrom patients. Only 22% of the high-risk group subsequently displayed violence producing a false positive rate of 3.-6:1.

An analagous scale was developed by Pruesse and Quinsey (1977). Examining a group of 206 patients from the maximum security mental hospital at Penetanguishene, Ontario a 0–5 point scale was developed to include such variables as the presence or absence of a diagnosis of personality disorder and length of time spent in mental hospitals. When the association between the scale and readmission was tested, it was statistically significant. When violent behavior was used as the dependent variable, however, there was no relationship.

The two other works relevant to the questions of statistical prediction of dangerous behavior both employed the statistical analysis used by Hedlund and coworkers (1973), stepwise discriminant function analysis. The first is the work on the *Dixon* case discussed earlier (Thornberry & Jacoby, 1974; Jacoby, 1975). They found that this type of analysis substantially reduced the level of false positives evident in the clinical predictions. Their discriminant analysis correctly categorized 279 of the 432 patients as either not dangerous or dangerous. Assuming that the reason for the detention of the *Dixon* patients was that they were deemed by psychiatrists and administrators as too dangerous, then only 64 of the 432 patients (15%) were identified accurately by clinicians, i.e., only 64 were subsequently violent. Thus, the clinical false positive rate was 5.5:1 while the discriminant function analysis classified 173 as dangerous, of whom 40 were for a false positive rate of 3.3:1.

Recently this same type of analysis was applied to a group of incompetent felony defendants (Steadman & Cocozza, 1978c). As seen in Table 5–2, in this sample, also, there was improvement over the clinical predictions. Working with a set of 53 possible independent variables, ranging from height and weight through a history of drug or alcohol abuse, the discriminant analysis with the optimum prediction power for in-hospital assaults used seven factors. Of the 257 defendants, 80 were predicted to be dangerous. Of these, 43 were assaultive, producing a false positive rate of .86:1, which means that for every 10 persons correctly identified, 8.6 were incorrectly predicted to be dangerous. Of the 177 predicted not to be assaultive, 58 were indeed assaultive while hospitalized. Thus, the overall accuracy

Table 5–2   Accuracy of Clinical and Statistical Predictions
of Assaultiveness While Hospitalized

| | Clinical prediction | | | | Statistical prediction | | | |
| | Not dangerous | | Dangerous | | Not dangerous | | Dangerous | |
Actual groups	N	Percent	N	Percent	N	Percent	N	Percent
Not assaultive while hospitalized	63	61.2	75	48.7	119	67.2	37	46.2
Assaultive while hospitalized	40	38.8	79	51.3	58	32.8	43	53.8
TOTAL	103	100.0	154	100.0	177	100.0	80	100.0

rate of the statistical prediction was 63%. This compares with the overall accuracy percentage of 46% by the psychiatrists and their false positive rate of .95:1.

When the same 53 variables were used to discriminate on the assaultiveness in the community, the statistical predictions were more impressive than for hospital violence. As seen in Table 5–3, the increase in predictive accuracy between the statistical and clinical predictions was moderate. Whereas the clinical predictions were accurate 59% of the time, 13 correctly identified as dangerous and 77 identified as not dangerous, the statistical predictions were accurate in 70% of the cases, with 10 persons incorrectly identified as not dangerous and 36 inaccurately predicted to be assaultive. Thus, the statistical false positive rate is 2.4:1 compared to the 3.8:1 clinical rate.

Where much greater improvement is evident between the level of accuracy of statistical predictions and clinical ones is in subsequent

Table 5–3   Accuracy of Clinical and Statistical Analysis
Predictions of Assaultiveness in the Community

| | Clinical prediction | | | | Statistical prediction | | | |
| | Not dangerous | | Dangerous | | Not dangerous | | Dangerous | |
Actual groups	N	Percent	N	Percent	N	Percent	N	Percent
Not assaultive in community	77	86.5	50	79.4	91	90.0	36	70.6
Assaultive in community	12	13.5	13	20.6	10	10.0	15	29.4
TOTAL	89	100.0	63	100.0	101	100.0	51	100.0

arrest of violent crimes, as is seen in Table 5–4. While the psychiatrists incorrectly predicted 57% of the cases, (83 they diagnosed as dangerous who were not subsequently arrested for a violent crime, and 11 they evaluated as not dangerous who were), the statistical predictions were inaccurate in only 25% of the cases (33 predicted to be dangerous who were not, and nine predicted to be not dangerous who were subsequently arrested for a violent crime). Thus, overall, the statistical analysis correctly identified 124 of the 166 defendants and displayed a false positive rate of 2.2:1 (33 predicted wrongly to be dangerous and 15 correctly predicted to be dangerous) as compared to the false positive rate of 6.4:1 (83 to 13) experienced by the psychiatrists in their predictions.

In sum, it is clear from the statistical prediction studies reviewed that: (1) in every case where comparisons were made, statistical prediction was superior to clinical prediction; (2) in most cases, statistical predictions offered somewhat more accuracy than simple probabilities based on the base rates of the dangerous behaviors in question; (3) in all cases, the statistical predictions reduce the false positive rate of clinical predictions; and (4) the most accurate predictions of dangerous behavior remain those who say no one will be dangerous. Related to this fourth point, it must be noted that all clinical predictions analyzed were actual decisions about groups of patients thought to be unusually dangerous. On the other hand, none of the statistical studies were actually used in detention decisions. Thus, the latter predictions were unimpeded by the ever-present and strong political pressures to err in a conservative direction by over-predicting who will be dangerous. Nevertheless, given the clear superiority of statistical prediction and inaccuracy of clinical predictions, there are serious questions about any patient's right not to be a false positive.

Table 5–4   Accuracy of Clinical and Statistical Predictions
of Subsequent Arrest for Murder, Manslaughter, or Assault

	Clinical prediction				Statistical prediction			
	Not dangerous		Dangerous		Not dangerous		Dangerous	
Actual groups	N	Percent	N	Percent	N	Percent	N	Percent
No subsequent violent arrest	59	84.3	83	86.5	109	92.4	33	68.8
Some subsequent violent arrest	11	15.7	13	13.5	9	7.6	15	31.2
TOTAL	70	100.0	96	100.0	118	100.0	48	100.0

IMPLICATIONS

It should be clear by this time that the research evidence on the prediction of dangerous behavior is consistent, but sparse. There is simply not that much evidence. What there is tends to be almost exclusively one type: follow-ups of groups for whom clinical predictions were made and then who spent substantial time institutionalized before some type of judicial intervention occurred requiring less restrictive settings. Monahan (1978b) has raised some probing questions about the adequacy of the available evidence to reach the conclusions that are being accepted about psychiatric inabilities to predict dangerous behavior. He suggests that some of the most important issues about clinical predictions relating to emergency commitment have yet to be addressed. Most of the research evidence, he argues, is not definitive because of the large amount of time between when predictions are made and the validating behaviors occur. Also in most of the research, even where the amount of time between the prediction and the follow-up is shorter, such as in Cocozza and Steadman (1978) and Levinson and Ramsey (1979), treatment occurs. Thus, many serious gaps exist in the research evidence on clinical predictions.

Likewise, there has not been very extensive work in the statistical prediction of dangerous behavior. What was done has been as consistent in its findings of improved accuracy over clinical predictions as have the clinical studies been consistent in showing little predictive expertise by clinicians. In every instance, overall, the statistical predictions have been more accurate than the clinical prediction, particularly in reducing the false positive rates. This reduction is important, not only for the moral and ethical issues that Wilkins addresses, but also in terms of program costs. In many instances, evaluations of dangerousness result in placement in higher security facilities, which typically cost more to construct, have higher staff-patient ratios, and, as in the case in New York, have higher paid ward staff than the regular security facilities. Thus, identification procedures, which constantly overpredict, not only have implications in terms of patient rights, but also in terms of public expenditures. Nevertheless, as the data reviewed above indicate, there are severe restrictions in the ready application of the statistical predictions methods. These range from their inherent limitations in accuracy, through the complexity of the statistical applications themselves, to their limited testing and the ethics of detaining any individual because of statistical probabilities for groups into which their characteristics place them.

In examining the issues of predicting dangerous behavior and the application of the dangerousness standard, it may be productive to turn around the usual questions. That is, rather than asking what evidence is there that psychiatrists, or other clinicians, cannot accurately predict dangerous behavior, ask instead what evidence is there that they *can?* When the question is phrased in this manner, the answer is unequivocal. *There is none.* Nowhere in the research literature is there any documentation that clinicians can predict dangerous behavior beyond the level of chance. While there continue to be assertions of the viability of clinical judgment (Kinzel, 1975) that assure the listeners of accurate predictions and efficacious treatment to deter violence, there exists no empirical documentation. Clearly, as Monahan has pointed out, the range of research needed to assess the full range of relevant situations adequately has barely been tapped. Nevertheless, there is not a single piece of empirical evidence that accurate predictions under any circumstances are made by clinicians. There may be many instances in which they are quite accurate, but they have yet to demonstrate empirically that they can. At this time, it would seem appropriate to switch the burden of proof, given the consistency of the limited research evidence to the contrary.

It would appear that the legal activism that is most appropriate is demanding more from the predictors of dangerous behavior in the way of further specification of the factors that lead to their predictions, the time limits of their predictions, the behaviors that are being predicted, and how these behaviors seen as dangerous are logically derived from the clinical evidence. Monahan (1978), for example, has argued that if one takes the 48-hour period that in many jurisdictions is the limit of emergency commitment, the clinician may be quite competent to make accurate assessments. This is, of course, an open question, but one for which there are no data. However, when the predictions are extended to 60 days, months, or years, it becomes meaningless in most instances. Likewise, if a person is considered dangerous because he deals in hard drugs, as was the case in one of the incompetent felony defendants in our research, and is about to be committed to a maximum security facility where drugs are not expected to be available for sale, he is not likely to be dangerous in that particular setting. Thus, the development of clear definitions of the behaviors to be entered as evidence, as well as the specific behavioral expectations and the time frames of these predictions, are important for due process protections in both the mental health and criminal justice systems.

This issue of due process protections is the key to understanding the predictions of dangerous behavior and right not to be a false positive. Kittrie (1971) has noted that dangerousness is a key concept of therapeutic state in that it masks, as is common with many treatment modalities, the actual use of the police power of the state under a *parens patriae* rationale for state intervention into an individual's life. The real issue in the commitment of the person for dangerousness is the state's justifiable right to protect its members. However, it is usually done as though it were in the best interest of the person committed, which it may also be. Because of this confusion between the rationales for involuntary commitment and the use of dangerousness, Wilkins' conceptualization of the right not to be a false positive becomes extremely important.

Since the use of predictions of dangerousness is really a product of the state's right to protect its citizens, the question arises as to how often the state can be justified in detaining persons as dangerous who would not actually display the predicted behavior. That is, what is an acceptable false positive rate? That is, of course, a social policy question that frequently parades as a medical question of clinical judgment. Wilkins' suggestion is that this question should not be posed unilaterally. In this way, the moral trade-offs of inappropriate detention versus perceived needs for protection might be differentially applied to persons based on their history of prior violent behavior. In addition to any penalties of detention or fines, a price of criminal conviction, or documented assaults that resulted in hospitalization, would be an increase in the level of error that was acceptable. For example, if there is no history of violence, the level of error that would be tolerated might be none, as Wilkins suggests, or five in 100, or the like. With one prior incident, this acceptable level might be 15 errors in 100 predictions. With mulitple prior incidents, it would increase to 25 to 100 and so forth. As U.S. laws now stand, it would appear that the basic assumption is that no errors are being made, or, at least, there are very few. While criminal evidentiary standards, as converted into mathematical probabilities (Cocozza & Steadman, 1976) do allow some errors, these clearly depend on the seriousness of the resulting penalty. Thus the "more likely than not" standard, or 51% level of certainty, is not an acceptable standard in a capital punishment case. In such instances, the level of certainty must be "beyond a reasonable doubt" at about a 95% or 99% certainty. As yet, the application of such varying evidentiary standards has not been discussed, let alone implemented, in the area of predicting dangerous behavior. Given the evidence presented here, it is clear that such discussions are core clarifications needed in an area of muddled clinical and social policy debate. The evidence is limited, but consistent. False positive rates are high, greatly exceeding any accepted criminal law evidentiary standards. Whether or to what extent a person may have a right not to be a false positive is a question that clearly emerges from the data. Not only must a wider range of research be designed to address the scope of circumstances in which predictions of dangerous behavior are relevant, but also policy analyses must begin to demarcate the scope of a patient's right not to be a false positive in the application of the dangerousness standard.

References

Bloom, B. L., Lang, E. W., & Goldberg, H. Factors associated with accuracy of prediction of posthospitalization adjustment. *Journal of Abnormal Psychology,* 1970, *76*(2), 243–249.

Cocozza, J. J. Dangerousness. *Psychiatric News,* August 1973, *15,* 2.

Cocozza, J. J., & Steadman, H. J. The failure of psychiatric predictions of dangerousness: Clear and convincing evidence. *Rutgers Law Review,* 1976, *29*(5), 1084–1101.

Cocozza, J. J., & Steadman, H. J. Prediction in psychiatry: An example of misplaced confidence in experts. *Social Problems,* 1978, *25*(3), 265–276.

Ennis, B. J., & Litwack, T. R. Psychiatry and the presumption of expertise: Flipping coins in the courtroom. *California Law Review,* 1976, *62,* 693–752.

Fagin, A. The policy implications of predictive decision-making: "Likelihood" and "dangerousness" in civil commitment proceedings. *Public Policy,* 1976, *24*(4), 491–528.

Halpern, A. L. Review of *Careers of the criminally insane. Bulletin of the American Academy of Psychiatry and the Law,* 1975, *4*(2), 187–191.

Hedlund, J. S., Sletten, I. W., Altman, H., & Evenson, R. C. Prediction of patients who are dangerous to others. *Journal of Clinical Psychology,* 1973, *29*(4), 443–447.

Jacoby, J. E. *Prediction of dangerousness among mentally ill offenders.* Paper presented at annual meeting of the American Society of Criminology. Toronto, Ontario: 1975.

Kinzel, A. Confronting and identifying dangerousness. *American Journal of Psychiatry,* 1975, *132,* (12), 1331.

Kittrie, N. *The right to be different.* Baltimore: Penguin Books, 1971.

Koppin, M. *Age, hospital stay, and criminal history as predictors of postrelease danger.* Pueblo, Colorado: Colorado State Hospital, 1977.

Kozol, H., Boucher, R., & Garolfalo, R. The diagnosis and treatment of dangerousness. *Crime and Delinquency,* 1972, *18,* 371–392.

Laves, R. G. The prediction of "dangerousness" as a criterion for involuntary civil commitment: Constitutional considerations. *The Journal of Psychiatry & Law,* 1975, *3*(3), 292–326.

Levinson, R. M., & Ramsay, G. Dangerousness, stress, and mental health evaluations. *Journal of Health and Social Behavior,* 1979, *20* (2), 25–37.

Maryland's Defective Delinquency Statute—A Progress Report. Department of Public Safety and Correctional Services. Unpublished manuscript, State of Maryland, 1973.

Megargee, E. I. The prediction of dangerous behavior. *Criminal Justice and Behavior,* 1976, *3*(1), 3–22.

Mesnikoff, A. M., & Lauterbach, C. G. The association of violent dangerous behavior with psychiatric disorders: A review of the research literature. *The Journal of Psychiatry & Law*, 1975 (Winter), 415–445.

Monahan J. Social policy implications of the inability to predict violence. *Journal of Social Issues*, 1975, *31*(2), 153–164.

Monahan, J. The prediction of violent criminal behavior: A methodological critique and prospectus. In National Academy of Science, *Deterrence and Incapacities: Estimating the Effects of Criminal Sanctions on Crime Rates*. Washington, D.C., 1978. (a)

Monahan J. Prediction research and the emergency commitment of dangerous mentally ill persons: A reconsideration. *American Journal of Psychiatry*, 1978, *135*(2), 198–201. (b)

Peele, R., Chadoff, P., & Taub, N. Involuntary hospitalizations and treatability: Observations from the District of Columbia experience. *Catholic University Law Review*, 1974, *23*, 744–753.

Pruesse, M., & Quinsey, V. L. The dangerousness of patients released from maximum security: A replication. *Journal of Psychiatry & Law*, 1977, (Summer), 293–299.

Rubin, B. Prediction of dangerousness in mentally ill criminals. *Archives of General Psychiatry*, 1972, *27*, 397–407.

Scheff, T. *Being mentally ill.* New York: Aldine, 1966.

Scheidemandel, P. L., & Kanno, C. K. The mentally ill offender: A survey of treatment programs. The Joint Information Service of the American Psychiatric Association and the National Association for Mental Health. Washington, D.C., 1969.

Shah, S. A. Dangerousness: Some definitional, conceptual, and public policy issues. In B. Sales (Ed.), *Perspectives in Law and Psychology*. New York: Pergamon, 1977.

Shah, S. A. Dangerousness: A paradigm for exploring some issues in law and psychology. *American Psychologist*, 1978, (March), 224–238.

Sheldon, R. B. *Assessing dangerousness in the criminally insane.* Paper presented at the American Psychological Association meeting, San Francisco, 1977.

Steadman, H. J. A new look at recidivism among Patuxent inmates. *Bulletin of the American Academy of Psychiatry and the Law*, 1977, *5*(2), 200–209.

Steadman, H. J., & Cocozza, J. J. *Careers of the criminally insane*. Lexington, Massachusetts: Lexington Books, 1974.

Steadman, H. J., & Cocozza, J. J. Psychiatry, dangerousness, and the repetitively violent offender. *The Journal of Criminal Law & Criminology*, 1978, *69* (Summer), *2*, 226–231. (a)

Steadman, H. J., & Cocozza, J. J. *The dangerousness standard & Psychiatry: A cross national issue in the social control of the mentally ill.* Paper presented at the 9th World Congress of Sociology, Uppsala, Sweden, 1978. (b)

Steadman, H. J., & Cocozza, J. J. The prediction of dangerousness—*Baxstrom: A case study. The Role of the Forensic Psychologist* G. Cooke (Ed.) Springfield, IL: Charles Thomas. 1980.

Stone, A. A. *Mental health and law: A system in transition.* Rockville, Maryland: National Institute of Mental Health, 1975.

Thornberry, T. P., & Jacoby, J. E. *The uses of discretion in a maximum security mental hospital: The Dixon case.* Paper presented at the Annual Meeting of the American Society of Criminology, Chicago, 1974.

Treffert, D. *Dying with your rights on.* Paper presented at the annual meeting of the American Psychiatric Association, Detroit, May, 1974.

Wenk, E., & Emrich, R. Assaultive youth: An exploratory study of the assaultive experience and assaultive potential of California Youth Authority wards. *Journal of Research in Crime and Delinquency,* 1972, *9,* 171–196.

Wenk, E., Robinson, J. O., & Smith, G. W. Can violence be predicted? *Crime and Delinquency,* 1972, *18,* 393–402.

Wilkins, L. T. Current aspects of penology: Directions for corrections. *Proceedings of the American Philosophical Society,* 1974, *118*(3), 235–247.

Chapter 6

ANTISOCIAL BEHAVIOR OF DISCHARGED MENTAL[1] PATIENTS:
Research Findings and Policy Implications

Judith Godwin Rabkin, Ph.D.
Arthur Zitrin, M.D.

The history of the care of the mentally ill is a chronicle of neglect and apathy, punctuated by periodic outcries for reform when tranquility, convenience, or comfort of the public are threatened or disturbed by the insane in its midst. Demands for reform are also heard when the public conscience becomes sufficiently troubled after some scandalous events bring the plight of the mentally ill into open view. We are now in such a time of public concern.

The movement toward community based care for the chronically mentally ill matured in the late 1950s as a result of a number of influences operating simultaneously: the development of psychotropic drugs; a concern for civil rights of mental patients as a part of the general civil rights movement; a prevailing view in the mental health establishment that such patients could be treated more effectively in the community; and, crucially, the mistaken belief, principally among legislators, that such community treatment would save money.

In recent years, no single topic related to the care of the mentally ill has received more attention in the lay press and in scientific publica-

[1]This chapter is a revised and expanded version of a paper by J. G. Rabkin entitled, "Criminal behavior of discharged mental patients: A critical appraisal of the research." *Psychological Bulletin*, 1979, 86, 1–27, copyright © 1979 by the American Psychological Association. Reprinted with permission.

tions than the policy of *deinstitutionalization* and its effects on discharged patients and the communities to which they are returned. The relevant statistics have been widely publicized: nationwide, the number of resident patients at one point in time in state and county mental hospitals declined from a peak of 558,922 in 1955 to 193,436 patients in 1976 (*GAP Publication No. 102,* 1978). Although these figures show that far fewer patients are now hospitalized at any one time, hospital admissions and rates of mental illness have not declined, so that evidently many more patients are living in the community.

While it may seem, in terms of numbers of discharged patients, that the "deinstitutionalization movement" has been successful, this view is not widely shared either by mental health professionals or members of the public who live in areas where many expatients have settled. Instead, the movement has brought to the fore debates about the quality of the community experience for these patients and the community's experience with these patients—the burdens and the costs.

Few commentators are satisfied with the typical conditions of daily living of expatients, or the extent to which they are in fact participating community members (e.g., Aviram & Segal, 1973; Talbott, 1979). Many discharged patients do not live independently but rather in some form of sheltered-care facility, where community involvement may be restricted or discouraged (Segal & Aviram, 1976). Talbott (1978) has estimated that 44% or 407,000, of those living in homes for the dependent and elderly have some form of mental disability. Thousands more live in concentrated numbers in transitional or deteriorated urban areas. In New York City alone, about 60,000 patients are discharged from psychiatric hospitals *annually* (Meznikoff, 1979). While many recover sufficiently to resume normal patterns of living, the chronically ill seldom do. Large numbers live in substandard single-room-occupancy (SRO) hotels, often in high-crime areas, of which few receive systematic supervision or treatment or have access to recreational, vocational, or socialization programs (Koening, 1978). For these deinstitutionalized patients, the care they receive is often illusory; they may have less community and less care where they live than they had in their state hospitals, where at least food, clothing, shelter, and the presence of other people were routinely available (Bassuk & Gerson, 1978; Holden, 1978).

It has long since become clear that adequate community programs are much more expensive than many policy makers had been led to expect, and that such programs are now seriously underfunded. The mentally ill and their advocates have never been a constituency with much power and influence, and in the competition for public funds, their cause has not had a high priority. It is generally agreed that if the community mental health movement is not to be a reform that failed, the deficiency of inadequate funding will have to be remedied.

However, even where funds have been available to develop community facilities, there is public resistance to having them established in residential neighborhoods. It is widely believed by community members that mental patients are likely to display impulsive, violent, assaultive, and otherwise socially disruptive behavior. In public meetings held to consider the applications of new psychiatric facilities in the neighborhood, many community spokespersons openly express such fears (Carmody, 1975; Wykert, 1975). The vast majority of mental health professionals respond to community opposition by declaring that such fears are groundless, that mental patients are actually less likely than other people to commit crimes, and that the local opponents are speaking from prejudice rather than fact. Indeed, in such settings, spokespersons for the mental health establishment have condemned as uncharitable and reactionary the attitudes of the communities who have expressed resistance to new psychiatric facilities.

In contrast to these community views, most mental health professionals do believe that mental patients have relatively few encounters with the law, and that, on the infrequent occasions when they are arrested, it is for minor offenses like vagrancy, loitering, or public intoxication. It is furthermore assumed that such charges largely stem from socially inept and unacceptable behavior, like urinating on lampposts or wandering aimlessly in the street, rather than purposive criminal acts such as robbery. Psychiatric textbooks, general medical magazines (Farnsworth, 1977), and psychiatric reviews (Gulevich & Bourne, 1970) generally concur in their evaluation of the scientific literature on the criminal behavior of the mentally ill. This literature is regarded as sparse and inconsistent but overall supporting the position that patients commit fewer crimes than the general population. This seems to be the prevailing belief, not only among mental health professionals, but also among many with a liberal ideological orientation.

It is our belief that only by evaluating the validity of these concerns, and by adjusting administrative policies where necessary, can local treatment programs successfully be established to meet the long-range goal of community care of the mentally ill. Accordingly, this review was undertaken to examine the available research evidence regarding the extent and nature of antisocial behavior of discharged mental patients. The questions to be considered concern the prevalence of arrests among formerly hospitalized and former outpatients treated for psychiatric disorders, in comparison to arrest rates of the general public. A separate literature on the prevalence of mental illness among criminals is not included, nor is a review of efforts to predict dangerousness among mental patients, criminal defendants, or the criminally insane. The studies included for review are epidemiological prospective studies, and each is addressed to one or more of the following questions:

1. Do discharged mental patients currently have higher arrest rates than members of the general population?
   A. Have these rates changed over time?
   B. What factors have contributed to such changes, if observed?
2. What are the best predictors of postdischarge arrests?
3. What is the association between arrest risk and diagnostic category?
4. Are discharged mental patients more likely to be arrested for certain types of crime?
5. Does hospitalization reduce the probability of recidivism among patients with prior arrest records?

After consideration of pertinent methodological issues, each study is briefly cited in chronological order (see Rabkin, 1979, for a more detailed analysis of each study).

Cumulative findings are then summarized according to the questions posed, and the state of the evidence for each is evaluated. Finally, some implications are drawn with respect to the relevance of these findings for the further development of community psychiatry programs.

METHODOLOGICAL CONSIDERATIONS

The question here under consideration is a deceptively simple one: Are formerly hospitalized mental patients engaged in criminal activity with lesser or greater frequency than other people? The appropriate research design is necessarily a prospective one (sometimes called a *cohort design*): Two groups of people, one with a history of psychiatric hospitalization and one without, but otherwise similar, are followed for equal periods of time, in order to obtain for each group counts of police encounters, arrests, convictions, and incarcerations. Because it has been claimed that mentally disturbed citizens are treated differently by the criminal justice system than are other defendants, a retrospective or case-control design, in which the histories of convicted offenders are searched for evidence of mental illness, is not as effective, although it is considerably simpler and less costly. This review therefore focuses on prospective studies.

Since arrests for criminal acts are comparatively rare events, and because the expected incidence of arrests was unknown at the start, investigators have been obliged to study a large number of people at risk. Among the studies reviewed, samples have ranged from 310 to nearly 100,000 patients discharged from the same or similar hospitals within a one- or two-year time span. Frequency of arrests within a specified follow-up period, ranging from 1½ to 5½ years, have been computed from police records, and then annual arrest rates have been compared with figures compiled at the catchment, county, state, or national level for the general population of similar age. Comparative rates of arrests for patients and the general population have served as the basis for conclusions about the relative incidence of criminal activity among discharged mental patients.

A number of methodological problems become apparent in the course of reviewing studies in this field. Some problems, such as lack of equivalence in the demographic and psychiatric characteristics of patient samples, are more or less unavoidable when one considers together any series of studies conducted by different people in different places at different times. Moreover, such heterogeneity may be regarded as an asset in the sense that replicated findings can be generalized to a broader segment of the population of patients. Other difficulties, such as extrapolating rates based on few cases, are common to any epidemiological study of rare events, and can be dealt with by collapsing categories to enlarge the number of cases used to generate rates, and to seek patterns rather than focus on separate rates by specific category.

Apart from such general considerations, there are a number of problems specific to the field under study that warrant mention. One issue concerns the differential probability that mentally disturbed and other people will be arrested, sent to jail, convicted, and incarcerated. (Studies in this review excluded from consideration those defendants who are hospitalized by court order for psychiatric observation, as well as those classified as criminally insane.) It has been argued that convictions and even arrests are inadequate measures of crime among mental patients because the seriously disturbed defendant and those with histories of hospitalization are rehospitalized instead of arrested. Recent evidence supports this contention. Both Levine (1970) and Lagos, Perlmutter, and Saexinger (1977) found extremely high rates of violent or illegal behavior preceding and precipitating hospitalization in the admission notes of randomly selected inpatients. Levine reported that 71 of 100 patients had committed illegal acts, including 23 judged to be felonies, in the course of episodes leading to their hospitalization, none of which were prosecuted. Similarly, Lagos and colleagues found that 36% of 321 patients manifested some form of violent behavior in the episode leading to hospitalization, of whom only 2.6%

were prosecuted. Despite validity problems in these data sources, including the possibilty that admitting personnel unduly empahasize violence in order to justify the decision to admit, it does seem that many dangerous, violent, and illegal acts, commited by distressed, distraught people, lead to hospitalization rather than arrest. As a result, arrest rates may underestimate frequency of violence among the mentally ill.

Another source of error in use of arrest and conviction rates to represent frequency and type of illegal behavior of the mentally ill concerns the response of the criminal justice system. If indeed charged instead of hospitalized, the disturbed defendant may be acquitted on grounds of insanity. Alternatively, the charge may be reduced. In some states, defendants accused of serious crimes (felonies) cannot be committed to a psychiatric hospital except for brief observation if an insanity plea is under consideration. A common solution is the reduction of a charge to a lesser offense (a misdemeanor) to enable commitment of a disturbed defendant (Paull & Malek, 1974). This procedure applies only to psychotic individuals; sociopathy, alcoholism, and drug abuse are not legally acceptable grounds for either acquittal or reduction of charges for commitment purposes. One result is to lower overall arrest rates for the mentally ill. Another is to reduce the severity of charges pressed against schizophrenics who then appear less prone to criminal acts than nonpsychotic diagnostic groups.

In an effort to obtain less biased measures of criminal activity of mental patients, one may seek to enumerate all police contacts, rather than just those culminating in arrests. Apart from the practical difficulties of obtaining such information, however, one cannot equate police contact with criminal activity. Firstly, most police contacts do not lead to arrests. The FBI *Uniform Crime Reports* (1978) indicates that only 21% of index crimes were "cleared" during 1977. A crime is cleared when law enforcement agencies have identified the offender, have sufficient evidence to charge the person, and actually take him or her into custody. Clearance rates vary widely by type of offense, ranging from 75% of murder offenses to 15% of motor vehicle thefts. Police clear a high percent of crimes against the person, both because of the more intense investigative effort made and because of the greater availability of witnesses to identify the perpetrator and to testify against him. In their review of dispositions of encounters between discharged mental patients and the police, Giovannoni and Gurel (1967) also found that only a minority of police encounters culminate in arrests. Although this reflects to some extent limitations of law enforcement resources and procedural constraints, not all police encounters will lead to arrests, since several people may be suspected in the same case, and only one is ultimately charged.

Another objection to the use of police contacts as an index of criminal activity is the possibility of differential "whistle blowing" behavior for exmental patients and other citizens. Former patients may be more likely to be under police surveillance because of their known status; their social ineptness may heighten their visibility; or unfriendly neighbors may call the police with complaints for purposes of harassment. A more basic difficulty is the definition of criminal activity, which is necessarily determined only by a judge in court, so that police contacts may be interesting to study, but are insufficient evidence in themselves.

A similar argument may be made with respect to arrest records. Here, also, the defendant may be innocent. It seems likely, however, that a sufficient number of mental patients are taken out of court channels before completion of trial and passage of a verdict, so that use of conviction rates alone gives a misleadingly low estimate of the criminal activity of the mentally ill (Zitrin, Hardesty, Burdock, & Drossman, 1976). In all of the studies reviewed here, with one exception, measures of criminal behavior are based on arrest rates. The exception: a pair of studies conducted by Sosowsky (1974) found that conviction and incarceration rates highly correlated with arrest rates.

Another problem concerns computation of crime rates by specific category. There is no national criminal code, and definitions and classifications of offenses vary between jurisdictions and over time within a given jurisdiction. A particular offense may be a felony in one state and a misdemeanor in another, or it may be reclassified as one or the other 5 or 10 years hence. It is therefore difficult to compare arrest rates, for example, for concealed weapons between Wyoming and New York. One solution is to consider broader categories of crime rather than specific offenses, although here the problem becomes what system of classification to use in developing such categories. It may be to circumvent such difficulties that the majority of recent investigators chose to emphasize the relative occurrence of violent crimes, defined as homicides plus assaults, where the charges are less ambiguous, the proportion of arrested perpetrators is comparatively high, and the task of classification is less difficult.

The foregoing issues have been related to the task of defining and counting cases, which constitute the numerator of a rate. There are also problems in selecting an appropriate *denominator*, which is defined as all cases at risk for the event in the numerator. Almost all investigators have computed the denominators of their patient rates as the number of discharged patients in their sample. Because of the large sample sizes used in most studies, the size of error in using this denominator is probably minor, especially if the sample is not broken down into subgroups. Some patients, however, die, move to other states, or spend time away from the community in jails, mental or medical hospitals, nursing homes, or elsewhere. In each instance, they are no longer "at risk" for arrest. In just one study (by Giovannoni & Gurel, 1967) was an effort made to determine the actual population at risk; others overestimated the denominator size and, thus, obtained lower arrest rates. Another prevalent error is the inclusion of patient arrests in general population figures derived from FBI records. Only Sosowsky (1974) excluded treated patients from his population arrest rates.

An additional source of error is lack of genuine equivalence between patient and general population groups. No one has ever claimed that state hospital patients (who constitute the vast majority of patients studied in this field) are representative of the general population. At best, they represent the less fortunate members of society, who may be collectively described as lacking social status, financial resources, occupational skills, and often family ties. If mental patients in public facilities were compared to their peers along these variables, each of which is associated with the distribution of both arrests and mental illness in the geneal population, fewer differences might be found.

While it is true that studies in this research area are individually and collectively incomplete, and in many respects insufficient in their designs and analyses, their review appears warranted on several grounds. Firstly, they represent the only available empirical evidence in an area of tremendous public concern. At the present time, intense policy debates are being conducted regarding the relative rights of patients and of communities into which they are discharged. The cumulative evidence to be derived from these studies may help to clarify major elements in these debates. In addition, analysis of this literature should serve as a guide to future research by indicating important unresolved questions and suggesting more fruitful methods for their investigation.

In our opinion, the methodological issues raised here are both relevant and significant, but probably are not major sources of weakness in the group of studies to be reviewed here. The direction of bias is not consistent. While no study is flawless, no problem was universal, so that agreement of results across studies lends strength to their conclusions, the foregoing difficulties notwithstanding.

LITERATURE REVIEW

Early Studies

Between 1922 and 1955, four studies were conducted regarding the subsequent arrest rates of paroled or discharged mental patients.

Ashley (1922) wrote a brief report on the later careers of 1,000 patients paroled from his hospital in New York State during the preceding 10 years. In 1938, Pollock published a study of the legal offenses committed by over 5,800 patients paroled during fiscal 1937 from all state hospitals in New York. Cohen and Freeman (1945) conducted a follow-up study of 1,676 patients paroled or discharged from one of three state hospitals in Connecticut between 1940 and 1944. The last and perhaps most influential in this series of early investigations was conducted for the New York State Department of Mental Hygiene by Brill and Malzberg (1962). Their report, based on 10,247 male patients discharged from New York state hospitals during fiscal 1947, was circulated within the department but not otherwise disseminated until 1962.

These four studies consistently found that discharged psychiatric patients had lower total arrest rates than did members of the general population. Cohen and Freeman (1945) and Brill and Malzberg (1962) both observed that a history of arrests prior to psychiatric hospitalizaton was a useful predictor of the probability of postdischarge arrests. In particular, the data of Brill and Malzberg show that mental illness and psychiatric hospitalization do not raise the probability of subsequent arrest above that existing before hospitalization, and do not create such a tendency if it did not previously exist. This is an observation of major and enduring significance, and is perhaps ultimately all that must be said on the subject of crime and mental illness. Their data demonstrate that crime rates for expatients without arrest records are lower than for the general population, and are inflated by the presence of patients with police records. In 1947, and, as we shall see, even more so today, persons with arrest records constitute a larger proportion of the patient population than of the general population, and it is this fact that contributes to the higher arrest rates of mental patients when they are considered as one group.

These four studies together constitute the foundation for psychiatric reassurances that former mental patients are no threat or danger to their neighbors. In fact, the first two studies concur in their results and interpretations, while the third and fourth identify the major factor contributing to higher arrests among discharged patients, providing a framework within which to integrate the apparently contradictory findings of studies published before and after 1965.

The first three studies are difficult to evaluate since so little information was provided with respect to record sources, case representativeness and selection, and computation of rates. Nevertheless, even if the authors minimized patient arrests and used high estimates of population arrest rates to yield an exaggerated contrast, it seems reasonably certain that mental patients discharged before World War II were less often arrested than were members of the general public.

Recent Studies

Since 1965, eight American studies involving nine separate samples were designed to contribute further empirical evidence to the question of dangerousness of discharged mental patients. In terms of temporal sequence, the studies of Rappeport and Lassen (1965, 1966) serve as a bridge between the earlier studies and contemporary ones, since they investigated arrest rates of patients discharged from all Maryland psychiatric hospitals during the fiscal years of 1947 and also 1957. Their total samples consisted of 708 men and 693 women in 1947, and 2,152 men and 2,129 women in 1957. Arrests were recorded for only five offenses, all of which were violent crimes against persons. For each of these offenses, patient rates were found to be equivalent to or higher than those of the Maryland population.

The next study, conducted by Giovannoni and Gurel (1967), is distinguished by the national distribution of its sample of 1,142 chronic schizophrenic male patients discharged from Veterans Administration neuropsychiatric hospitals. They found patient arrest rates to be higher for several violent crimes against persons. In California, Sosowsky (1974, 1978) undertook a statewide analysis of arrest, conviction, and incarceration rates for violent crimes (homicide and aggravated assault) of 99,361 former state hospital patients and outpatients at state-supported facilities, compared to those of the nontreated population of California. He also studied the criminal records of a cohort of 301 state hospital patients in San Mateo County compared to those of the nonhospitalized county residents. Sosowsky found that, even when age, sex, and ethnic membership were controlled, patients had much higher arrest and conviction rates for violent crimes than their counterparts in the general population.

An investigation of patient arrest rates conducted at Bellevue Psychiatric Hospital by Zitrin et al. (1976) and Durbin, Pasewark, and Albers' (1977) study of Wyoming state hospital patients continued to find that patient arrest rates exceeded those of the general population. The most recent investigation of arrest rates of two cohorts of discharged patients was conducted in New York State by Steadman, Melick, and Cocozza (1977) and Steadman, Cocozza, and Melick (1978) with comparable results. In their study, as in all others that examine such data, a history of arrest before hospitalization emerged as the best single predictor of postdischarge arrests. In general, while each study has some limitations, and not all provide equivalent data, they are cumulatively persuasive in their evidence that patterns of arrests among former mental patients are very different from and far higher than those reported earlier, both in absolute terms and in comparison to those of the general public.

Evaluating the Evidence

In this section, we summarize cumulative findings to clarify what answers have been provided by the foregoing studies, and what remains learned.

1. Do mental patients currently have higher arrest rates than members of the general population? Today, and over the past 20 years, mental patients discharged from public facilities *as a group* have total arrest rates for all crimes that equal or exceed public rates with which they have been compared. Arrest and conviction rates for the subcategory of *violent* crimes were found to exceed general population rates in every study where they were measured. The certainty of these findings must be tempered by consideration of design limitations, including nonequivalent comparison groups and lack of attention to variables such as age and social class.

1a. Have these rates changed over time? The arrest rates of paroled and discharged patients based on pre-1950 records consistently were found to be lower than those reported for the general population. There has been a pronounced relative as well as absolute increase in arrests of mental patients since then. That is, while arrest rates for both patients and the general public have increased, the rate of acceleration for patients has been much greater.

1b. What factors have contributed to this upward trend in arrest rates? At least two developments may account for the observed changes, both of which are fundamentally related to the evolving social role of the mental hospital in our society. First is the change in hospital policies regarding involuntary admission and retention of patients, and the likelihood and timing of a patient's discharge. In the past, it was easier to have patients involuntarily committed. Recent legal reforms have largely restricted such commitment to situations where the prospective patient is perceived as potentially dangerous to himself or others. Although psychiatric predictions of dangerousness are admittedly inaccurate (APA TAsk Force, 1974; Cocozza & Steadman, 1978; Dix, 1976; Steadman, 1973; Stone, 1975), it does seem probable that these restricted criteria alter the nature of the patient population and enhance the probability that discharged patients may be at greater risk for subsequent dangerous behavior.

Duration of commitment and discharge policies have also changed. Forty years ago, committed patients were often hospitalized for long periods of time in large state facilities, physically removed from their communities of origin. As Pollock (1938) described in detail, patients who were released had to meet a series of requirements, not only with respect to their psychiatric status and social functioning, but also regarding available familiar resources. Once recovered, these socially acceptable, cooperative patients with welcoming and protective friends and relatives were paroled, and their progress was monitored by an elaborate, extensive,and *compulsory* system of home and clinic visits. If parole authorities were notified of a change in status, the patient could be rehospitalized at once. While New York State's hospital system may have been more cautious about discharges than others, this general system prevailed nationally (Giovannoni & Gurel, 1967).

Today in New York State facilities, as elsewhere, the average patient stay is 60 days. In acute-care units, patients are usually discharged within two weeks. Nationally since 1950s, hospital stays have become progressively shorter, and hospital populations have declined, although admissions have not, leading to far more discharged patients in the community. Since the late 1960s, heavy emphasis has been placed on community based treatment on a voluntary basis. As soon as the acute symptoms of hospitalized patients subside, usually with the help of psychotropic medication, patients are discharged. There is no compulsory aftercare or follow-up. In short, virtually all patients admitted in the past several years are promptly returned to the community. The state mental hospital's traditional role as a "warehouse for the unwanted" has been transformed into a brief way-station for the most acutely disturbed.

The second major change concerns a shift in the way the civil machinery distributes disruptive members of the community. More today than in the past, offenders who appear to be mentally disturbed, or who have a history of psychiatric hospitalization, tend to be diverted to the mental health rather than the criminal justice system. Overcrowding in the courts may encourage the use of hospitalization as an alternative method of removing disturbing people from the community. A reciprocal relationship between the sizes of mental hospital and prison populations was noted some time ago by Penrose (1939), and in Britain this has come to be known as "Penrose's Law" (Gunn, 1977).

Since an increasing number of mental patients have prior police records, and since all patients are now quite promptly discharged, it is not surprising that mental patients returning to the community will, as a group, have a higher arrest rate than in the past when the patient population had a different composition. As Giovannoni and Gurel have stated the point: "It is primarily in the way mental hospitals are utilized by the community, and particularly as this influences the kinds of patients admitted and the number and kinds of patients released, that one is likely to find the major sources of variation in expatient crime rate" (1967, p. 151).

2. *What are the best predictors of postdischarge arrests?* It has been repeatedly and convincingly demonstrated that a small subset of patients, who have prior criminal records, accounts for the large majority of postdischarge arrests. A record of prior arrest is the single best predictor so far identified. Young age is also a good predictor. Other variables significantly associated with postdischarge arrests, but not large in their effect, include male sex and unmarried status. Short hospital stay and diagnoses of alcoholism, drug abuse, and personality disorder are also associated with arrest risk when analyzed separately, but their predictive value seems to be largely accounted for by their relationship to sex and age, as Steadman and colleagues (1977) demonstrated in their multivariate analyses. Despite the consistency with which these predictors have been identified, their predictive power is weak. Much remains to be learned in the prediction of disruptive, illegal behavior by mental patients after their return to the community.

3. *What is the association between arrest risk and diagnostic category?* It is generally believed that patients diagnosed as personality disorders, alcoholics, and drug abusers are most likely to display antisocial and aggressive behavior. There is less consensus about whether these three diagnostic labels describe mental illness. In some epidemiological studies of true prevalence rates, investigators systematically exclude these categories (e.g., Gove & Tudor, 1973) and focus exclusively on neuroses and functional and organic psychoses. In addition, states vary in their policies of admitting patients more than once to state facilities with a primary diagnosis of alcoholism, so that their proportions of the total population vary by area as a function of administrative policy.

In those studies that generated interpretable findings about crime rates of different diagnostic groups in relation to their size in the patient sample under study, alcoholics, addicts, and personality disorders were in each case found to have excess rates (Brill & Malzberg, 1962; Durbin et al., 1977; Steadman et al., 1977; Zitrin et al., 1976). The consistency of these results lends them credibility. The effects of age and sex must be considered, however, in view of Steadman's observations regarding their associations. Since two of the four studies dealing with diagnostic differences were based on male samples only (Brill & Malzberg, 1962; Durbin et al., 1977), sex is evidently not a critical factor. The role of age remains uncertain. Giovannoni and Gurel found, in their group of older chronic schizophrenic males, that nearly three quarters of those arrested had drinking problems. More direct evidence would be available by studying differential diagnostic rates in an age-stratified sample to see if the differences prevail at various ages. At present, we may conclude that patients with diagnoses of personality disorders, alcoholism, and drug dependency have disproportionate arrest rates. Whether this is caused by the nature of their disorders or by demographic characteristics associated with their distribution in the general population remains unclear.

Evidence is less consistent regarding the subsequent criminal activity of patients diagnosed as schizophrenic. In those studies where schizophrenics constituted half or less of the patient sample, their arrest rates have *not* been disproportionately high. In the most detailed analysis of arrests by diagnostic group, conducted by Zitrin and colleagues, schizophrenics were found overrepresented among those patients who committed violent crimes with bodily harm, but not in terms of overall arrest rates for all crime categories combined. In two samples in which all or most of the patients were schizophrenic (Giovannoni & Gurel, 1967; Sosowsky, 1974), arrest rates were much higher for patients than for control populations, especially for violent crimes. That is, schizophrenic samples had the same excess of crimes, compared to control groups, that characterized samples with predominantly nonschizophrenic patients. From the preliminary evidence available, it seems that arrest rates of schizophrenics do not exceed those of other diagnostic groups, with the possible exception of violent crimes (homicides and assaults) where their rates may be higher. Critical and uncontrolled are the factors of age and social class, which require evaluation before firmer conclusions can be derived.

4. Are mental patients more likely to be arrested for certain types of crime? Traditionally, it was believed that mental patients, when arrested at all, were charged with minor offenses such as loitering, vagrancy or public intoxication. It was an unpleasant surprise to learn that not only were patient arrest rates the same or greater than those of the general population in recent years, but this excess was particularly pronounced in the category of felonies, and, specifically, of violent crimes or "crimes against persons." Six investigators, using eight patient samples, found higher arrest (and/or conviction) rates for the crimes of homicide and assault among patients than control groups. The magnitude of this excess ranged from 1½ to 29 times greater than general population rates. No studies reported contrary findings. The consistency and size of the differences across patient samples varying in time, place, and diagnostic composition make them convincing. It seems reasonable to conclude that mental patients are more likely to be arrested for assaultive and sometimes homicidal behavior than are other people.

No clear pattern emerges regarding the relative frequency with which other crimes are charged against mental patients. Rappeport and Lassen (1965, 1966) found highest rates for robbery by males, and aggravated assault by females. Giovannoni and Gurel reported that after violent crimes, which accounted for 27% of police contacts among their patients, the next most common offenses were drunkenness (23%), motor vehicle theft (13%), and crimes against property (12%). Durbin et al. (1977) reported a high incidence of drug offenses among his predominantly alcoholic clientele, while Steadman and colleagues found the most common offenses in their 1968 sample to be drug, property, and violent crimes, and property, sex, and violent crimes in their 1975 sample. In short, apart from assaultive behavior, mental patients are apparently no more likely to be arrested for some crimes than others, judging from the limited evidence at hand.

5. Does hospitalization reduce the probability of arrest recidivism among patients with prior arrest records?   The question is interesting because a positive finding would provide support for the notion of a causal association between mental status and crime, in contrast to the opinion of several investigators that disturbed and criminal behaviors may coexist but are causally independent. However, this would require demonstration that recidivism rates of discharged patients with prior police records are lower than those of nonhospitalized offenders— either placed on probation or incarcerated—who are otherwise equivalent in terms of salient social, historical, and demographic variables. Alternatively, people arrested for a second time could, in theory, be randomly assigned to one of three conditions: psychiatric hospitalization, probation, or incarceration in correctional facilities. The matched design has never been attempted. The random assignment design cannot be undertaken, and is offered only to illustrate the difficulties entailed in the acquisition of necessary evidence to answer the question posed about the effects of hospitalization on recidivism.

Despite the absence of such conclusive evidence, several of the authors whose studies are reviewed here have discussed the issue of recidivism among discharged patients. Cohen and Freeman (1945) were the first to suggest that hospitalization may reduce recidivism, based on their finding that only 26% of patients arrested before being hospitalized were also arrested after discharge. The only others to be impressed with a decline in arrests after hospitalization among patients with records were Durbin and his colleagues (1977). Of the 43 men in the sample who were arrested in the five years before hospitalization, only 8, or 19%, were also arrested within five years after discharge. They concluded that "factors associated with hospitalization . . . may have influenced the reduction in arrest rates after hospitalization" (p. 83).

Other investigators who discussed recidivism disagreed. Rappeport and Lassen (1965) stated, "As best we can interpret our data, there was a tendency toward recidivism not unlike that seen in the general community." Brill and Malzberg (1962) and Steadman and colleagues (1977) interpreted their findings similarly. Zitrin et al. (1976) only reported recidivism rates for the 85 patients in their sample arrested for crimes of violence for two years before or after the hospitalization under study. Of the 64 patients arrested before hospitalization, 36 were also arrested after discharge, producing a total recidivism rate of 56% among patients who committed one or more crimes of violence.

In summary, reported recidivism rates for arrests among discharged mental patients in the foregoing studies ranged from 19% to 56%. These rates were derived from different periods of record surveillance, include different crime categories, and were gathered over a period of 30 years. In contrast, only 2% to 4% of patients without prior arrest records were arrested within five years after discharge.

Until now, no data were available regarding arrest rates of released offenders, so that the recidivism rates reported in studies of discharged mental patients were difficult to interpret. Recently completed research by Steadman, Vanderwyst, and Ribner (1978) fills this gap. They selected from their 1968 and 1975 patient samples those who were residents of Albany County (Ns of 307 and 204, respectively), and compared their arrest rates during the next 18 months with those of Albany County residents released from state and county prisons during the same calendar years (N = 167 and 252, respectively). With this combined data set, they were able to answer several major questions heretofore unresolved in the literature.

Comparison of total arrest rates for the general public with those of allpatients and all offenders showed that, while rates for both incarcerated groups exceed those of the public, exprisoners had higher rates than expatients. Patients with no police records had rates indistinguishable from those of the general public, while those of offenders continued to exceed those of patients with the same number of previous arrests. Refining his categories further, Steadman compared arrest rates within age group with number of prior arrests held constant. In these comparisons, results were inconsistent, which may be at least partly due to the small number of cases in each category.

Since the offenders, as a group, were on the average over 10 years younger than offenders among the general public, and included many more males and nonwhite members, their higher arrest rates seemed attributable, at least in part, to demographic factors. Fortunately, in his second study, Steadman (1978) undertook a multivariate analysis of such variables, generating evidence to evaluate the contribution of each variable to the prediction of subsequent arrest. Two variables, those of age and number of prior arrests, accounted almost entirely for the explained variance (about .33 for the patient sample and .25 for offenders). Sex, ethnicity, number of prior hospitalizations, and number of days previously hospitalized did not materially improve prediction of subsequent arrest for either group beyond that accounted for by age and prior arrests. Not only are these findings intrinsically interesting, but they suggest that the lack of control over ethnicity, sex, and prior hospitalization found in most of the studies were reviewed may not after all have led to misinterpretation of findings.

Steadman's data permit us to conclude that expatients have lower recidivism rates than exoffenders. Whether this difference is directly attributable to the impact of the hospital experience is still not demonstrable in the absence of evidence that the two cohorts (patients and offenders) are otherwise the same except for the nature of their incarceration. However, the available evidence is consistent with the possibility that hospitalization is a better deterrent to recidivism than imprisonment, or that hospitalization may indeed reduce the probability of recidivism in a causal manner.

Conclusions Drawn From the Research Evidence

In this review, arrest history, age, and diagnosis have emerged as the variables that best predict the probability of illegal or dangerous behavior after hospital discharge. It must be emphasized that these variables are statistically related to the outcome variable, but are not powerful predictors even with group data. On an individual basis, neither they nor any other variable or set of variables studied to date are useful predictors of future illegal or dangerous behavior.

From the information currently available, it seems that discharged mental patients as a group are not significantly less likely than others to exhibit dangerous behavior. At this time, there is no evidence that their mental status as such raises their arrest risk; rather, antisocial behavior and mental illness apparently coexist, particularly among young, unmarried, unskilled, poor males of whom a disproportionate number belong to ethnic minorities. It is unlikely that most people would care to have such neighbors, even in the absence of a history of psychiatric hospitalization.

The major factor associated with increases in arrest rates of discharged mental patients in recent years is the increased proportion of mental patients who have arrest histories before their hospitalization. For males in New York State, for example, this proportion has risen from 15% to 40% in the past 30 years.

Arrests are fairly infrequent events, even when mental patients are inappropriately considered as a single group. In the 18 months after discharge from New York State hospitals in 1975, for example, 90% of patients were *not* arrested. When patients with arrest histories, primary diagnoses of substance abuse, and personality disorders are considered separately, the remainder of the patient group appears to be no more dangerous and possibly less so than are those members of the general public who are not mentally ill.

POLICY IMPLICATIONS

Implications for Admission Criteria

As noted earlier, general concern about the civil rights of oppressed and minority groups during the past 20 years has led to revision of standards for involuntary hospitalization and retention of mental patients. In many jurisdictions, such confinement is now limited to times when patients are "dangerous" or "gravely disabled." The principle of the choice of the "least restrictive environment" has been incorporated into many laws. "Right to treatment" and "right to freedom" decisions by the courts have combined with more restrictive admissions policies to swell the numbers of chronically mentally ill in the community. The possibility that such persons are more likely than the general public to commit crimes has sharpened the controversy over standards for admission to and discharge from mental institutions.

The criterion of "dangerousness" for involuntary hospitalization has sparked a debate over the ability to apply such a standard. Paradoxically, the "dangerousness" standard has been adopted largely because of the criticism from outside of psychiatry that most commitment procedures violate civil rights of patients. Yet, as we have noted, those same critics and most psychiatrists agree that predictions of future dangerousness of hospitalized patients are highly unreliable.

Despite these recent developments, attitudes of the general public regarding the balance between patient rights and community safety remain tilted toward the latter. As Shah (1978) has pointed out, widespread apprehension about and indifference toward the mentally ill have led to tolerance of the preventive detention of many "false positives" in order to protect the community from the risk of release of "false negatives," those who do engage in violent behavior despite the expectations to the contrary. Shah also noted that other groups who are more predictably dangerous to society, such as drunken drivers and those convicted of three or more felonies, are not subjected to preventive confinement for the community's protection.

A more basic issue than the difficulty of predicting dangerousness in the mentally ill is that the determination of what kinds of harmful behaviors justify confinement is one that should be made by the courts. By judicial default this responsibility has fallen to the specialty of psychiatry, whose members have tried to carry it out in good faith. Predictably, however, psychiatrists have not been up to the task and have been severely criticized for this failure. We believe that psychiatry should reject this role and limit its function to the area of its traditional responsibility, concern for the welfare of patients, leaving the protection of the community to the police and the judicial system.

In additon to problems of prediction and violation of patients' civil rights, a serious consequence of the application of the "dangerous" standard for involuntary hospitalization is that those mentally ill who are most likely to benefit from such care and who are rarely dangerous are least likely to receive it. At the same time, hospitals admit those dangerous persons with a diagnosis of mental illness who are most refractory to treatment (e.g., sociopaths, character disorders, and substance abusers). We agree with Peszke (1975) that "to commit a mentally ill individual to a hospital simply because he fulfills the criterion of dangerousness, while not committing a nondangerous mentally ill individual who is incapable of making rational decisions and could benefit from treatment, is analagous to not hospitalizing an unconscious accident victim who is unable to ask for help but is not dangerous" (p. 827).

Discharge Policies

If statutory standards for involuntary admission of mental patients are often imprecise or difficult to comply with, the criteria for discharge are even more vague. When mentioned at all, the conditions under which patients can be released are stated tautologically in terms of their not requiring further hospitalization. For example, the New York Law (Chapter 27, Article 29, Section 29.15) states that, "A patient may be discharged . . . if . . . such patient does not require active inpatient care and treatment."

Such a general standard is inevitable, and perhaps even desirable, since no specific standards can govern the variety of circumstances that are represented by any hospital population: different types and degrees of illnesses and amenability to treatment; availability of treatments in the hospital; social setting and situations to which the patient will return; opportunities for aftercare, etc. However, lack of specific standards has led to considerable confusion and uncertainty about when patients should be discharged from the hospital.

It is unlikely that we shall in the near future see the financing and coordination that would make possible the extensive aftercare and rehabilitation services that are essential ingredients of successful community mental health care, and on which the policy of deinstitutionalization was premised. While working toward such a goal, a number of constructive changes in discharge policies can be implemented. We believe that wider use of a system of conditional discharges for certain categories of mental patients, with mandatory attendance at outpatient clinics and frequent periodic monitoring by mental health workers, would increase the likelihood of patients receiving better posthospital care and making a more successful social adjustment, while minimizing the possibility of violent or socially disruptive behavior.

Our review indicates that patients who are young, with prior arrest records, and who are substance abusers are particularly likely to engage in criminal behavior. Such persons are probably also least likely to attend aftercare clinics voluntarily. A parole system could make possible timely intervention that might prevent criminal behavior, or abort full clinical relapses. The first year after discharge is a particularly important period for close supervision, since criminal behavior or rehospitalization is more likely to occur during that time. Such conditional releases should include the right of the hospital to order the rehospitalization of the patient, if required attendance at a clinic is not complied with or if the patient's mental condition deteriorates and meets the standard for involuntary admission. Safeguards, such as notice and opportunities for hearing, would be observed, as in the case of any involuntary hospitalization. Conditional releases should be based on an evaluation of the patient's prognosis and needs irrespective of the voluntary or involuntary status of the patient. Implicit in such a program is the obligation of the hospital to formulate specific and detailed aftercare plans for conditionally released patients before their discharge, and to allocate adequate resources for their implementation.

CONCLUSIONS

In conclusion, we would like to reiterate our finding that, while patients considered *as a group* do have higher arrest rates than nonpatients *as a group*, it is largely because the patients include in their midst a disproportionate share of people with prior police records.

The "dangerousness' criterion for involuntary hospitalization, now widely used, results in a concentration of patients in mental institutions who display antisocial and disruptive behavior that is generally refractory to treatment, while selectively excluding severely ill but nonthreatening persons who are more likely to benefit from hospital care. It is likely that many of the "dangerous" patients were formerly cared for in the criminal justice system and have in recent years been increasingly diverted to mental hospitals and clinics. The elimination of the dangerousness standard would alter the composition of the hospitalized population and reduce the rate of criminal activity among discharged mental patients. Short hospitalization and rapid turnover of psychiatric patients with inadequate follow-up care also may put many patients at higher risk for antisocial behavior when discharged than was the case when hospital stays were longer and discharge criteria more stringent.

Our suggestions regarding revisions in discharge policies are designed to more closely supervise discharged patients in order to reduce the probability of disruptive behavior in the community. This is particularly indicated for those patients with prior criminal records. While it is difficult to balance the civil rights of patients regarding confidentiality of prior police records and mandatory aftercare with community demands for protection, an equilibrium of some kind must be sought for the well-being of both.

REFERENCES

American Psychiatric Association Task Force on Clinical Aspects of the Violent Individual. *Clinical aspects of the violent individual.* Washington, D.C.: American Psychiatric Association, 1974.

Ashley, M. C. Outcome of 1,000 cases paroled from the Middletown State Hospital. *State Hospital Quarterly* (New York), 1922, *8,* 64–70.

Aviram, U., & Segal, S. P. Exclusion of the mentally ill: Reflection of an old problem in a new context. *Archives of General Psychiatry,* 1973, *29,* 126–31.

Bassuk, E. L., & Gerson, S. Deinstitutionalization and mental health services. *Scientific American,* 1978, *238,* 46-53.

Brill, H., & Malzberg, B. Statistical report based on the arrest record of 5,354 male expatients released from New York State mental hospitals during the period 1946–48. (1954 mimeo.) *Mental Hospital Service (APA) Supplement No. 153,* August 1962.

Carmody, D. Saving a West Side block. *The New York Times,* 12–30-75, p. 29.

Cocozza, J. J. & Steadman, H. J. Prediction in psychiatry: An example of misplaced confidence in experts. *Social Problems,* 1978, *25,* 265–276.

Cohen, L. H., & Freeman, H. How dangerous to the community are state hospital patients? *Connecticut State Medical Journal* 1945, *9,* 697–700.

Dix, G. "Civil" commitment of the mentally ill and the need for data on prediction of dangerousness. *American Behavioral Scientist*, 1976, *19*, 318–334.

Durbin, J. R., Pasewark, R. A., & Albers, D. Criminality and mental illness: A study of arrest rates in a rural state. *American Journal of Psychiatry*, 1977, *134*, 80–83.

Farnsworh, D. Dangerousness. *Psychiatric Annals*, 1977, *7*, 55–70.

Federal Bureau of Investigation, *Uniform crime reports for the United States, 1977*. Washington, D.C.: U.S. Government Printing Office, 1978.

GAP Publication No. 102 The chronic mental patient in the Community. Vol. X, May, 1978.

Giovannoni, J. M., & Gurel, L. Socially disruptive behavior of exmental patients. *Archives of General Psychiatry*. 1967, *17*, 146–153.

Gove, W. R., & Tudor, J. Adult sex roles and mental illness. *American Journal of Sociology*, 1973, *78*, 81:2–835.

Gulevich, G., & Bourne, P. Mental illness and violence. In D. Daniels, G. Mapshall, & F. Ochberg (Eds.), *Violence and the struggle for existence*. Boston: Little Brown, 1970.

Gunn, J. Criminal behaviour and mental disorder. *British Journal Of Psychiatry*, 1977, *130*, 317–329.

Holden, C. The plight of the "deinstitutionalized" mental patient. *Science*, 1978, *200*, 1366.

Koenig, P. The problem that can't be tranquilized. *The New York Times Magazine*, 1978, May 21, 14.

Lagos, J. M., Perlmutter, K., & Saexinger, H. Fear of the mentally ill: Empirical support for the common man's response. *American Journal of Psychiatry*, 1977, *134*, 1134–1137.

Levine, D. Criminal behavior and mental institutionalization. *Journal of Clinical Psychology*, 1970, *26*, 279–284.

Mesinkoff, A. M. A solution to metropolitan mental-health problems. *Psychiatric Annals*, 1979, *9*, 67–79.

Paull, D., & Malek, R. Psychiatric disorders and criminality. *Journal of the American Medical Association*, 1974, *228*, 1369.

Penrose, L. Mental disease and crime: Outline of a comparative study of European statistics. *British Journal of Medical Psychology*, 1939, *18*, 1–15.

Peszke, M. A. Is dangerousness an issue for physicians in emergency commitment? *American Journal of Psychiatry*, 1975, *132*, 825–828.

Pollack, H. M. Is the paroled patient a threat to the community? *Psychiatric Quarterly*, 1938, *12*, 236–44.

Rabkin, J. G. Criminal behavior of discharged mental patients: A critical appraisal of the research. *Psychological Bulletin*, 1979, *86*, 1–27.

Rappeport, J. R., & Lassen, G. Dangerousness-arrest rate comparison of discharged patients and the general population. *American Journal of Psychiatry*, 1965, *121*, 776–783.

Rappeport, J. R., & Lassen, G. The dangerousness of female patients: A comparison of the arrest rate of discharged psychiatric patients and the general population. *American Journal of Psychiatry*, 1966, *123*, 413–419.

Segal, S. P., & Aviram, U. Community-based sheltered care. In P. Ahmed & S. Plog (Eds.), *State mental hospitals.* New York: Plenum, 1976.

Shah, S. A. Dangerousness: A paradigm for exploring some issues in law and psychology. *American Psychologist*, 1978, *33*, 224–236.

Sosowsky, L. *Putting state mental hospitals out of business—the community approach to treating mental illness in San Mateo County.* Berkeley, Calif.: Graduate School of Public Policy, University of California, duplicated report, July 1974.

Sosowsky, L. Crime and violence among mental patients reconsidered in view of the new legal relationship between the state and the mentally ill. *American Journal of Psychiatry*, 1978, *135*, 33–42.

Steadman, H. J. Some evidence on the inadequacy of the concept and determination of dangerousness in law and psychiatry. *The Journal of Psychiatry and Law*, 1973, 409–426.

Steadman, H. J. *Patterns of arrest among exmental patients and offenders: Implications for a therapeutic state.* Unpublished manuscript, 1978. (Available from: 44 Holland Avenue, Albany, N.Y. 12229.)

Steadman, H. J., Cocozza, J. J., & Melick, M. E. Explaining the increased arrest rate among mental patients: The changing clientele of state hospitals. *American Journal of Psychiatry*, 1978, *135*, 816–820.

Steadman, H. J., Melick, M. E., & Cocozza, J. J. *Arrest rates of persons released from New York State Department of Mental Hygiene psychiatric centers.* Report to the Commissioner of Mental Hygiene, 1977.

Steadman, H. J., Vanderwyst, D., & Ribner, S. Comparing arrest rates of mental patients and criminal offenders. *American Journal of Psychiatry*, 1978, *135*, 1218–1220.

Stone, A. Comment, *American Journal of Psychiatry*, 1975, *132*, 829–831.

Talbott, J. *The death of the asylum.* New York: Grune & Stratton, 1978.

Talbott, J. Care of the chronically mental ill—Still a national disgrace (editorial). *American Journal of Psychiatry*, 1979, *136*, 688–689.

Wykert, J. Community resistance to centers. *Psychiatric News*, 1975, *10*, 1 and 27.

Zitrin, A., Hardesty, A. S., Burdock, E. I., & Drossman, A. K. Crime and violence among mental patients. *American Journal of Psychiatry*, 1976, *133*, 142–149.

Chapter 7

PRIVACY, CONFIDENTIALITY, AND INFORMED CONSENT IN PSYCHOTHERAPY

John O. Noll[1,2]
Catherine E. Rosen[3]

The foundation for the current recognition of and the debate surrounding the rights of mental patients was provided by the pioneer work of psychiatrist Thomas Szasz (*The Myth of Mental Illness,* 1961; *Law, Liberty, and Psychiatry,* 1963; etc); and the writings of Goffman (1961), Kittrie (1971), and Scheff (1966, 1975) among others. As Redlich and Mollica recently stated, "With some shame, we state that most of the changes in establishing patient's rights were not brought about primarily by psychiatrists but by civil libertarians led by lawyers, and that the most important decisions were made by enlightened judges" (1976, p. 129).

[1]Professor and Director of Clinical Psychology Program, University of North Dakota.

[2]Appreciation is extended to Thomas M. Lockney, Law School, University of North Dakota, for his invaluable stimulation over the years and for reviewing an early version of this chapter; to Steve Podrygula, for bringing to my attention several of the studies discussed in this chapter; and to John D. Tyler for his helpful suggestions during the final preparation of the manuscript.

[3]Department of Educational Psychology. University of Georgia.

Questions of involuntary deprivation of freedom are involved only rarely with outpatients, and these patients generally initiate therapy on their own behalf. It is our belief, however, that most of the two to three million psychotherapy clients in the United States (Westin, 1976) have had and will continue to have their rights violated by therapists regardless of the context in which therapy occurs.

Barring exceptionally heroic efforts (Ennis, 1972), the future social-political-economic opportunities of those individuals who have been subject to mental hospitalization are severely limited. What is easily overlooked is that many of these opportunities are narrowed for the psychotherapy client. Whether or not psychotherapy clients benefit from therapy, they may suffer repression as a result of having been in psychotherapy as compellingly demonstrated by Weinstock and Haft (1974). Their study revealed that an individual's prospects for employment were reduced substantially if it were known that an applicant was a psychotherapy client.

This chapter will deal with privacy-confidentiality issues as they relate to psychotherapy. It will be readily apparent, however, that these issues have an impact far beyond the psychotherapy relationship. A review of the admittedly rather sparse research in these areas will illustrate the ways in which the ethical position of the psychotherapist influences his/her perception and interpretation of privacy-confidentiality issues. Also, the particular action that a psychotherapist may take regarding privacy-confidentiality issues will have obvious and not so obvious impact upon the client and client expectations for good or ill and also upon society and societal expectations. An examination of the literature reveals that client rights are frequently violated by the psychotherapist, by the institutional context in which the pscyhotherapist may practice, and by the myriad of third party involvements with the psychotherapy relationship. Finally, a "theory" of informed consent to psychotherapy is proposed that will provide a means to correct currently prevalent practices and that will be promotive of greater client choice and autonomy.

THE RIGHT TO PRIVACY AND CONFIDENTIALITY—SOME OF THE ISSUES

There is a nationwide concern about the invasion of individual privacy in many important aspects of American life (Westin, 1976; *Personal Privacy in an Information Society,* 1977). No longer may a potential client's sensitivities about the degree of privacy of the psychotherapy relationship be dismissed as a reflection of an individual's "defensiveness." There is a growing public awareness of privacy-confidentiality issues in psychotherapy. A salesman revealed to a colleague of one of us that he "has had the inclination on occasion to talk to a professional, but with everything getting so bureacratic these days, I might be blackballed somewhere along the line if I did." Rosen (1977) noted that 24% of one of her client samples expressed concern that personal information sent to state offices might somehow be used against them in the future.

Knowlton (1977) found that the most critical dimension affecting people's attitudes toward nine different professions plus "Best Friend," was a trustworthy/untrustworthy dimension. This trustworthy dimension was: (1) the single best predictor of future behavioral intention regarding with whom a person might consult for a mental health problem, (2) the best predictor of overall attitude toward these professions and, (3) with the exception of best friend, minister was rated significantly more trustworthy than all of the other professions in the following order: doctor, nurse, counselor, social worker, clinical psychologist, psychiatrist, attorney, and psychologist, (Knowlton, 1976). Stevens and Shearer (1978) suggested that trustworthiness may be correlated with a profession's reputation for maintaining confidentiality.

Definitions of Terms

Because there may exist some misunderstanding of the concepts of confidentiality, privileged communications, and privacy, perhaps some clarification of these terms might be helpful. For a fuller treatment of these concepts, the reader is referred to Shah (1969, 1970a, 1970b).

Confidentiality. This is the most familiar concept to psychotherapists, other professionals, such as lawyers and physicians, and to laypersons. Essentially, confidentiality refers to the psychotherapist's ethical obligation not to reveal to others anything said by a client-patient or to acknowledge the existence of the relationship. There are circumstances, however, under which psychotherapists may breach the confidential relationship. Those circumstances represent situations in which psychotherapists may "in the client's best interest" inform authorities or a client's relatives of a client's dangerousness to self or others. More typically, psychotherapists release confidential information about clients irrespective of possible untoward consequences for the client when the client consents to such a release or requests the psychotherapist to do so. The principle of confidentiality as a general ethical obligation is incorporated in the ethical codes of psychiatrists, psychologists, and social workers.

Privileged Communications. Privileged communications refers to the legal protections provided the client by statute or by the court in legal matters relating to a client. Theoretically, at least, the psychotherapist is *legally* obligated to retain the confidences of the client in legal proceedings, unless the client has waived his or her right to the privilege, or as part of a lawsuit has entered his or her emotional condition as an important element in the litigation. Under these latter circumstances, the psychotherapist is obligated to testify or risk being found in contempt of court.

It was once believed by many that privileged communications statutes represented the royal road to legally protected communications in psychotherapy, and some apparently still entertain that notion (Meyer & Smith, 1977). The growing number of exceptions attached to most privilege statutes has led one experienced observer to note: "Like the Roman God Janus, the law on privilege faces in opposite directions at the same time ... Virtually nothing is shielded by the shield. In every jurisdiction, the exceptions and implied waivers are so many and so broad that it is difficult to imagine a case in which the privilege applies" (Slovenko, 1974, p. 656).

Other variants of the concepts of confidentiality and privilege that have been discussed are the concepts of *absolute confidentiality* (Segal, 1977; Szasz, 1963) and *absolute privilege* (Dubey, 1974; Slawson, 1969). These concepts have a long history going back to the Hippocratic oath. In effect, these concepts, the former an ethical one and the latter a legal one, assume the position that the client's communications will be held in confidence by the psychotherapist under any and all circumstances. That is, the psychotherapist will not break confidentiality any more than one would expect a priest to break the confidentiality of the confessional.

For centuries, the Catholic church has recognized the crucial importance of confidentiality to penitents with regard to the latter's communications in the confessional. The priest is committed to the proposition that what he hears in the confessional (under the seal) has the status of absolute confidentiality. Even the identity of the person is presumed to be unknown, anonymous to the priest, so that the penitant speaking or revealing himself may not be inhibited (Haas, 1978).

With the advent of psychoanalysis, the first modern systematic form of secular psychotherapy, psychoanalysts have enjoyed the reputation of being most conscientious about protecting the confidentiality of the relationship between themselves and their clients (Plaut, 1974; Slovenko, 1974). Some have exercised extreme discretion with respect to note and record keeping, if any, in order to safeguard the privacy and confidentiality of the relationship (Hollender, 1965; Slovenko, 1974). When the Watergate "plumbers" broke into Daniel Ellsberg's psychotherapist's office, they found nothing of value; even the billing addresses were kept at the psychiatrist's home.

Privacy. This concept generally refers to the right of individuals to have control over personal information and to be free of intrustions into their lives.

Margulis (1977a) points out that the "legal concept of privacy is not a recent legal innovation. Instead, this concept, appearing as 'damage by viewing,' has been an integral part of Jewish law (the Talmud) for at least 1500 years" (p. 2). He suggested the following definition of privacy: "Privacy as a whole or in part, represents the control of transactions between person(s) and other(s), the ultimate aim of which is to enhance autonomy and/or to minimize vulnerability" (Margulis, 1977b, p. 10).

PRIVACY-CONFIDENTIALITY: PROFESSIONAL ATTITUDES AND PRACTICES

Until recently, research of many privacy-confidentiality issues has been quite minimal. One may safely predict, however, that there will be considerably more study of them in the future.

One of the earliest studies proved to be paradigmatic of research that was to follow, both in method and in the pattern of results obtained. Little and Strecker (1956) used a questionnaire consisting of nine hypothetical situations to which they sought responses from a small group of psychiatrists. A few of the questions asked and the responses to them were as follows:

> "What is your ethical responsibility when a patient tells you her husband is mentally ill and is planning to kill her, and you have reason to believe this is true, but she will not permit commitment or help from the police, and forbids you to interfere?"

In response, 32% would report to legal authorities, 18% would seek commitment of either the patient or the spouse, 13% would seek consultation from a colleague, 3% would refuse to continue with the patient unless she became more cooperative, and 34% felt that their responsibility was to continue to work with the patient only.

> "What is your ethical responsibility when one of your patients takes out a large insurance policy, and plans to suicide as soon as the suicide clause is fulfilled, and he does not accept your recommendations for treatment?"

In response, 47% felt that their responsibility was to attempt to continue working with the patient and to respect his confidences, 26% would inform the family, 5% would insist on commitment, 5% would report it, 8% would inform the insurance company, one only if he committed suicide, 3% would stop treatment, and 5% would consult with others.

> "What is your ethical responsibility when a patient whom you have had in treatment for some time reveals acts of disloyalty and sabotage against the United States and demands that you keep such information secret by his right of privileged communications?"

In response, 89% felt an ethical responsibility to report such information, although 35% felt that they would personally evaluate the seriousness of such acts before they would report them. Eight percent would do nothing, and one respondent did not wish his reply to be used.

These responses illustrate and illuminate that with the exception of the third situation (disloyalty and sabotage) the lack of unanimity of response is quite clear. Furthermore, it is apparent that those who would make or advocated extra-therapeutic-intervention responses were imposing ethical considerations that were clearly in violation of the client's expressly stated wishes.

Wiskoff (1960) reported the results of a "divided loyalty" or a "client vs. society" study with psychologists as respondents. They represented three divsions of the American Psychological Association (APA): Clinical Psychology, Industrial Psychology, and Counseling Psychology.

Of the 22 hypothetical incidents portrayed, one dealt with homicide, one with suicide, and one with treason, incidents similar to those used by Little and Strecker (1956).

With regard to the three critical incidents, it was found that 64% would release information in the homicide incident, 42% would release information in the incident depicting a suicidal threat, and that 45% would release information in the treason incident.

These results are considerably different from those found by Little and Strecker (1956), the most divergent being the situation dealing with treason. The incidents portraying the suicidal and homicidal threats were also markedly different between the two studies, although these differences are masked by the manner in which Wiskoff summarized the data given earlier. Further analysis revealed that clinical psychologists would break confidentiality significantly less often than would the other groups.

Wiskoff (1960) noted that, "If all psychologists in the sample viewed the three incidents as imminent danger and followed APA's recommendations, there should have been unanimous release of information" (p. 659). We will continually find that individuals respond to a number of ethical-confidentiality issues in terms of how they perceive their own role and function vis-à-vis the client, society, and professional identity.

Jagim, Wittman, and Noll (1978) found that 98% of the professionals in their study agreed that the therapist has an ethical obligation to maintain confidentiality, and 98% believed that confidentiality was essential to maintaining a positive relationship.

Interestingly, a professional's position on confidentiality was not predictive of his/her responses to a legal requirement to disclose child abuse or the so-called duty to warn third parties in the event of a client threatening to harm (*Tarasoff,* 1976). Sixty-three percent indicated to varying degrees their obligation to the legal requirement to report child abuse, and 76% emphasized disclosure to third parties rather than confidentiality, even though *Tarasoff* has precedential value only in California. There were no significant differences relating to professional affiliation, place of employment, or private practice.

Rosen (1976) presented professionals and graduate students in both psychology and social work with 10 critical ethical issues. The research question was, Would they uphold the client's right to privacy or would they jeopardize privacy rights by reporting illegal behaviors? A sample of well-educated laypersons was presented with the same critical situations and was asked to predict the behavior of the professional in each incident.

Although the results indicated that professionals state they would uphold their clients' rights to confidentiality to a significantly greater degree than the laypersons' predictions, when the responses of the two samples were compared, over 70% of both samples would ignore client's rights of privacy when the client's behavior jeopardized the well-being of others.

The rationales for both groups' decisions were rated and professionals were judged to be more client oriented while laypersons expected the professionals to be more society oriented.

The results of the more recent studies of Jagim et al. (1978) and Rosen (1976) differ from the Wiskoff (1960) study. These later studies suggest that, over the past two decades, psychotherapists may have become more inclined to function as agents of social control and, further, that laypeople expect them to function in this manner. If these trends are confirmed by further research, potential consumers of psychotherapy services will indeed be in peril, as may be the perception of psychotherapists as individuals who will respect their client's privacy.

In their study of privacy issues with a large group of psychoanalysts, Szasz and Nemiroff (1963) found that only 12% replied *never* to a question about exchanging information about "office patients" with others, including professional colleagues. Only 16% responded *never* when asked about communicating with a colleague who was seeing a spouse of one's patient. Only 16% chose *never* to the question, "Do you give your patients letters or statements for use with draft boards, schools, courts, etc., affirming that in your opinion they are in need of psychiatric or psychoanalytic treatment, mentally ill (or words to that effect)?" Furthermore, 71% of these analysts agreed that training analysts should communicate with officers of the training institutes concerning their patient-candidates. Further erosion of client privacy, in psychoanalytic practice has occurred with the emergence of the third party payer (Chodoff, 1974; Gibson, 1977).

A study conducted by the *Yale Law Journal* (1962) found that the great majority of samples of marriage counselors, psychiatrists, psychologists, and social workers favored a privileged communications statute.

These results were supported in a study by Suarez and Balcanoff (1966). Ninty-two percent of their respondents favored a privileged communications statute. There was a wide divergence of opinion expressed, however, regarding the exceptions to confidentiality to be included in a statute.

They concluded, "As expected, the psychiatric profession is largely in favor of a protective statute, and the reasons offered revolve around the basic theme that a *proper and productive psychotherapeutic relationship can only exist in a climate of absolute confidentiality*" (p. 622, emphasis added). One may inquire however, how it is possible to provide a climate of absolute confidentiality when there are numerous exceptions built into most privilege statutes?

Taken together, the results of the studies discussed thus far demonstrate that professionals do believe that confidentiality is very important or even crucial to the practice of psychotherapy and to the client. These results also demonstrate that, while professionals generally "believe in" the necessity for privacy and confidentiality on the one hand, the large majority definitely believe that some things are, in fact, more confidential than others. Many therapists will or say that they they will intervene in their clients' lives, even though some of their clients may expressly forbid interference. Such practices flatly contradict the often-proffered statement that early in a psychotherapeutic relationship "the patient is assured of privacy, confidentiality, and moral neutrality" (Korchin, 1976, p. 285). In practice, contrary to expressed theory, only a relatively small percentage of professionals appear to be fully committed to these principles. One implication of this discussion seems clear—what is to one psychotherapist a rational, defensible ethical position is to another a position of ethical and/or legal irresponsibility. This may be one of the reasons why professional organizations find it difficult and perhaps impossible to arrive at a clear-cut ethical position regarding confidentiality (*APA Monitor,* 1977).

There emerges a clear implication for the client as well, caveat emptor: let the buyer beware. A potential client might well find it to his/her advantage and best interests to query prospective psychotherapists about the limits, if any, to confidentiality.

PRIVACY-CONFIDENTIALITY: CLIENT AND NONCLIENT ATTITUDES

With the exception of Rosen's recent study (1977a), only a few early studies were found in which clients or former clients have served as participants in privacy-confidentiality research, but there are available some contemporary social science research findings using nonclients.

In their study of client expectations regarding psychotherapy, Garfield and Wolpin (1963) included seven items dealing with privacy, three of which were related to other individuals having knowledge of their being in psychotherapy. The modal responses of this group indicated that they had minimal concern about relatives, friends, or employers knowing of their involvement in psychotherapy. Lewis & Worman (1964) studied former counseling center clients' reactions to *authorized* and *unauthorized* release of confidential information and found that in the unauthorized conditions education-vocational clients would allow more categories of individuals to receive information about themselves than would clients who had sought counseling for personal problems. Similar results were obtained in the authorized condition.

Simmons (1968) conducted a similar counseling center study using only the condition of releasing information *without consent.* Two-thirds of the clients indicated that counselors may release some kinds of information, but release was related to type of client problem, kind of information released, the recipient of the information, and sex of client. However, 33% did not agree to unauthorized release.

These studies suggest that many former clients readily acquiesce to counselor requests and that former clients may be overly trusting of their counselors.

There are several studies in which questions relating to confidentiality were addressed to nonclients. In the *Yale Law Journal* study (1962), a sample of laypeople was asked whether or not a privileged communication statute would have any effect upon their willingness to disclose personal information. The authors concluded that, "Our survey shows that for every two laymen who claim they would not be affected by the lack of a privilege for communications with a psychiatrist, psychologist, marriage counselor, or social worker, nearly five claim they would be less likely to make full disclosure" (p. 1255).

Singer's (1978) study gives us greater understanding of the role of consent forms and the value of confidentiality in eliciting personal information from people. Singer measured the impact of various informed consent procedures upon response rates and response quality in social surveys of such sensitive areas as drinking, marijuana use, etc., in addition to more conventional questions.

An assurance of confidentiality appeared to affect the rate of nonresponse to individual questions. Respondents who were told that their answers would remain completely confidential had the lowest refusal rate. The promise of absolute confidentiality also enhanced the quality of response to sensitive questions.

The introduction of a consent form into the situation appears to sensitize individuals and they begin monitoring what they say about themselves. More complete and valid responses result when the interviewee is convinced of the sincerity of the promise of confidentiality and of the person making the promise.

The importance of privacy maintenance to self-disclosure was underscored in a recent study. Spinner (1978) found that subjects would be more willing to disclose intimate matters when a dyadic boundary was relatively secure and little likelihood existed of the disclosed information being revealed.

Strassburg, Anchor, Cunningham, and Elkins (1978) reported that clients rated as improved were seen as more self-disclosing during psychotherapy than nonimprovers. If intimate self-disclosure is important for successful therapy, and if self-disclosure varies as a function of the security of the dyadic boundary, then it is essential that personal information revealed during therapy be protected.

Rosen (1977b) found that 83% of a large sample of school teachers and administrators who were pursuing advanced degrees would not want personally identifying information sent to state offices if they were to apply to a local mental health center for services. Only 38% would resist granting permission if their refusal to do so would preclude the obtaining of service; most would relinquish their right to privacy under the latter circumstances.

Stevens and Shearer (1978) surveyed college students to assess their views about confidentiality. Conclusions based upon their survey included: (1) before communicating with any third party, written consent should be obtained from the client, (2) therapists should not reveal information to authorities, even if this posture would be in defiance of the courts, (3) an exception to the maintenance of complete confidentiality would be a threat to harm a third party, and (4) therapists, during the first client contact, should employ informed consent procedures that state their exceptions to complete confidentiality.

These students were virtually unanimous that, "It is important to be able to say anything to a counselor without fear that he/she will tell anyone else." There is no doubt, that both professionals and laypeople support many of the values attributed to the importance of confidentiality in psychotherapy relationships.

Are clients more trusting, more willing to allow professionals to assume control over them, more vulnerable, and, therefore, less likely to inquire about or to assert their rights? Rosen's study (1977a) indicates that this may be true. She demonstrated that clients experience subtle forces to relinquish their rights to privacy. In Phase I of her study, all new mental health clients at four mental health centers were presented with a form to sign during the intake interview. The form consented to having their identified records released to the state. Of 962 new clients, there was 100% compliance. During Phase II, the same form was given to new clients, but in two clinics, an additional statement was read to each client explaining the purpose of the form and what consent would mean. In these two clinics, compliance was again 100%.

In the other two clinics, the statement was also read, but it was followed by an assurance that they would receive services whether or not the release was signed. In one of the two clinics where the statement was read, compliance dropped to 41%. In the other, compliance dropped to 20%.

That the importance of privacy of their psychotherapy cannot be underestimated is attested to by the fact that 3% to 4% of those individuals possessing insurance coverage for psychotherapy do not use it and, while 55% of psychoanalytic patients have some form of health insurance (Marmor, 1975), 10% of these clients do not use their insurance coverage (Gibson, 1977). As to why this is so, Marmor's best guess "is that in most instances the patient fears significant losses of one kind or another if the fact that undergoing psychiatric therapy gets onto some official record" (Marmor, 1975, p. 107). Would not a greater number of clients opt for this alternative, i.e., pay out of pocket, if they were aware of such potentially harmful records (Noll, 1976)?

Those assessing group insurance plans for mental health care have noted that when given a choice between clinic services or fee for service from private sources, the latter option is most frequently chosen (Avnet, 1969; Glasser & Duggan, 1969). Grossman (1971) reported that those who have experienced both types of services emphasized their concern with privacy as the basis for their preference for the private fee option.

Professionals also believe that their clients anticipate that their communications will be confidential and the presence or absence of confidentiality will facilitate or inhibit client communications (*Yale Law Journal,* 1962), a belief receiving confirmation from nonclients (Singer, 1978; Spinner, 1978). Jagim et al. (1978) found that 95% of the professionals sampled felt that clients believe their communications will remain confidential.

SOURCES OF VIOLATION OF PRIVACY-CONFIDENTIALITY RIGHTS

In the preceeding sections of this chapter, areas of potential violation of client privacy-confidentiality rights by psychotherapists were amply demonstrated. There are, however, numerous other violations of client rights that are more subtle and perhaps are even more pernicious in their effects. The primary means by which client rights violations and client repression occurs is through the compilation and subsequent distribution, primarily by psychotherapists, of information about individuals and their alleged illnesses, the use of this information by the psychotherapist's institutional affiliations, if any, and by numerous third parties who request information from psychotherapists about the latter's clients or former clients.

The growth of the mental health center, the expansion of psychiatric services in general hospitals, the advent of the third party payer, and the numerous requests for information from other third parties have sown the seeds for the development of many privacy rights problems (Grossman, 1977). The Advisory Committee on Automated Personal Data Systems noted in its report *Records Computers and the Rights of Citizens* (1973) that: "The new criminal justice information network can be used in conjunction with the vast private and government computer dossiers being compiled by credit bureaus, insurance companies, welfare agencies, mental health units, and others. Cumulatively, these files threaten an 'information tyranny' that could lock each citizen into his past; they signal the end of a uniquely American promise—that an individual can shed past mistakes and entanglements and start out anew" (p. 224–225).

The manner in which the psychotherapist's institutional affiliation may violate client privacy rights may be illustrated by the results of a study by Noll and Hanlon (1976). In a survey of mental health centers and state and territorial directors of mental health, they found that

51% of the mental health centers reported one or more personal identifiers (name, address, and social security number) to their state directors. Sixty percent of the state directors reported receiving one or more of the identifiers. Importantly, 36% of the centers acknowledged that they provided their directors with such information *without the knowledge of their clients.* Predominately, centers required the permission of their clients prior to releasing client information to third parties. Some centers, however, automatically released information about certain classes of clients to referral agencies or when clients were referred from specific sources. As Rosen (1977a) has clearly demonstrated, clients sign away their rights rather easily under certain circumstances, so the fact that mental health centers report the use of signed release forms does not necessarily imply that their clients are exercising voluntary choice when they comply with the request for their signatures. Noll and Hanlon (1976) also found that 81% of the centers stored client records indefinitely.

A provocative article by Kelley and Weston (1974) dealt with violations of the civil liberties of mental health center clients. They propose guidelines to accommodate the competing interests between privacy vs. accountability, and they present several sound recommendations and actions that mental health center personnel may take that would result in greater client privacy protections. Westin (1976) also proposes guidelines for mental health centers.

Increasing pressures have been leading to the development of peer review committees (Langsley and Lebaron, 1974). Consequently, professional organizations have been rapidly forming *Professional Standards Review Organizations* (PSROs) within the various states (Gibson, 1977; Sullivan, 1974). The development of PSROs is primarily a result of pressure from third party payers and of the expectations professions have that their services will be increasingly included in insurance coverage for mental health services either by private insurers or by a national health insurance plan.

In short, the PSRO will, when requested by the third party payer, review whether the cost, the length of time, and the procedures employed for the presenting problems of a client are compatible with local professional standards. Presumably, if potential clients are aware of the existence of such committees, they too may address similar questions to them. Depending upon the candor of psychotherapists with their clients, clients may be completely unaware that such an eventuality may occur or that his/her case may be currently under review by the committee. The PSRO guidelines suggested by the Department of Health, Education, and Welfare cited in Westin (1976) would require the therapist to inform the client of such a review.

Consequences of Violations of Privacy-Confidentiality Rights

Some of the sources for requests for information by third parties were revealed by a 1970 survey of California psychiatrists reported in *Personal Privacy in an Information Society* (1977). "Of the 346 respondents, 89% reported that they had been asked for medical-record information by insurance companies, 56% by schools, 49% by employers" (p. 281).

The factors that contribute to employers' decisions regarding applicants, the manner in which admissions committees of professional schools use the psychological-psychiatric-personality data they may have in their possession about candidates, etc., contribute to a kind of mystification as to just what occurs. Furthermore, it might be quite difficult to "prove" that a given candidate was refused employment, an insurance policy, or admission to a professional school because of having been a client. Occasionally, an individual reveals that his application for an insurance policy had been rejected because he had acknowledged his previous status as a psychotherapy patient (Sorrels, 1977).

The results of the Weinstock and Haft (1974) study represent a dramatic example of the severely negative consequences that may be the result of having been a psychotherapy client. In a survey of industrial physicians, a questionnaire was employed covering a variety of physical illnesses, such as myocardial infarction, angina pectoris, diabetes mellitus, etc., and psychiatric illness.

The respondents' replies to the category "psychiatric illness" are of considerable interest because, with the exception of the "aortic stenosis on treatment" category, a person currently in psychotherapy received the highest rejection rate of any other illness category for a managerial position; only 14% of the respondents offered an unqualified approval for employment, while 63% gave an unqualified rejection. For employment at the clerical level, an individual in psychotherapy was rejected by 56%, with only 23% giving an unqualified yes; virtually these same results were obtained for maintenance jobs.

These results indicate the degree of stigmatization that is borne by those individuals who may be in psychotherapy. These individuals are perceived as having an affliction more dire in its consequences than would be found with those having a serious chronic physical illness. Implications from this study are clear: acknowledgment of having been a participant in and/or recipient of "mental health care" may reduce opportunities for employment in many sectors of the economy to virtually zero.

To have one's application rejected by a school, an insurance company, or an employer obviously may have drastic consequences for one's life chances. The question is basically one of relevant criteria for rejection, not one of psychotherapy client status or even of diagnosis of a mental condition (Hollender, 1960). Psychotherapists do not have sufficient knowledge of the variety of criteria for successful prediction in most areas (Ennis & Litwack, 1974; Ziskin, 1977). Even if they did possess such expertise, should psychotherapists acquiesce to such requests?

Furthermore, whenever a psychotherapist responds to a request from a third party (with the client's permission to do so), the psychotherapist is assuming the position of a double agent (Halleck, 1971; Noll, 1974; Szasz, 1967). As Mariner prophetically commented, "Unless *therapists* make their positions known, the problem [of third party requests] will inevitably become greater as more and more organizations become accustomed to compliance with their requests for therapists' opinions" (1967, p. 72, emphasis in original).

THE PSYCHOTHERAPISTS' DILEMMAS

The evidence clearly shows that client rights are violated daily, and yet these practices continue. It is difficult to contest Shaw's observation that "all professions are conspriacies against the laity" (Shaw, 1962, p. 110), when professional organizations themselves do not assume and promulgate an ethical stance regarding client rights among their members, particularly when these organizations and the members are well aware that these violations do occur.

Is there any way out? Are there any viable alternatives to the more traditional modes of dealing with these problems? Can psychotherapists make some hard choices that, when once made, may serve more clearly their own and their client's ultimate best interests? It seems clear that it devolves upon the individual psychotherapist to develop his/her own moral, ethical stance regarding many client rights issues, a conclusion reached by others (Grossman, 1973; Hollender, 1965; Jagim et al., 1978; Little & Strecker, 1956; Siegel, 1976; Szasz, 1963.)

ABSOLUTE CONFIDENTIALITY AS A SOLUTION

Absolute confidentiality of client communications has been advocated as the appropriate ethical position to protect both client and therapist rights. Recently, Dubey (1974) put it this way: "When the therapist is asked, 'Doctor, is what I tell you confidential?' he must be able to answer, 'What you tell me, I will keep confidential, even if you decide that you don't want me to' " (p. 1093). In part, this statement echoes Hollender's comment that: "Therapists engaged in society-oriented or patient-oriented psychotherapy agree on the need to protect the individual patient, and, hence, they favor privileged communication; therapists engaged in patient-oriented psychotherapy go one step further: they maintain that *absolute confidentiality under all circumstances*—whether the patient wants it or not—is essential" (Hollender, 1965, pp. 4–5, emphasis added). Further, "Privilege as a right of the patient should exist to protect the individual patient; privilege as a right of the psychiatrist [psychotherapist] is needed to protect the practice of psychotherapy" (p. 1).

But, did Hollender mean what he said? Apparently not, for when he was queried about the possibility of a patient presenting a serious suicidal threat, he replied: "You would have to dissolve the patient-oriented type of relationship and you would not return to it. . . . The patient himself would no longer be engaged in therapy in which he would make the decisions about changes in his life, etc." (p. 7).

If the absolute position does not contain the concept of *total* privacy on the part of the therapist, then it is obvious that the confidence is not absolute and that the therapist has implicitly reserved the right to unilaterally break the contract with the client under certain conditions or circumstances.

THE STATUS OF THIRD PARTY INQUIRIES AND THE ABSOLUTE POSITION

A therapist assuming an absolute position will not respond to a third party inquiry, whether the client desires it or not, although the client is free to do with his or her privacy as he/she may choose (Szasz, 1963).

This position also requires that the therapist refuse to testify in court, if subpoenaed. Some critics of the absolute position assert that such therapists put themselves above the law. Perhaps it is more a reflection of the therapist's commitment to his/her role and a willingness to assume the consequences of it, rather than an assertion that "I am above the law!" It is not unknown that newspaper reporters challenge the court's right to know the reporter's sources, or for that matter, for psychiatrists to refuse to testify (*In Re Liftshutz*, 1970).

The advent of the third party payer threatens to breach the absolute privacy barrier, and does so when the client and therapist agree to submit reimbursement for cost of therapy forms to an insurance carrier. These forms typically request a diagnosis and statements about the client's presenting and ongoing problems. This threat need not materialize if the psychotherapist were to decline to make his/her services available under third party payer programs. Financial considerations usually represent an irresistible pressure, however. Chodoff (1972) has articulated the rather widespread implications inherent in this form of financial arrangement, such as issues of confidentiality, therapists' allegiance, the appearance of professional identity confusions "as the therapist becomes less a priest and more a business man," and the organizations to which he belongs become involved increasingly with guild and political concerns, etc. Kovacks (1975) has expressed doubt that by 1984, there will exist anything approximating a private consulting room. Furthermore, as Wohl (1974) has elucidated, insurance carriers are not the only source of third party payers; spouses and parents, for example, are frequently represented as third party payers, and due consideration must be given to this reality when a therapist negotiates a contract under such circumstances.

Suppose, however, that a client or former client is confronted with a question regarding his or her current or past contact with a psychotherapist, e.g., having been "under psychiatric care." As demonstrated by the Weinstock and Haft (1974) study, the way an individual responds to this question could have rather significant life outcomes.

INFORMED CONSENT TO PSYCHOTHERAPY AS A PROTECTION OF CLIENT RIGHTS

Let us assume that a present or former client responds affirmatively to a question concerning his/her mental health status, i.e., to a question on an application form that inquires whether or not the client has ever consulted a psychiatrist or psychologist. Typically, such application forms include a waiver for the applicant to sign that permits the company to request information about the client from the client's present or past therapist. If the psychotherapist maintains an absolute position on confidentiality, he/she will not acknowledge the inquiry.

If the therapist holds a relative or the more usual position regarding confidentiality, he/she will respond to an inquiry because the permission to release form, or copy thereof, will accompany the request. What the company or admissions committee may do with the information obtained will, in part, be a reflection of the therapist's attitude toward the client. In any event, if the therapist does supply information, the therapist has assumed a double-agent role (Noll, 1974), because, to paraphrase Halleck (1971), if the therapist can enumerate a sufficient number of positive statements about the client, the client *may* be employed or *may* be granted an insurance policy, etc.

Clients typically have not been informed of the possibility of negative consequences accruing from inquiries regarding their mental health status. Clients may be completely unaware of their stigmatized status for having been a psychotherapy client. These consequences can be grave, especially in view of the computerization of health records and the accessibility of health records to the insurance industry. For example, if a person is rejected for a life insurance or health insurance policy for "psychiatric reasons," that information will be made available to the insurance industry through the Medical Insurance Bureau located in Boston, Massachusetts (Westin, 1976). This represents the kind of paper trail that some seek to avoid by paying for their own psychotherapy, rather than by exercising their option for payment through their insurance coverage.

Noll (1974, 1976, 1977) has argued that a client's rights are violated whenever the client has not been informed of untoward potential consequences *prior* to those occasions when a client may be confronted with inquiries possessing the potential for client self-incrimination. Furthermore, such questions should be considered as violations of an individual's right to privacy. In effect, Noll has argued for the application of informed consent procedures to psychotherapy on ethical grounds as a means of protecting the rights of clients. This position may be seen as analogous to the potential long-term side effects of a treatment or procedure in medicine. Bersoff (1976) has noted the need for informed consent to psychotherapy, specifically with regard to informing clients that the therapist "has a duty to warn" third parties whom the client may seriously threaten to harm. Plaut (1974) earlier suggested that clients be informed of the therapist's limits to confidentiality, a position that Robitscher (Noll, Robitscher, & Wolpert, 1977) agrees as necessary to avoid client entrapment.

The concept of informed consent to treatment is a relatively new and rapidly expanding one. Some of the functions served by informed consent include the promotion of individual autonomy and self-determination, the protection of the individual's status as a human being, the avoidance of fraud and duress, and the fostering of rational decision making (Capron, 1974). Two relatively recent court decisions have hastened concern about the implementation of informed consent to medical treatment: *Canterbury* v. *Spence* (1972) and *Cobbs* v. *Grant* (1972). In *Cobbs,* the court held that, in the absence of the patient's consent to treatment or if a treatment were applied other than that to which the patient consented, the physician is liable under the *battery theory.* Where the patient consented to the procedure but an undisclosed-but-known risk materialized, liability of the physician would come under the *negligence theory.* The court noted, "The trend appears to be categorizing failure to obtain informed consent as negligence" (p. 8).

The court in *Canterbury* v. *Spence* (1972) rejected the view that the "physician's obligation to disclose is either germinated or limited by medical practice" (p. 783). The court, instead, required disclosure of material risks. Risks were deemed material when a reasonable person in the patient's apparent position "would likely attach significance to the risk or cluster of risks in question in deciding whether or not to forego the proposed therapy" (p. 787). In other words, the court adopted a reasonable-person standard and rejected the usual professional community standard of disclosure.

The question we would like to pose is this: "Do the various forms of repression to which a psychotherapy client may be exposed represent 'material risks'?" Because of the evidence presented in this chapter, we believe the answer to be in the affirmative. If this theory is found to be legally valid, numerous psychotherapists could be found legally negligent because of their failure to provide adequate informed consent procedures to their clients.

Psychiatrists have begun to attempt to formulate informed consent guidelines applicable to some aspects of psychiatric practice (Gross, 1975; Lebensohn, 1975; Meisel, Roth, & Lidz, 1977; Shlensky, 1977). Gross (1975), reporting for a California Medical Association panel on psychiatry and informed consent, expressed concern about the potential impact of informed consent procedures on the psythotherapy client and on the therapeutic relationship.

Alexander and Szasz (1973) and Schwitzgebel (1975) have advocated the use of a contractual model, a model that most therapists use either implicitly or explicitly, although there may be some differences in opinion regarding what parameters are necessary and sufficient to constitute a contract (Greenfield, 1976; Parker, 1976). Schwitzgebel (1975) does not find the use of the concept of informed consent a very positive one. Nevertheless, he seems to recommend a combination of informed consent procedures and a contract.

It appears to us that the distinction that Schwitzgebel attempts to draw between informed consent, on the one hand, and the contractual model, on the other, is largely an artificial one, because appropriately formulated informed consent procedures constitute the contract; whereas a contract, per se, does not necessarily include the informed consent parameters about which Bersoff (1976), Noll (1974, 1976, 1977), Plaut (1974), and others have expressed concern.

While psychiatrists appear to be opposed to written informed consent procedures to psychotherapy (Gross, 1975; Noll et al., 1977), we feel that written information is much more protective of the rights of all concerned. Information provided might plausibly include the intervention techniques anticipated or contemplated, the limits, if any, to confidentiality, i.e., the circumstances under which the therapist, if not an absolutist, will break confidentiality, the potentially untoward consequences of acknowledging having been a client (the politico-socio-economic side effects of having transactions with a psychotherapist), and client access to and/or the destruction of client records. The frequency of contacts, fees, responsibilities of each participant, probable improvement, and alternatives to therapy may be incorporated in the verbal contract between the therapist and client.

There are a number of advantages to providing information in writing and in a form that the client may keep. The primary advantage is the opportunity it affords the client for independent review, free from the stresses that clients frequently experience under such circumstances (Rosen, 1977). The client may wish to review the information at his/her leisure and address the various issues immediately or as they may become relevant during the period of obtaining assistance. Furthermore, a written statement allows the psychotherapist to devote more attention to the client, rather than engaging in a lengthy presentation of a *Miranda*-type warning (Bazar, 1978). A written format also has the advantage of presenting relevant information in a factual manner.

Such procedures will also be protective of the psychotherapist's rights and potential liability as well. Schwitzgebel (1975) offers the following example: "If the therapist contracts with the patient or his family to prevent suicide, then he ought to be allowed to use the force necessary to conduct his treatment and be held liable under his contract. Conversely, if the therapist chooses to use no coercion or restraint and clearly makes no provision to prevent suicidal acts, then the therapist ought not to be held liable" (pp. 819–820).

CONCLUSION

Client privacy and confidentiality have been examined and, with relatively rare exceptions, they have been found to be to a great extent illusory, whether psychotherapy is sought from a public agency or a private practitioner. To be sure, clients enjoy a much greater degree of protection of their privacy rights in the private sector, and espcially in the absence of a third party payer and a position of absolute confidentiality on the part of the therapist. If psychotherapists wish to be serious about protecting their clients' and their own rights and options, however, psychotherapists, wherever they may practice their art, bear a heavy responsibility to employ full and informed consent-contractual procedures with their clients. To do otherwise continues to perpetuate practices that are demeaning, depreciating, unethical, and violative of individual choice and autonomy.

REFERENCES

Alexander, G. J., & Szasz, T. S. From contract to status via psychiatry. *Santa Clara Lawyer,* 1973, *13,* 537–559.

APA Monitor, 1977, *3,* 22–23.

Avnet, H. H. Psychiatric insurance—ten years later. *American Journal of Psychiatry,* 1969, *126,* 667–674.

Bazar, J. New threats to confidentiality. *APA Monitor,* 1978, *7,* 4.

Bersoff, D. N. Therapists as protectors and policemen: New roles as a result of *Tarasoff. Professional Psychology,* 1976, *7,* 267–273.

Canterbury v. Spence, 464 F 2d 772 (D.C. Cir.); cert denied 409 US 1064 (1972).

Capron, A. M. Informed consent in catastrophic disease research and treatment. *University of Pennsylvania Law Review,* 1974, *123,* 340–438.

Chodoff, P. The effect of third party payment on the practice of psychotherapy. *American Journal of Psychiatry,* 1972, *129,* 540–545.

Cobbs v. Grant, 8 Cal 3d 229, 104 Cal Rptr 505, 502 P 2d 1 Cal 1972.

Dubey, J. Confidentiality as a requirement of the therapist: Technical necessities for absolute privilege in psychotherapy. *American Journal of Psychiatry,* 1974, *131,* 1093–1096.

Ennis, B. J. *Prisoners of psychiatry.* New York: Harcourt Brace Jovanovich, Inc., 1972.

Ennis, B. J., & Litwack, T. R. Psychiatry and the presumption of expertise: Flipping coins in the courtroom. *California Law Review,* 1974, *3,* 693–752.

Garfield, S. L., & Wolpin, M. Expectations regarding psychotherapy. *Journal of Nervous and Mental Disease,* 1963, *4,* 353–362.

Gibson, R. W. (Ed.). *Professional responsibilities and peer review in psychiatry.* Washington, D.C.: American Psychiatric Association, 1977.

Glasser, M. A., & Duggan, T. Prepaid psychiatric care experience with UAW members. *American Journal of Psychiatry,* 1969, *126,* 675–681.

Goffman, E. *Asylums: Essays on the social situation of mental patients and other inmates.* Garden City, N.Y.: Anchor Books (Doubleday & Co., Inc.), 1961.

Greenfield, L. On contracts between analyst and analysand. *American Psychologist,* 1976, *31,* 615–616.

Gross, G. A. Guidelines for patient consent in psychiatry. *Clinical Psychiatry News,* October 1975, *3*(10).

Grossman, M. Insurance reports as a threat to confidentiality. *American Journal of Psychiatry,* 1971, *128,* 64–68.

Grossman, M. The psychiatrist and the subpoena. *The Bulletin of the American Academy of Psychiatry and the Law,* 1973, *4,* 245–253.

Grossman, M. Confidentiality in medical practice. *Annual Review of Medicine,* 1977, *28,* 43–55.

Halleck, S. L. *The politics of therapy.* New York: Science House, Inc., 1971.

Haas, L. W. (Pastor, Newman Center, University of North Dakota). Personal communication, May 10, 1978.

Hollender, M. H. The psychiatrist and the release of patient information. *American Journal of Psychiatry*, 1960, *116*, 828–833.

Hollender, M. H. Privileged communication and confidentiality. *Diseases of the Nervous System*, 1965, *26*, 169–175.

In Re Lifschutz, 2 Cal 3d 415, 467 P. 2d 557, 85 Cal. Rptr. 829 (1970).

Jagim, R. D., Wittman, W. D., & Noll, J. O. Mental health professionals' attitudes toward confidentiality, privilege, and disclosure to third parties. *Professional Psychology*, 1978, *9*, 458–466.

Kelley, V. R., & Weston, H. B. Civil liberties in mental health facilities. *Social Work*, 1974, *19*, 48–54.

Kittrie, N. N. *The right to be different.* Baltimore, Maryland: The John Hopkins University Press, 1971.

Knowlton, D. D. *An assessment and analysis of the general public's attitudes toward helping professionals.* Unpublished master's thesis, University of North Dakota, August 1976.

Knowlton, D. D. *An assessment and analysis of the general public's attitudes toward helping professionals.* Paper presented at the Midwestern Psychological Association, Chicago, May 1977.

Korchin, S. J. *Modern clinical psychology.* New York: Basic Books, Inc., Publishers, 1976.

Kovacs, A. L. Economic legitimacy for professional practitioners. *American Psychologist*, 1975, *30*, 1160–1162.

Langsley, D. G., & Lebaron, G. I. Peer review guidelines: A survey of local standards of treatment. *American Journal of Psychiatry*, 1974, *131*, 1358–1362.

Lebensohn, Z. M. Problems in obtaining informed consent for electric shock therapy. In R. Allen, E. Ferster, & J. Rubin (Eds.), *Readings in Law & Psychiatry* (2nd Ed.) Baltimore, Maryland: 1975.

Lewis, E. C., & Warman, R. E. Confidentiality expectations of college students. *Journal of College Student Personnel*, 1964, *6*, 7–11.

Little, R. B., & Strecker, E. A. Moot questions in psychiatric ethics. *American Journal of Psychiatry*, 1956, *113*, 455–460.

Margulis, S. T. Introduction: Privacy as a behavioral phenomenon. *The Journal of Social Issues*, 1977, *33*, 1–4. (a)

Margulis, S. T. Conceptions of privacy: Current status and next steps. *The Journal of Social Issues*, 1977, *33*, 5–21. (b)

Mariner, A. S. The problem of therapeutic privacy. *Psychiatry: Journal for the Study of Interpersonal Processes*, 1967, *30*, 60–72.

Meisel, A., Roth, L. H., & Lidz, C. W. Toward a model of the legal doctrine of informed consent. *American Journal of Psychiatry*, 1977, *134*, 285–289.

Meyer, R. G., & Smith, S. R. A crisis in group therapy. *American Psychologist*, 1977, *32*, 638–643.

Noll, J. O. Needed . . . A bill of rights for clients. *Professional Psychology*, 1974, *4*, 3–12.

Noll, J. O., & Hanlon, M. J. Patient privacy and confidentiality at mental health centers. *American Journal of Psychiatry*, 1976, *133*, 1286–1289.

Noll, J. O. The psychotherapist and informed consent. *American Journal of Psychiatry*, 1976, *133*, 1451–1453.

Noll, J. O. On the other hand. *APA Monitor*, 1977, *4*, 3.

Noll, J. O., Robitscher, J., & Wolpert, E. (Discussants). *Today in Psychiatry Series, Special Edition: Contemporary Conflicts*. Chicago, Illinois: Abbott Laboratories, 1977.

Parker, K. A. On a contract model for treatment. *American Psychologist*, 1976, *31*, 257–258.

Personal privacy in an information society. The Report of the Privacy Protection Study Commission. Washington, D.C.: Superintendent of Documents, U.S. Government Printing Office, July 1977.

Plaut, E. A. A perspective on confidentiality. *American Journal of Psychiatry*, 1974, *131*, 1021–1024.

Records computers and the rights of citizens. Report of the Secretary's Advisory Committee on Automated Personal Data Systems. Washington, D.C.: U.S. Department of Health, Education, and Welfare, July 1973.

Redlich, F., & Mollica, R. F. Overview: Ethical issues in contemporary psychiatry. *American Journal of Psychiatry*, 1976, *133*, 125–136.

Rosen, C. E. *Professionals' responses and layperson expectations regarding clients' rights to privacy*. Unpublished manuscript, Northeast Georgia Community Mental Health Center, Athens, Georgia, 1976.

Rosen, C. E. Why clients relinquish their rights to privacy under signaway pressures. *Professional Psychology*, 1977, *8*, 17–24. (a)

Rosen, C. E. *Do potential community mental health center clients want privacy?* Unpublished manuscript, Northeast Georgia Community Mental Health Center, Athens, Georgia, 1977. (b)

Scheff, T. J. *Being mentally ill: A sociological theory*. Chicago: Aldine Publishing Co., 1966.

Scheff, T. J. *Labeling madness*. Englewood Cliffs, N.J.: Prentice-Hall, 1975.

Schwitzgebel, R. K. A contractual model for the protection of the rights of institutionalized mental patients. *American Psychologist*, 1975, *30*, 815–820.

Shah, S. A. Privileged communications, confidentiality, and privacy: Privileged communications. *Professional Psychology*, Fall 1969, pp. 56–59.

Shah, S. A. Privileged communications, confidentiality, and privacy: Privacy. *Professional Psychology*, Spring 1970, pp. 243–252. (a)

Shah, S. A. Privileged communications, confidentiality, and privacy: Confidentiality. *Professional Psychology*, Winter 1970, pp. 159–164. (b)

Shaw, B. The doctor's dilemma. In *Bernard Shaw complete plays with prefaces*, Vol. I. New York: Dodd-Mead & Co., 1962.

Shlensky, R. Informed consent and confidentiality: Proposed new approaches in Illinois. *American Journal of Psychiatry*, 1977, *134*, 1416–1418.

Siegal, M. Confidentiality. *The Clinical Psychologist*, 1976, *30*, 1.

Simmons, D. D. Client attitudes toward release of confidential information without consent. *Journal of Clinical Psychology*, 1968, *24*, 364–365.

Singer, E. Informed consent: Consequences for response rate and response quality in social surveys. *American Sociological Review*, 1978, *43*, 144–162.

Slawson, P. F. Patient-litigant exception. *Archives of General Psychiatry*, 1969, *21*, 347–352.

Slovenko, R. Psychotherapist-patient testimonial privilege: A picture of misguided hope. *Catholic University Law Review*, 1974, *23*, 649–673.

Sorrells, J. Therapists as patients. *APA Monitor*, August 1977, p. 17.

Spinner, B. *Privacy and self-disclosure.* Paper presented at the American Psychological Association, Toronto, Canada, September 1978.

Stevens, C., & Shearer, S. L. *An assessment of nonprofessionals' views on confidentiality.* Unpublished manuscript, University of North Dakota, 1978.

Strassberg, D. S., Anchor, K. N., Cunningham, J., & Elkins, D. *Client self-disclosure and outcome in individual psychotherapy: The therapist's perspective.* Paper presented at the American Psychological Association, Toronto, Canada, August 1978.

Suarez, J. M., & Balcanoff, E. J. Massachusetts psychiatry and privileged communication. *Archives of General Psychiatry*, 1966, *15*, 619–623.

Sullivan, F. W. Professional standards review organizations: The current scene. *American Journal of Psychiatry*, 1974, *131*, 1354–1357.

Szasz, T. S. *The myth of mental illness: Foundations of a theory of personal conduct.* New York: Hoeber-Harper, 1961.

Szasz, T. S. *Law, liberty and psychiatry: An inquiry into the social uses of mental health practices.* New York: Macmillan, Inc., 1963.

Szasz, T. S. The psychiatrist as double agent. *Trans-Action*, October 1967, pp. 16–24.

Szasz, T. S. *The ethics of psychoanalysis.* New York: Dell Publishing Co., 1969.

Szasz, T. S., & Nemiroff, R. A. A questionnaire study of psychoanalytic practices and opinions. *The Journal of Nervous and Mental Disease*, 1963, *137*, 209–221.

Tarasoff vs. Regents of University of California, 13, C 3rd 177, 118 Cal. Rptr. 129, 529 P. 2d 553, *Vacated*, 131 Cal. Rptr. 14, 551 P. 2d 334 (1976).

Weinstock, M., & Haft, J. I. The effect of illness on employment opportunities. *Archives of Environmental Health*, 1974, *29*, 79–83.

Westin, A. F. Computers, health records, and citizen rights. *NBS Monograph 157.* Washington, D.C.: U.S. Department of Commerce, 1976.

Wiskoff, M. Ethical standards and divided loyalties. *American Psychologist*, 1960, *15*, 656–660.

Wohl, J. Third parties and individual psychotherapy. *American Journal of Psychotherapy*, 1974, *4*, 527–543.

Yale Law Journal. Functional overlap between the lawyer and other professionals: Its implications for the privileged communication doctrine. *Yale Law Journal*, 1962, *71*, 1226–1273.

Ziskin, J. *Coping with psychiatric and psychological testimony* (2nd Ed.) 1977 Pocket Supplement. Law and Psychology Press, Beverly Hills, California, 1977.

Chapter 8

COMMUNITY TREATMENT AS THE LEAST RESTRICTIVE ALTERNATIVE:
Costs and Benefits

Susan Makiesky Barrow
Linda Gutwirth

INTRODUCTION

The recent movement toward placing mental patients in community settings that are "less restrictive" than the traditional custodial institutions is the product of a complex interplay of social, economic, legal, and clinical factors. These convergent developments, which have altered public and professional attitudes toward hospitalization, now find succinct expression in the slogans "shorter is better" and "out is better than in" (Glick & Hargreaves, 1979).

Historically, *moral treatment,* the reform movement of the 1840s, removed the mentally ill from communities and placed them in remote asylums. The concept of returning mental patients to community life, however, emerged as early as 1855 with Galt's plan for accommodating "some lunatics . . . those of quiet demeanor . . . laboring under chronic insanity" in the household of "a farmer and his family" (Galt, 1855, cited by Weinberg, 1978).

Although Galt's plan met with opposition, Massachusetts eventually passed a law in 1885 authorizing the boarding out of "insane persons of the quiet chronic class"; and in the first 20 years of the program, 762 patients were so accommodated. Despite the program's success, Massachusetts remained for many years the only state to provide such placement. Interest in various forms of community care for the mentally ill came and went in the United States, and it was not until the 1960s that it became a national priority.

Friedman and Yohalem (1978) have recently noted that "the principle of delivering services in the least restrictive alternatives to total institutions is the legal counterpart to the concepts of normalization and deinstitutionalization." They have further observed that the right to treatment in the least restrictive setting, while relatively simple in theory, can become complex to apply in practice.

Underlying this complexity are a number of specific issues having to do with the costs and benefits of community placements for patients, for those close to them, and for the wider community and society. From a clinical perspective, the most critical question is how the right to treatment in the least restrictive environment relates to current clinical understandings of what constitutes effective treatment. We can identify contrasting positions that have been taken on the question of the clinical costs and benefits of community care: In one view, while long-term hospitalization is to be avoided, the mental hospital continues to have a critical role to play in the treatment system. Brief hospitalization, followed by aftercare, is seen as the treatment of choice for most severely disturbed patients. The role of the institution, in this view, is to stabilize the symptoms—usually through medication—and return patients to the community as quickly as possible.

Adherents to a contrasting perspective seek to avoid all hospitalization, favoring a range of community-based alternatives that have developed as model or experimental programs. The social deficits associated with psychiatric disabilities are viewed as the primary targets of treatment efforts, and community-oriented programs aim at helping patients develop, *in vivo*, the skills needed to live as normally and independently as possible.

While proponents of these views tend to focus on the clinical rationale for them, there are other issues at stake as well: Does the patient's right to treatment in the least restrictive setting conflict with the rights of families and others close to the patient by placing undue burdens on these significant others? And what impact does the patient's right to the least restrictive form of psychiatric treatment have on the communities in which patients are placed? Finally, what is the relative cost of institutional and community placement in monetary terms? Does the community treatment of the mentally ill cost less than institutional care—or does it merely shift the cost from the state hospitals to other treatment facilities and the social service and criminal justice bureaucracies?

An accumulating body of empirical work has begun to shed light on these issues, and the remainder of this chapter will be devoted to reviewing the relevant findings. The legal focus on less restrictive alternatives to institutionalism has developed in the context of United States legal processes and a movement in this country to protect patients' civil rights. We have thus limited our discussion here to community care efforts in the United States. However, the phasing down of mental institutions is an international phenomenon. England and Canada in particular have developed approaches to noninstitutional treatment, which may have important implications for community care in this country. For details of the English experience, see the work of Wing (1978), Bennett (1978), Grad and Sainsbury (1968), and Hoenig and Hamilton (1969). For a description of the Saskatchewan plan in Canada, see Lafave, Stewart, and Grunberg (1968).

The next section examines the outcome of efforts to reduce the length of hospital stays through the provision of community residences, and psychiatric and rehabilitative aftercare programs. Following that we focus on efforts to avoid hospitalization entirely, and conclude with a discussion of some of the implications of the findings for mental health policy.

Ex-patients in the Community:
Deinstitutionalization, Brief Hospitalization, and Aftercare

The deinstitutionalization of long-term residents of mental institutions is a phenomenon that by now has largely been accomplished. With the emptying and closing of state hospitals in various parts of the country, thousands of mentally disabled individuals have poured into local communities. After years of custodial care, however, many have lost most if not all of the family relationships and basic coping and self-care skills they may once have possessed. For the most part, these patients have been absorbed into such semiinstitutional residential environments as nursing homes and board-and-care facilities.

In states such as California, where deinstitutionalization was carried out through rapid, massive closing of state institutions, private entrepreneurs moved quickly to fill the need for sheltered "community" placements for former state hospital residents. A flourishing industry in board-and-care homes developed. By and large, these facilities have been privately owned, profit-making enterprises. They have arisen in the private sector as a response to the emergence of a "market" for such services. Despite efforts to control the worst abuses (see Atkinson, 1975), these facilities have continued to reflect the failure of the mental health system to meet the needs of chronic patients.

A number of exposés of board-and-care facilities have shown living conditions in many of them to be worse than those in the state hospitals they replaced (Atkinson, 1975). Moreover, rehabilitation programs designed to integrate former patients into community life have been inadequate or nonexistent. In fact, Lamb and Goertzel (1971), who investigated a variety of alternatives for the long-hospitalized chronic patient, questioned whether residents of such facilities were really "in" the community. Erickson (1975) also reviewed the literature on some of these "special settings" and suggested that the benefits of low cost and nonhospital housing might be offset by the high prices exacted in terms of the patients' well-being. He cited evidence of high rates of adjustment regression (Ellsworth, 1968; Epstein & Simon, 1968), but also of the positive effects that were produced when active treatment programs were introduced into these settings (Lamb & Goertzel, 1971, 1972; Wilder, Kessel, & Caulfield, 1968).

Many former patients have been discharged to foster care—a form of home placement in which a responsible adult, paid to care for one or more ex-patients, receives varying amounts of supervision from the hospital staff. Carpenter (1978) has suggested that foster care warrants more attention from researchers than it has received—in view of the large role it has played in discharge planning. Positive values have been found to be associated with multiple placements in a home (Sculthorpe, 1960); the development of intense relationships with the caretaker has been reported (Chouinard, 1975); and entire foster communities have been successfully mobilized to receive discharged patients (Keskiner & Zalcman, 1974; Keskiner, Zalcman, Ruppert, & Ulett, 1972).

Halfway houses have constituted another approach to sheltered care. Most halfway house programs, like board-and-care facilities and foster homes, have served as posthospital residences for patients whose severe impairment or lack of adequately supportive natural environments have precluded independent living. Defined as nonmedical residences in the community, they have been designed to encourage patients to participate in community life with the hope that they may eventually move on to more "normal" living arrangements. Sometimes, these houses have constituted an alternative to hospitalization (Mosher, Menn, & Matthews, 1975) or, on occasion, a permanent placement (Cannon, 1975; Lamb, 1979). Halfway houses have varied greatly in selection of residents, staffing, program, and financing (Carpenter, 1978).

In comparison with more traditional residential placements, the lodge societies developed by Fairweather and his colleagues (Fairweather, Sanders, Maynard, & Cressler, 1969) represented an ambitious attempt to deal with the chronic patient's return to the community. The emphasis here was on employment, with lodges running their own businesses (Daggett, 1971; Fairweather et al., 1969; Shean, 1973).

Accommodations going beyond the halfway houses or lodges toward more independent living have included supervised apartments and independent apartment living (Chien & Cole, 1973; Easton, 1974; Kresky, Maeda, & Rothwell, 1976; Orndoff, 1975; Richmond, 1969–70).

Variations in goals, patient populations, types of staffing, and so on make an overall assessment of sheltered placements difficult. Assessment is further complicated by differences in the amount of information contained in studies of community placement. In particular, outcome measures have varied from study to study. Mosher and his colleagues (Mosher et al., 1975) adopted a few standardized scales in their study of acute patients in a halfway house, and Stein, Test, and Marx (1975) developed instruments for the purpose of evaluating community alternatives to hospitalization. Finally, Trute and Segal (1976), in attempting to measure the social integration of ex-patients living in sheltered care facilities in two different geographic areas, developed an instrument that seems likely to be useful in comparative studies. They explored the amount of time an individual spent in his or her residence, as well as access to goods, services, places, and social contacts in the community. By relating this information to census tract data, they found that ex-patients became more integrated into communities that were not marked either by strong social cohesion or by severe social disorganization. Carpenter (1978) suggested that prediction of successful residential programs and fruitful comparison of facilities would require the development and use of instruments designed to measure the effects of transitional living arrangements in diverse parts of the country and with different patient populations. All types of transitional facilities have been found to be less costly than hospitalization, and patients prefer them (Carpenter, 1978).

The loss of social-living skills resulting from lengthy institutionalization has necessitated the placement of many deinstitutionalized patients in sheltered, semi-institutional environments. But the number of long-stay patients has diminished dramatically, as hospital policies have mandated the return of patients to the community as quickly as possible.

A number of studies have compared outcomes for patients hospitalized for brief and for longer periods (Caffey, Galbrecht, & Klett, 1971; Caffey, Jones, Diamond, Burton, & Bowen, 1968; Glick, Hargreaves, Drues, & Showstack, 1976a, 1976b, 1976c, 1977; Hargreaves, Glick, Drues, Showstack, & Feigenbaum, 1977; Herz, Endicott, & Spitzer, 1975, 1976; Mattes, Rosen, & Klein, 1977; Mendel, 1966; Reibel & Herz, 1976; Rosen, Katzoff, Carillo, & Klein, 1976; Singer &

Grob, 1976). Many of these studies suffer from such methodological problems as the diagnostic heterogeneity of study samples, the failure to control other potentially consequential variables, idiosyncratic definitions of short and long stays, and the confounding of the effects of hospital and posthospital treatment. In general, however, the studies have found that the outcomes for briefly hospitalized patients have differed little from the outcomes of longer hospital stays. Caffey and his colleagues (Caffey et al., 1971) studied 201 schizophrenic men from 14 Veterans Administration hospitals and found that, while short-stay patients were more symptomatic at discharge than long-stay patients, there were no significant differences between the groups in incidence of readmissions, time out of the hospital before first readmission, or community adjustment during the year-long follow-up period.

Herz and his coinvestigators (Herz et al., 1975, 1976) similarly discovered no deleterious consequences of shorter hospital stays. In fact, their studies found that briefly hospitalized patients spent less time as inpatients, showed less psychopathology, and evidenced less impairment in role functioning than standard-stay patients after two years.

In the one major set of studies that found some disadvantages to shorter stays for schizophrenic patients (Glick et al., 1976a, 1976b, 1976c, 1977), the researchers failed to control for aftercare use and, in fact, long-stay patients received more outpatient care after discharge than short-stay patients. Moreover, differences in socioeconomic status, education, and premorbid adjustment favored the long-stay group, making it difficult to interpret the finding that long-stay patients showed slightly superior functioning at the one- and two-year follow-up periods.

Reissman, Rabkin, and Streuning (1977), who have reviewed the literature on brief hospitalization, concluded that there are feasible and cost-effective alternatives to standard hospitalization, and the burden must now be on clinicians to justify the use of hospital stays of more than 60 days. But clinical and economic benefits of briefer stays must be weighed against the consequences for the families and others close to the patients. Does the patient's early return to the community place intolerable burdens on those with whom the patient resides?

Many studies have found that the families of psychiatric patients —particularly those with chronic disabilities—have been heavily burdened by their responsibilities to the patient. The one set of studies that specifically addressed the question of family burden for briefly hospitalized patients (Herz et al., 1976; Herz, Endicott, & Gibbon, 1979) found that, regardless of the length of the patient's stay in the hospital, the families of patients reported many problems. These included worry about the future, subjective distress, coping with the patient's irritability and anger, and concern about the patient's failure to contribute to family support. These studies found, however, that patients were more likely to be rehospitalized because of psychopathology and impaired functioning than because of family burden. Moreover, while there were few differences between brief- and long-stay groups in the amount of burden experienced by family members, brief hospitalization had some positive effects on families. The patient's earlier return to the community meant an earlier resumption of occupational roles and, consequently, less financial burden for the families. Negative effects on children were rare. They occurred, however, only when patient-parents were at home, and the investigators have emphasized the importance of monitoring the possible deleterious effects on children when patients who are parents are discharged before they are able to perform well in parental roles.

In general, then, the limited literature on the consequences of brief hospitalization policies for patients' families indicates a need for greater attention to the difficulties experienced by the families of patients regardless of the length of hospital stay. Given adequate support and monitoring of family problems, however, brief hospitalization need not add to family burden and may in fact reduce it.

Although methodological problems in many studies have made it difficult to disentangle the effects of brief hospital and posthospital treatment, most investigators have stressed that short-term hospitalization requires follow-up with aftercare treatment. Similarly, the success of efforts to "deinstitutionalize" long-term mental hospital residents has been shown to be affected by the availability in the community of psychiatric and social services and their use by former patients. Psychosocial and pharmacological therapies, social skills training, and vocational rehabilitation were all shown to be important in enabling former mental patients to develop the skills and autonomy needed for survival in the communities to which they returned.

Mosher and Keith (1979) have reviewed the evidence for the effectiveness of antipsychotic drug treatment and psychosocial therapies in preventing or delaying rehospitalization and in improving social functioning in the community. They concluded that effective community treatment has entailed a combination of drug treatment and additional psychosocial services (Hogarty, Goldberg, & Schooler, 1973; Kirk, 1976; Serban & Thomas, 1974). It should be noted, however, that research evaluating different modes of psychosocial treatment has been limited, so the results are inconclusive. Moreover, patients' participation in psychiatric aftercare treatment cannot be assumed. Underutilization of psychiatric aftercare was found to be associated with such ecological and systems factors as family attitudes toward treatment, diagnosis and severity of pathology (Henisz, Flynn, & Levine, 1977; Udell & Hornstra, 1975), communication problems between inpatient and outpatient facilities (Raynes & Warren, 1971; Wooley & Kane, 1972), and, for some patients, lack of awareness of their needs for outpatient treatment (Serban & Gidynski, 1974). Attempts to account for increasing hospital readmission rates have implicated lack of regular psychiatric aftercare treatment as a major factor in rehospitalization (Serban & Thomas, 1974; Serban & Gidynski, 1974).

Vocational rehabilitation should play an important role in the community treatment of the psychiatrically disabled, since employment appears to be one factor that reduces the likelihood of rehospitalization (Anthony, Buell, Sharrett, & Althoff, 1972). Studies of the effects of hospital milieu therapy programs have suggested that helping a patient adapt to a work situation that is not similar to a real work situation will probably only prepare him or her for sheltered employment (Anthony et al., 1972). The effectiveness of programs that approach the "real" work situation has been described (Brown, 1970; Colten, 1971). The payment of at least minimum hourly wage has been mentioned as a factor of demonstrated importance (Brennan, 1968): Some vocational rehabilitation programs have promoted independent job-seeking skills (Pumo, Sehl, & Cogan, 1966); others have helped former patients deal with their hospitalization when applying for jobs (Anderson, 1968). Unfortunately, there is too little research as yet available to permit assessment of the effects of vocational rehabilitation on ex-patients' functioning.

In sum, policies of deinstitutionalization, and of brief hospitalization with aftercare treatment, have reduced the patient census on mental hospital wards and replaced the prospect of long-term incarceration that formerly faced many chronically disabled individuals with a condition that has been called *intermittent patienthood* (Friedman, Von Mering, & Hinko, 1966). Posthospital treatment programs have generally been designed to maintain former patients in the community and forestall relapse, and, when compared with the outcomes of *no* treatment, they have demonstrated some success. Few, however, have been geared to treat the episodic decompensation that characterizes the course of many chronic psychiatric illnesses, and the very concept of *after*care reveals the prominence of the hospital in this formulation of community treatment. Yet whether intermittent patienthood is an inevitable fact of life for people with chronic psychiatric disabilities remains an open question. The remainder of this chapter explores some of the major efforts that have been made to answer it.

ALTERNATIVES TO HOSPITALIZATION: NONPATIENTS IN THE COMMUNITY

Recent court rulings have upheld the individual's right to treatment in the least restrictive setting, and have required that less restrictive treatment alternatives be explored before resorting to involuntary hospitalization. But can individuals with severe chronic psychiatric disabilities be treated effectively in the community without being hospitalized at all? Clinical opinions vary, and, indeed, the question of community alternatives to hospitalization raises a host of issues: What do we mean by community alternatives? Are they necessarily "less restrictive" than psychiatric institutions? What kinds of individuals do well in what kinds of community placements? What are the relevant outcome criteria? How do clinical outcomes relate to other consequences of community care, such as family burden and economic cost? What role, if any, should hospitalization play under a policy of community care?

None of these questions can be answered definitively at this point. With a few exceptions, community treatment programs designed as alternatives to hospitalization have been experimental and small in scale. Long-term follow-up findings are not yet available for the newer programs. Moreover, variability in the rigor of research methodologies employed in evaluating community treatment efforts, the populations served, and the outcome measures used has made it difficult to compare results across studies or to reconcile conflicting conclusions. But within these limits, a picture of some of the potential benefits and costs of variously conceived programs of community treatment is beginning to emerge from the research findings.

We will focus on several controlled evaluation studies that have examined community-based alternatives to hospital treatment of mental illness. This is not intended to be a comprehensive survey of current efforts to shift the locus of treatment from inpatient facilities to community settings. Rather, we draw on our best information to date regarding the outcome of efforts to treat severe mental illness without resorting to hospitalization.

Bachrach's (1976) analysis of deinstitutionalization has directed attention to the multiple—though often unacknowledged—functions that psychiatric institutions have served. She has emphasized the need not only to provide community alternatives to the *treatment functions* served by the institution, but also to confront the fact that a major function of institutionalization has been the *custodial care* of hospital residents. Experimental programs designed as alternatives to hospitalization have varied along both dimensions—treatment and shelter—and can be characterized in terms of how they have dealth with both.

The *residential alternatives* provided in these programs have ranged from sheltered residential environments, such as Soteria House (Mosher & Menn, 1978), through family placements, as in the early experiments in Louisville (Davis, Dinitz, & Pasamanick, 1974; Pasamanick, Scarpitti, & Dinitz, 1967) and Denver (Langsley & Kaplan, 1968; Langsley, Machotka, & Flomenhaft, 1971), to the kinds of group and foster placements implemented in Philadelphia by Weinman and his colleagues (Weinman & Kleiner, 1978; Weinman, Kleiner, Yu, & Tillson, 1974). Finally, community programs in Southwest Denver (Polak, 1978; Polak, Kirby, & Deitchman, 1979) and in Wisconsin (Marx, Test, & Stein, 1973; Stein & Test, 1978; Stein, Test, & Marx, 1975; Test & Stein, 1978) have adapted their interventions to a whole range of patient living environments, including independent residence.

Variations in the residential dimensions of these programs have been crosscut by treatment alternatives, which have varied in the kinds of individuals they have treated, in the extent to which they have used professional versus nonprofessional or indigenous community treatment staff, and in their emphasis on the individual "patient" versus family and social context.

Research designs have also varied. Most studies have randomly assigned subjects to experimental or control groups, but they have differed in the kinds of programs of hospital treatment they have used for control subjects, as well as in sample sizes, length of follow-up, and outcome measures used. We will briefly describe each of these major experimental programs before discussing the study designs, procedures, and findings.

The Programs

Among the earliest controlled experiments with noninstitutional care for the psychiatrically disabled were two programs of *home treatment,* one in Louisville, Kentucky, and the other in Denver, Colorado. The Institute Treatment Center (ITC) in Louisville was established in 1961 as an experimental program for treating acutely psychotic schizophrenic patients in their homes (Pasamanick et al., 1967). Schizophrenic individuals between 18 and 60 years of age presented for admission to the state hospital and a local mental health center were taken into the study if they were not homicidal or suicidal, resided in the Louisville area, and had families who would accept them back and provide supervision at home. Study subjects were randomly assigned to one of three treatment alternatives: usual hospital treatment, home on drugs, and home on placebo. Treatment focused on ensuring provision for patients' basic life needs, providing support and services for family members, and medication maintenance. The treatment program was carried out through home visits by public health nurses, who visited patients weekly at first but with diminishing frequency over time. The nurses dispensed medication prescribed by the project psychiatrist and talked with the patient and family members on each home visit.

Another program that attempted to avoid hospitalization by treating disturbed individuals in the family context was established in Denver (Langsley & Kaplan, 1968; Langsley et al., 1971). Individuals who lived with families and were judged to be in need of immediate hospitalization were randomly assigned to outpatient *Family Crisis Therapy* (FCT) or to hospitalization. The focus of the experimental FCT treatment was to improve the ability of patients and their families to handle family problems. This was done by working intensively with all family members to reduce the tension surrounding the current crisis, returning the family to precrisis levels of functioning.

The early studies in Louisville and Denver limited their focus to individuals living with families. Yet for many of the chronically mentally disabled, the family is not an available treatment resource. For others, the family environment is seen rather as contributing to or exacerbating the disabled person's inability to cope with life's exigencies. For such individuals, community-based treatment must include some alternative living environment as well. In recent years, a number of experimental programs have emerged in response to this need.

One of the most innovative hospital alternatives, Soteria House, was developed in the San Francisco area (Mosher & Menn, 1978a, 1978b; Mosher, Menn, & Matthews, 1975). Soteria's philosophy has run counter to the current emphasis of many community programs on treatment in the natural environment, and has provided instead a sheltered residential setting where schizophrenic individuals can experience their psychosis in a supportive context. It has been unique among alternative programs in a variety of other ways as well. Firstly, it has aimed at early intervention in the course of an individual's psychosis in order to interrupt the development of chronic mental illness and prevent the start of a cycle of hospitalization and rehospitalization. Secondly, the philosophy of Soteria House has been explicitly nonmedical. This perspective has been directed at discouraging the development of a patient identity and the consequent negative expectations that have often emerged from the medical focus on sickness rather than health. One reflection of Soteria's nonmedical approach has been the use of nonprofessional staff. In addition, the program has attempted to minimize the use of drugs, so as to avoid suppressing the psychotic experience, fostering physician control, or emphasizing the clinical aspects of the illness rather than the social context in which the individual experiences it.

Soteria House has worked with a selected group of people who are young, unmarried, and have had only minimal previous hospitalization for schizophrenia. At any given time, Soteria House can accommodate only six residents and two paid, nonprofessional staff, who share household tasks among themselves. Formal structuring of roles has been minimized. Instead, emphasis has been placed on staff "being with" the residents and responding in a personal way to the behavioral and experiential aspects of psychosis.

The work in Southwest Denver by Polak and his colleagues (Polak, 1978; Polak et al., 1979) focused on treatment in the patient's home environment, but the innovation in this case was system-wide, and treated patients in a variety of living arrangements. The target of treatment was intervention in the small social system around the patient, rather than the patient's illness per se. Both initial evaluation and subsequent treatment were carried out in the patient's own social settings—at home, at work, etc., and, to ensure continuity of care, the staff members who carried out intake and evaluation procedures were the primary therapists. The Southwest Denver system departed from traditional approaches to treatment, not only in treating patients in their own environments, but in the innovative system of alternatives that was developed for individuals who could not remain at home. Four conditions were specified under which individuals would be removed from the home environment: a threat to life (the patient's or others at home); when rest and respite were needed; when emotional support was required for individuals with no resources; and when the home environment was itself pathological. Under these conditions, a number of alternative arrangements might be employed: (1) some patients were taken into private homes of individuals who were untrained in special therapeutic techniques but were encouraged to use their natural skills; (2) an intensive observation apartment (the home of a staff couple) provided a noninstitutional environment with 24-hour observation for patients who were heavily medicated or were thought to be a danger to themselves or others; (3) home day-care, involving various activity programs, took place in the homes of family sponsors; and (4) hospital beds were available as backup for people in need of intensive medical treatment, sophisticated medical diagnostic procedures, or a brief period of control beyond what would be provided in the observation apartment.

Two other programs also addressed themselves to providing community-based care for chronic patients who could not be placed with relatives. Weinman and his colleagues (Weinman & Kleiner, 1978; Weinman et al., 1974) developed a program drawing on indigenous community members viewed as *social change agents* to assist patients from Philadelphia State Hospital in daily-life activities. The community members, called *enablers,* came from the same socioeconomic backgrounds as the patients, had high school education or less, received no special training, yet served in a major therapeutic capacity. All patients in the study had been hospitalized for at least one year; for various reasons, none could return to live with their families. Half of the experimental group were sent to live in the home of an enabler; the other half shared lodgings with a group of patients and were visited daily by an enabler. Half of the patients in each of these groups received direct treatment from professional staff, while, for the other half, the professional staff worked only with the enabler, and not with the patients directly. Control groups consisted of two samples of patients who remained in the hospital, one treated with traditional modes of care, the other with *socioenvironmental* hospital therapy.

In Wisconsin, a group of investigators (Marx et al., 1973; Stein & Test, 1978; Stein et al., 1978; Test & Stein, 1978) developed another program of community care that was not limited to patients living with families. The *Training in Community Living* (TCL) program was directed at helping patients make a satisfying life in the community—by providing material resources, *in vivo* training in coping skills, support to maintain motivation for remaining involved with life, freedom from pathological dependency relationships (whether in the hospital or family setting), and an assertive support system that actively helped patients attain these goals.

The TCL program took an unselected sample of adults who came to the hospital for admission. Rather than hospitalizing them, the program treated patients through participation in a full schedule of daily living activities, with support from staff members who accompanied them, teaching and assisting with, for example, shopping, laundry, the use of transport, and job or sheltered workshop placement. In the initial phases, staff members might be constantly by the patient's side, but this intensive contact gradually diminished as the patient progressed.

TCL work with families was mainly directed at breaking pathological dependency ties—where necessary, by *constructive separation.* This involved curtailing and regulating family interaction with the patient, while providing family members with extensive support. Patients were assisted in finding alternative living arrangements when this seemed necessary. Hospitalization was used only in very specific circumstances. Patients who needed to be heavily medicated and required structure and nursing care might be hospitalized briefly, and hospitalization was also used for the protection of the individual and others against suicide or assault. Patients were *not* hospitalized when they used self-destructive behavior as a means of getting help, but they learned instead to break their dependency on the hospital as a refuge when life's problems became difficult.

The Studies: Procedures, Outcome Measures, and Findings

All of the programs described above were conceived as alternatives to hospitalization and were studied in relation to hospital treatment. Control groups were drawn from state hospitals, local facilities, or both, and a variety of measures were used to assess outcome for both experimental subjects and controls. Follow-up periods varied from four months, in Polak's (1978) study in Southwest Denver, to five years, in the Louisville home-care experiment (Davis, et al., 1974).

In the era of deinstitutionalization, the ability to keep patients out of the hospital has become a primary criterion of program success. All of the studies reviewed here reported hospital readmission rates during the treatment and follow-up periods. Differences in baselines used and lengths of follow-up make it difficult to compare readmission rates across studies. Within each study, however, experimental subjects treated in the community had lower rates of hospital admission during the course of experimental treatment and in the early posttreatment follow-up than did hospitalized controls (Langsley & Kaplan, 1968; Marx et al., 1973; Mosher & Menn, 1978a, 1978b; Weinman & Kleiner, 1978). These differences diminished with time, however, and in longer term follow-up became nonsignificant or disappeared (e.g., Davis et al., 1974).

The work of Polak and colleagues (Polak et al., 1979) is of particular interest with respect to rehospitalization. Unlike the other experiments cited, the Southwest Denver program was instituted on a system-wide basis. It has provided a full range of alternatives for the psychiatrically disabled, and "for more than four years this system has virtually supplanted the psychiatric hospital for all adult clients from Southwest Denver who are treated by public mental health services" (Polak et al., 1979, p. 49). Indeed, the entire catchment area of 100,000 persons used, over recent years, an average of about one hospital bed per year. This contrasts strikingly with the 1974–75 averages of 43 beds per 100,000 for the state of Colorado and 90 beds per 100,000 for the United States as a whole.

While these data indicate that a variety of community treatment approaches can be used to avoid hospitalization, Erickson (1975) has cautioned against measuring the success of treatment in terms of physical location (that is, treatment failures are in the hospital and treatment successes are in the community), and has urged instead a focus on restoring or improving psychosocial functioning. The studies of alternatives to hospitalization all employed a variety of measures of symptomatology, social adjustment, and social and instrumental performance and functioning.

Measures of psychopathology or mental status in general did not show marked differences between experimental and control groups either at discharge from treatment (Mosher & Menn, 1978a, 1978b; Weinman & Kleiner, 1978) or one year later (Mosher & Menn, 1978a, 1978b; Pasamanick et al., 1967). One exception occurred in the TCL program in Wisconsin, where significant differences were found between groups in global symptomatology and a number of specific symptoms at 4-, 8-, and 12-month follow-up (Stein & Test, 1978). In all cases, these differences favored the experimental subjects.

Measures of social functioning, social adjustment, and social participation produced more equivocal results. Individuals treated in the family context did not significantly differ from controls on such measures as domestic functioning and social participation (Pasamanick et al., 1967) or social adjustment and role functioning (Langsley et al., 1971), although experimental subjects in the Family Crisis Treatment program in Denver were better able than controls to handle family crises (Langsley et al., 1971). Follow-up on Soteria House residents found they were more likely than controls to be residing independently after one year, but resembled controls in psychosocial adjustment and time spent working. In contrast, at one-year follow-up, experimental subjects in the enabler program did better than the controls who received socioenvironmental hospital treatment on measures of instrumental and social performance (Weinman & Kleiner, 1978). Experimental subjects in the Wisconsin Training in Community Living program spent less time unemployed, earned more income, were more involved with trusted friends and in group social activities than controls, and were more likely to be residing independently (Stein & Test, 1978). Experimental subjects in the Southwest Denver program scored significantly better than controls on measures of goal attainment and self-disclosure (Polak, 1978).

Uniformly positive outcomes for experimental subjects were reported on measures of subjective responses such as self-esteem (Weinman & Kleiner, 1978), satisfaction with life situation (Stein & Test, 1978), satisfaction with treatment outcome, and depersonalization (Polak, 1978). And Mosher and Menn (1978a) reported a strong subjective impression of their own: Soteria House residents did not acquire the "look" of mental patients.

In sum, none of the studies of treatment alternatives reported negative consequences of community care as contrasted with hospital treatment, and the balance of outcomes favored avoiding hospitalization.

Unfortunately, differences in study populations and the multiplicity of measures used in different studies make it impossible to make valid comparisons between community treatment approaches investigated by different researchers. In the study of enablers in Philadelphia (Weinman & Kleiner, 1978), however, the experimental program was specifically designed to shed light on the effects of different approaches to community treatment. Of particular interest is the finding that clients who lived in the homes of enablers—a situation approximating group foster care—were dramatically less likely to be rehospitalized during the two-year follow-up period than clients with visiting enablers (4% versus 20%). Those with visiting enablers, however, showed significantly less psychopathology at the completion of treatment, and significantly greater instrumental behavior one year later than those living with enablers. It would seem, then, that while the foster care type of situation was particularly effective in extending community tenure, independent living with outreach services encouraged more effective levels of functioning.

A second contrast in the enabler study permits an assessment of the effects of using professional or nonprofessional staff as primary therapists. Professional staff members worked directly in this capacity with half of the experimental sample; for the other half of the experimental group, the enablers were trained by professionals to serve in this capacity. While rates of return to the hospital were not affected by these differences, the patients treated by enablers showed significantly less psychiatric disability than those treated by professional staff directly, suggesting that indigenous community members may, in fact, serve more effectively than professionals in some programs of community treatment.

The clinical outcomes of treatment approaches that abjured hospitalization, then, were generally positive. At least for the duration of the treatment, participants in such experiments tended to remain out of the hospital and, in some cases, showed greater improvements in symptomatology and social functioning than patients treated in traditional hospital settings. The short life of most of these experiments, however, makes it premature to rule out the possibility that an attention-placebo effect was responsible for the success of community treatment programs. Morever, where longer-term data were collected, they indicated that the positive effects of community care in avoiding hospitalization, reducing symptoms, and improving social adjustment and functioning rarely outlasted the life of the intervention (Davis et al., 1974; Mosher & Menn, 1978b; Test & Stein, 1978). As Beels (1979) has noted, "This result has caused discouragement because the conclusion has been advanced that 'schizoprenics don't learn'—they don't generalize from therapeutic experience" (p. 212). He suggests, however, that the real lesson to be drawn from these experiences is the importance of *present* social supports.

Two approaches to providing ongoing support for the psychiatrically disabled are suggested by findings from the experiments discussed. Test & Stein (1978) have recommended that programs such as Training in Community Living should "exist as an ongoing treatment modality that remains available to clients over an indefinite period of time." They have pointed out that the efforts and costs involved would be minimal, and the gains great. A rather different approach is implied by the enabler study. Weinman and Kleiner (1978) found that clients who lived in the home of an enabler experienced very low rates of rehospitalization in the two years *following the end of the experimental program.* In fact, two thirds of those clients had continued to reside in the homes of enablers after the treatment experiment ended. This suggests that when clients are effectively linked to indigenous community members—in this case, the enablers—professional intervention need not last indefinitely, nor will its withdrawal necessarily precipitate relapse. Community treatment may be most effective when it is done not only *in* the community, but *by* the community.

Given appropriate ongoing support, then, the evidence supports the clinical viability of alternatives to hospitalization. But the refusal to hospitalize individuals with serious psychiatric disabilities raises social issues as well as clinical ones. What are the consequences of community care for the families and communities in which the mentally ill reside?

Effects on Families

The home-care experiment of the ITC group in Louisville, Kentucky, is the only one of the hospital alternative programs described here that relied heavily on family members who were willing to have patients reside at home. Although no measures of family burden were reported, the investigators descriptively documented many difficulties encountered by the families of patients. In reporting on their five-year follow up study, Davis et al. (1974) stressed the importance of ongoing support by the treatment team to the family as well as to the patient.

An earlier study in England by Grad and Sainsbury (1968) specifically compared a community-oriented service with a hospital-oriented service in terms of family burden. They found that community care did entail more burden for families, although this was not the case for all groups of patients. In fact, the most severely burdensome patients were found in both services. The higher burden found for the community care patients was due to younger, psychoneurotic patients with one previous hospital admission. It should be noted, however, that these patients were not severely burdensome to their families in either service. Moreover, the families of these patients were found to have received less social work service and social support than the families of other patients. These findings reinforce the conclusion of the Louisville home-care study that effective community requires support for families as well as patients.

More recently, Hatfield (1978) suggested that professionals have often failed to see that families living with schizophrenia endure severe stress. Her research indicated that the psychological and physical resources of family caregivers were depleted to the point where personal efficiency was reduced and family life threatened. She found that the first priorities of family caregivers who were asked what kind of help would most relieve their stress were (1) information that would help them understand schizophrenia, and (2) practical management techniques.

Hatfield's findings are consistent with the results of British research (Creer & Wing, 1974; Wing & Olson, 1979), which reported that the principal complaints of relatives of schizophrenic patients were lack of advice from professionals on specific "difficulties of management" and lack of information about how services work and where to turn for help. Since printed information is quickly outdated, it has been suggested that an array of counseling and other services might be needed. Relatives should be consulted as to how to set up the services, so that they will be acceptable. A number of self-help groups and multiple-family groups—which reduce the social isolation of families living with schizophrenia—have already made promising starts in this direction (Beels, 1978; Lamb & Oliphant, 1979).

The Family Crisis Therapy experiment in Denver (Langsley & Kaplan, 1968) took a different approach to giving support to family members—one that included assisting in separating the patient from the family when that seemed indicated. Moreover, having defined mental illness as a problem for which the entire family had responsibility, the FCT team focused their treatment efforts on the family rather than the individual patient. For the families, consequences of this approach included reduction of tension, quick resumption of family functioning, and avoidance of shame associated with having to hospitalize a family member.

The other programs described above offered alternative living arrangements for individuals who could not reside with families or whose family relationships were viewed as pathological. In the Southwest Denver program (Polak, 1978), an emphasis on social systems intervention involved working intensively with family members when patients remained at home, but also provided a range of alternative settings permitting short- and long-term or permanent separation. Thus the policy of avoiding hospitalization need not require keeping the patient "home" at all cost.

Marx et al. (1973) also reported the value of work with family

members and the importance of *constructive separation* in breaking the
pathological dependency that characterized the relationship of some
patients to their families. While limiting the amount of contact between patients and families who needed to be constructively separated,
the TCL program staff were available to family members as well as
patients at all times. Using the Family Burden Scale to measure behavioral, economic, and subjectively experienced aspects of burden, Stein
and Test (1979) found a significant drop in the burden experienced
by the families of patients in the TCL program; no such decrease in
burden was found for the families of hospitalized controls.

In sum, the empirical research that has been addressed to the
consequences of community treatment alternatives for the families of
patients, along with more descriptive accounts, indicates that support
for family members is important whether or not patients are residing
at home. The availability of temporary or long-term alternative living
situations for patients seems to have benefits for both patients and
their families.

Studies that have assessed the relative costs of hospitalization and
alternative treatments, either for the families of patients or the wider
society, have shown that alternative programs need not be more costly
than hospital-based treatment (Mosher & Menn, 1978a; Stein & Test,
1979). Moreover, programs that improved work skills and resulted in
patients' spending more time employed (Stein & Test, 1979) may have
helped to prevent shifting the costs of caring for the mentally disabled
from the hospitals to the patients' families or the public assistance
system.

DISCUSSION AND POLICY IMPLICATIONS

The evidence of numerous studies seems to provide empirical
backing for an approach to hospitalization that reflects Glick and Hargreaves' (1979) slogans, "shorter is better" and "out is better than in."
We are, however, still far from being able to specify with any precision
the kinds of patients who will respond best to particular kinds of
interventions; and we still do not know how far we can generalize from
the relatively small experiments in community care that have been
carried out up to now. Continuing experimentation and research will
be needed to clarify these issues. Within the limits of our current
knowledge, however, some consistent patterns have begun to emerge,
suggesting some guidelines for the further development of community
care policies.

It is critical to recognize that shorter hospital stays or the refusal
to hospitalize at all have not in themselves produced clinical benefits

for patients. It is rather what happens to the patient in the community that determines whether the less restrictive alternatives to hospitalization are also more effective and humane. On the basis of the research reviewed here, it would seem that successful approaches to community treatment will depend upon the provision of *active and flexible programs* that emphasize *adaptation to the changing exigencies of real-life situations.* Such programs should ideally provide *ongoing support, promote self-sustaining links between patients and nonpatients* in the community, and give particular *attention to the needs of families* and others close to the patient. When community care is implemented on a *system-wide basis* that provides a comprehensive range of alternatives, the *hospital's role* in treatment can be sharply curtailed.

Active and Flexible Programs

The isolation and despair that have resulted from failures to ensure that community based services, support, and treatment are available to those who need them have been well documented in the popular media. To the extent that such failures stem from the organization of the service delivery system, they can be avoided in the future, given administrative commitments to doing so. But active programs of community care must also cope with the significant number of people who refuse available service, drop out of treatment programs, or fall through organizational cracks in the system. The nonparticipation in aftercare programs that bedevils professionals trying to serve schizophrenic patients has been attributed to the "lack of insight" (Serban & Gidynski, 1974) or "lack of social initiative" (Beels, 1979) that characterize chronic schizophrenia. Proposed remedies, such as conditional hospital discharges and compulsory aftercare (Serban & Gidynski, 1974), would be difficult to enforce and seem to run counter to efforts to provide the least restrictive form of treatment. It may be that the need for such extreme approaches can be averted through aggressive outreach—a concept that warrants more serious attention than it has been given. The TCL program, the visiting nurses used in the Louisville home care experiment, and the enabler program in Philadelphia all indicate the feasibility and effectiveness of outreach approaches.

Adaptation to Real-life Situations

Research has documented the failure of innovative hospital programs to produce improvements in patients' social adjustment and functioning after discharge (Erickson, 1975). Merely locating similar programs in the community should not be expected to produce strikingly different effects. More promising results have come from efforts to shift both the location and focus of treatment efforts to real community settings and situations. In the field of vocational rehabilitation, the effectiveness of programs that approximate "real" work situations—including payment of "real" rather than token wages—has been demonstrated (Brennan, 1968; Brown, 1970; Colten, 1971). This kind of approach has been successfully extended to training in "community survival skills" in Southwest Denver (Polak et al., 1979), while the Training in Community Living program (Stein & Test, 1978) has demonstrated the value of teaching basic social and coping skills in vivo—an approach that has produced enhanced levels of functioning among TCL program participants in contrast with controls during the course of the experiment.

Ongoing Support

The difficulty in sustaining the clinical gains of experimental programs has become a major concern for providers of community treatment. Although the need to offer ongoing services and support for people with chronic psychiatric disabilities seems to be clearly established, few programs have been designed—or funded—to do this. Most experiments in community treatment have been so brief, in fact, that their success may be attributable to an *attention-placebo* effect: any innovation produces improvements—for awhile. Even if this were the case, however, it need not lead to a rejection of the approach. It might, indeed, be more useful to consider how to sustain the effect—perhaps through such measures as ongoing internal program innovation, periodic reassessments of treatment goals and plans for individual clients, and continuous evaluation research.

The more serious consequence of the brevity of community treatment experiments has been the reversion of clients to "usual" patterns of chronic patienthood when the experiment ends. Test and Stein's (1978) proposal, to make support and services of the kind entailed by the TCL program available to patients indefinitely, offers one solution to this problem. The need for continuing professional support, however, should not be allowed to foster new dependencies for patients. Efforts should be made to develop or reinforce adaptive, naturally occurring social relationships. It may be that professionals can be most effective by offering support to these supporters.

Links Between Patients and Community Members

When treatment interventions emphasize effectively linking patients to indigenous community members, as opposed to program personnel, the support thus provided becomes self-sustaining and can be expected to have an ongoing effect. The successful involvement of nonprofessionals in major therapeutic roles has been reported in a number of studies (Mosher & Menn, 1978a; Polak, 1978; Weinman & Kleiner, 1978), but it may be that community members are most therapeutically effective when they also are linked to patients in such roles as neighbor, landlady, or friend, providing patients with an ongoing source of social support and social contacts. The findings of Weinman & Kleiner (1978), on the success of patients who continued to reside with their enablers after the experimental program ended, and the work by Keskiner & Zalcman (1974), on the integration of patients into foster communities, confirm the value of ongoing social ties in the community for sustaining positive outcomes.

The Needs of Families

The families of psychiatric patients experience considerable distress. Several studies have emphasized the importance of providing patients' families with such concrete services as information about the patient's illness, specific techniques for coping with disturbing behavior, and easy access to treatment personnel. This kind of support should be provided to families whether patients are hospitalized for extended periods, briefly, or not at all.

Research has shown, however, that in some cases the needs of both patients and their families were best met by temporary or permanent separation. In fact, findings from a recent study of deinstitutionalized patients in the U.S. (Schwartz, Spitzer, Muller, & Fleiss, 1979), along with British studies on the negative consequences of critical family attitudes to patients (Brown, Birley, & Wing, 1968; Vaughn & Leff, 1976) suggest that the availability of alternative living arrangements may affect the success of efforts to maintain patients in the community. Schwartz et al. (1979) found that patients whose families anticipated that their return from the hospital would be burdensome were significantly more likely to suffer early relapse than patients whose families welcomed their return. Programs that encouraged constructive separation of patients and families in some circumstances, however, have found that such separation did not obviate the need for ongoing support to family members.

System-wide Programs

Many of the programs reviewed here have been directed at specific subgroups, such as younger, first-break schizophrenic patients (Soteria House), or schizophrenic patients living with family members (the ITC home-care experiment and the Family Crisis Therapy program). Their generalizability may be limited. In contrast, approaches that entail the kind of flexible, individualized treatment planning exemplified by the Training in Community Living program have been shown to be effective for an unselected sample of psychiatric patients, and can, moreover, be adapted to patients' changing needs at different points in the life cycle and illness course. Programs that are system-wide, as in Southwest Denver, can offer the most comprehensive range of alternatives to hospital treatment.

The advantages of a system-wide approach to community care go beyond the extension of community treatment to larger numbers and different kinds of patients; when the system is well integrated, such comprehensive programming can foster continuity of care and a clear allocation of responsibility, preventing the hospitalization by default that sometimes occurs when community agencies lose track of clients.

The Role of the Hospital

Our review of the efforts to treat patients in community settings has indicated that most community care programs have continued to use hospital treatment in specifically defined circumstances. Stein and Test (1979) have suggested that "the more comprehensive the community program, the less the need to use the hospital" (p. 30). Their work and that of others, described earlier, demonstrated that the use of the hospital can be sharply curtailed without diminishing the adequacy of treatment or the quality of life for patients and their families. It was only in the system-wide program of Southwest Denver, however, where virtually no one was hospitalized, that community care essentially supplanted hospital treatment. Whether similar programs can feasibly be implemented in other settings warrants and invites further experimentation and investigation.

The conclusion that programs of community care *can be* at least as effective as hospitalization in the treatment of most psychotic patients seems inescapable. This does not mean, however, that all community treatment programs will succeed. Ongoing monitoring and evaluation of community alternatives will be required to ensure the continued convergence of least restrictive and most effective treatment approaches.

REFERENCES

Anderson, J. *Job-seeking skills project.* Minneapolis, Minnesota: Minneapolis Rehabilitation Center, 1968.

Anthony, W. A., Buell, G. J., Sharrett, S., & Althoff, M. E. Efficacy of psychiatric rehabilitation. *Psychological Bulletin,* 1972, *79,* 447–456.

Atkinson, R. M. Current and emerging models of residential psychiatric treatment, with special reference to the California situation. *American Journal of Psychiatry,* 1975, *132,* 391–396.

Bachrach, L. L. (National Institute of Mental Health). Deinstitutionalization: An analytical review and sociological perspective. *DHEW Publication No. (ADM) 76–351.* Washington, D.C.: Superintendent of Documents, U.S. Government Printing Office, 1976.

Beard, J. H., Pitt, R. B., Fisher, S. H., & Goertzel, V. Evaluating the effectiveness of a psychiatric rehabilitation program. *American Journal of Orthopsychiatry,* 1963, *33,* 701–712.

Beels, C. C. Social networks, the family, and the psychiatric patient. *Schizophrenia Bulletin,* 1978, *4,* 512–521.

Bells, C. C. Social networks and schizophrenia. *Psychiatric Quarterly,* 1979, *51,* 209–215.

Bennett, D. The Camberwell District psychiatric services 1964–1974. In L. I. Stein & M. A. Test (Eds.), *Alternatives to mental hospital treatment.* New York: Plenum Press, 1978.

Blumenthal, R. L., & Kreisman, D. *Postdischarge living arrangements and their consequences for rehospitalization.* Paper presented at Arden House conference, New York State Psychiatric Institute, 1977.

Brennan, J. J. Standard pay or token pay for rehabilitation of mental patients. *Journal of Rehabilitation,* 1968, *34,* 2, 26–27.

Brown, G. W., Birley, J. L. T., & Wing, J. K. The influence of family life on schizophrenic disorders: A replication. *Journal of Health and Social Behavior,* 1968, *9,* 203–214.

Brown, J. K. Mental patients work back into society. *Manpower,* 1970, *2,* 20–25.

Caffey, E. M., Galbrecht, C. R., & Klett, C. J. Brief hospitalization and aftercare in the treatment of schizophrenia. *Archives of General Psychiatry,* 1971, *24,* 81–86.

Caffey, E. M., Jones, R. D., Diamond, L. S., Burton, E., & Bowen, W. T. Brief hospital treatment of schizophrenia: Early results of a multiple-hospital study. *Hospital and Community Psychiatry,* 1968, *19,* 282–287.

Cannon, M. S. The halfway house as an alternative to hospitalization. In J. Zusman & E. F. Bertsch (Eds.), *The future role of the state hospital.* Lexington, Mass.: D. C. Heath & Company, 1975.

Carpenter, M. D. Residential placement for the chronic patient: A review and evaluation of the literature. *Schizophrenia Bulletin,* 1978, *4,* 384–398.

Chien, C., & Cole, J. Landlord-supervised cooperative apartments: A new modality for community-based treatment. *American Journal of Psychiatry,* 1973, *130,* 156–159.

Chouinard, E. Family homes for adults. *Social and Rehabilitation Record,* 1975, *2,* 10–15.

Colten, S. I. Institutional psychiatric rehabilitation. *Rehabilitation Research and Practice Review,* 1971, *2,* 1–6.

Creer, C., & Wing, J. K. *Schizophrenia at home.* Surrey, England: National Schizophrenia Fellowship, 1974.

Daggett, S. R. The lodge program: A peer group treatment program for rehabilitation of the chronic mental patient. *Rehabilitation Record,* 1971, *2,* 31–34.

Davis, A. E., Dinitz, S., & Pasamanick, B. *Schizophrenics in the new custodial community: Five years after the experiment.* Columbus, Ohio: Ohio State University Press, 1974.

Easton, K. Boerum Hill: A private long-term residential program for former mental patients. *Hospital and Community Psychiatry,* 1974, *25,* 513–517.

Ellsworth, R. B. *Nonprofessionals in psychiatric rehabilitation.* New York: Appleton-Century-Crofts, 1968.

Erickson, R. C. Outcome studies in mental hospitals: A review. *Psychological Bulletin,* 1975, *82,* 519–540.

Epstein, L. J., & Simon, A. Alternatives to state hospitalization for the geriatric mentally ill. *American Journal of Psychiatry,* 1968, *124,* 955–961.

Fairweather, G. W., Sanders, D. H., Maynard, H., & Cressler, D. L. *Community life for the mentally ill: An alternative to institutional care.* New York: Aldine, 1969.

Friedman, I., Von Mering, O., & Hinko, E. N. Intermittent patienthood: The hospital career of today's mental patient. *Archives of General Psychiatry,* 1966, *14,* 386–392.

Glick, I. D., & Hargreaves, W. A. Hospitals in the 1980s: Service, training, and research. *Hospital and Community Psychiatry,* 1979, *3,* 125–128.

Glick, I. D., Hargreaves, W. A., Drues, J., & Showstack, J. A. Short vs. long hospitalization, a controlled study, III: Inpatient results for nonschizophrenics. *Archives of General Psychiatry,* 1976, *33,* 78–83. (a)

Glick, I. D., Hargreaves, W. A., Drues, J., & Showstack, J. A. Short vs. long hospitalization: A prospective controlled study, IV: One year follow-up results for schizophrenic patients. *American Journal of Psychiatry,* 1976, *133,* 509–514. (b)

Glick, I. D., Hargreaves, W. A., Drues, J., & Showstack, J. A. Short vs. long hospitalization: A prospective controlled study, V: One year follow-up results for nonschizophrenic patients. *American Journal of Psychiatry,* 1976, *133,* 515–517. (c)

Glick, I. D., Hargreaves, W. A., Drues, J., & Showstack, J. A. Short vs. long hospitalization: A prospective controlled study, VII: Two year follow-up results for nonschizophrenics. *Archives of General Psychiatry,* 1977, *34,* 314–317.

Grad, J., & Sainsbury, P. The effects that patients have on their families in a community care and a control psychiatric service: A two-year follow-up. *British Journal of Psychiatry,* 1968, *114,* 265.

Hargreaves, W. A., Glick, I. D., Drues, J., Showstack, J. A., & Feigenbaum, E. Short vs. long hospitalization: A prospective controlled study, VII: Two-year follow-up results for schizophrenics. *Archives of General Psychiatry,* 1977, *34,* 305–311.

Hatfield, A. B. Psychological costs of schizophrenia to the family. *Social Work,* 1978, *23,* 355–359.

Henisz, J. E., Flynn, H. R., & Levine, M. Clients and patients of mental health services. *Archives of General Psychiatry,* 1977, *34,* 1345–1348.

Herz, M. I., Endicott, J., & Gibbon, M. Brief hospitalization: Two-year follow-up. *Archives of General Psychiatry,* 1979, *36,* 701–75.

Herz, M. I., Endicott, J., & Spitzer, R. L. Brief hospitalization of patients with families: Initial results. *American Journal of Psychiatry,* 1975, *132,* 413–418.

Herz, M. I., Endicott, J., & Spitzer, R. L. Brief vs. standard hospitalization: The families. *American Journal of Psychiatry,* 1976, *133,* 795–801.

Hoenig, J., & Hamilton, N. *Desegregation of the mentally ill.* London, England: Routledge & Kegan Paul, 1969.

Hogarty, G. E., Goldberg, S. C., & Schooler, N. R. Drug and sociotherapy in the aftercare of schizophrenic patients. *Archives of General Psychiatry,* 1973, *28,* 54.

Keskiner, A., & Zalcman, M. J. Returning to community life: The foster community model. *Diseases of the Nervous System,* 1974, *35,* 419–426.

Keskiner, A., Zalcman, M. J., Ruppert, F. H., & Ulett, G. A. The foster community: A partnership in psychiatric rehabilitation. *American Journal of Psychiatry,* 1972, *129,* 283–288.

Kirk, S. A. Effectiveness of community services for discharged hospital patients. *American Journal of Orthopsychiatry,* 1976, *46,* 646–659.

Kresky, M., Maeda, E. M., & Rothwell, N. D. The apartment program: A community living option for halfway house residents. *Hospital and Community Psychiatry,* 1976, *27,* 153–54.

Lafave, H. G., Stewart, A., & Grunberg, F. Community care of the mentally ill: Implementation of the Saskatchewan plan. *Community Mental Health Journal,* 1968, *4,* 37–45.

Lamb, H. R., & Goertzel, V. Discharged mental patients—are they really in the community? *Archives of General Psychiatry,* 1971, *24,* 29–34.

Lamb, H. R., & Goertzel, V. High expectations of long-term ex-state-hospital patients. *American Journal of Psychiatry,* 1972, *29,* 471–477.

Lamb, H. R., & Oliphant, E. Parents of schizophrenics: Advocates for the mentally ill. *New Directions for Mental Health Services,* 1979, *2,* 85–92.

Langsley, D. G., & Kaplan, D. M. *The treatment of families in crisis.* New York: Grune & Stratton, 1968.

Langsley, D. G., Machotka, P., & Flomenhaft, K. Avoiding mental hospital admissions: A follow-up study. *American Journal of Psychiatry,* 1971, *127,* 1391–1394.

Marx, A. J., Test, M. A., & Stein, L. I. Extro-hospital management of severe mental illness. *Archives of General Psychiatry,* 1973, *29,* 505–511.

Mattes, J. A., Rosen, B., & Klein, D. F. Comparison of the clinical effectiveness of "short" vs. "long" stay psychiatric hospitalization, II: Results of a three-year posthospital follow-up. *Journal of Nervous and Mental Disease,* 1977, *165,* 387–402.

Mendel, W. M. Effect of length of hospitalization on rate and quality of remission from acute psychotic episodes. *Journal of Nervous and Mental Diseases,* 1966, *143,* 226–233.

Mosher, L. R., & Keith, S. J. Research on the psychosocial treatment of schizophrenia: A summary report. *American Journal of Psychiatry,* 1979, *136,* 623–629.

Mosher, L. R., & Menn, A. Z. Lowered barriers in the community: The Soteria model. In L. I. Stein & M. A. Test (Eds.), *Alternatives to mental hospital treatment.* New York: Plenum Press, 1978. (a)

Mosher, L. R., & Menn, A. Z. Community residential treatment for schizophrenia: Two-year follow-up. *Hospital and Community Psychiatry,* 1978, *29,* 715–723. (b)

Mosher, L. R., Menn, A. Z., & Matthews, S. M. Soteria: Evaluation of a home-based treatment for schizophrenia. *American Journal of Orthopsychiatry,* 1975, *45,* 455–467.

Orndoff, C. R. Transitional living. In J. Zusman & E. F. Bertsch (Eds.), *The future role of the state hospital.* Lexington, Mass.: D. C. Heath & Company, 1975.

Pasamanick, B., Scarpitti, F. R., & Dinitz, S. *Schizophrenics in the community.* New York: Appleton-Century-Crofts, 1967.

Polak, P. R. A comprehensive system of alternatives to psychiatric hospitalization. In L. I. Stein & M. A. Test (Eds.), *Alternatives to mental hospital treatment.* New York: Plenum Press, 1978.

Polak, P. R., Kirby, M. W., & Deitchman, W. S. Treating acutely psychotic patients in private homes. *New Directions for Mental Health Services,* 1979, *1,* 49–64.

Pumo, B., Sehl, R., & Cogan, F. Job readiness: Key to placement. *Journal of Rehabilitation,* 1966, *32,* 5, 18–19.

Reibel, S., & Herz, M. I. Limitations of brief hospital treatment. *American Journal of Psychiatry,* 1976, *133,* 518–521.

Reissman, C. K., Rabkin, J. G., & Struening, E. L. Brief versus standard psychiatric hospitalization: A critical review of the literature. *Community Mental Health Review,* 1977, *2,* 2–10.

Richmond, C. Expanding the concepts of the halfway house: A satellite housing program. *International Journal of Social Psychiatry,* 1969–70, *16,* 96–102.

Rosen, B., Katzoff, A., Carillo, C., & Klein, D. F. Clinical effectiveness of short vs. long hospitalization. *Archives of General Psychiatry,* 1976, *33,* 1316–1322.

Schwartz, C. C., Spitzer, R. L. Muller, C., & Fleiss, J. Outcome of community care for chronic patients. Presented at the Annual Meeting of the American Psychiatric Association, Chicago, Illinois, 1979.

Sculthorpe, W. B. Multiple placements of psychiatric patients in foster homes. *Social Casework,* 1960, *41,* 517–523.

Serban, G., & Gidynski, C. Schizophrenic patients in the community. *New York State Journal of Medicine,* 1974, 1977–1981.

Serban, G., & Thomas, A. Attitudes and behaviors of acute and chronic schizophrenic patients regarding ambulatory treatment. *American Journal of Psychiatry,* 1974, *131,* 991.

Shean, G. An effective and self-supporting program of community living for chronic patients. *Hospital and Community Psychiatry,* 1973, *24,* 97–99.

Singer, J. E., & Grob, M. C. Short-term vs. long-term hospitalization in a private psychiatric facility: A follow-up study. *Hospital and Community Psychiatry,* 1975, *26,* 745–748.

Stein, L. I., & Test, M. A. An alternative to mental hospital treatment. In L. I. Stein & M. A. Test (Eds.), *Alternatives to mental hospital treatment.* New York: Plenum Press, 1978.

Stein, L. I., & Test, M. A. From the hospital to the community: A shift in the primary locus of care. *New Directions for Mental Health Services,* 1979, *1,* 15–32.

Stein, L. I., Test, M. A., & Marx, A. J. Alternatives to the hospital: A controlled study. *American Journal of Psychiatry,* 1975, *132,* 517–522.

Test, M. A., & Stein, L. I. Training in community living: Research design and results. In L. I. Stein & M. A. Test (Eds.), *Alternatives to Mental Hospital Treatment.* New York: Plenum Press, 1978.

Trute, B., & Segal, S. Census tract predictors and the social integration of sheltered-care residents. *Social Psychiatry,* 1976, *11,* 153–161.

Udell, B., & Hornstra, R. K. Good patients and bad: Therapeutic assets and liabilities. *Archives of General Psychiatry,* 1975, *11,* 389–393.

Vaughn, C. E., & Leff, J. P. The influence of family and social factors on the course of psychiatric illness. *British Journal of Psychiatry,* 1976, *129,* 125–137.

Weinman, B., & Kleiner, R. J. The impact of community living and community member intervention on the adjustment of the chronic psychiatric patient. In L. I. Stein & M. A. Test (Eds.), *Alternatives to mental hospital treatment.* New York: Plenum Press, 1978.

Weinman, B., Kleiner, R., Yu, J., & Tillson, V. A. Social treatment of the chronic psychiatric patient in the community. *Journal of Community Psychology,* 1974, *2,* 358–365.

Wilder, J. F., Kessel, M., & Caulfield, S. C. Follow-up of a "high expectations" halfway house. *American Journal of Psychiatry,* 1968, *124,* 1085–1091.

Wing, J. W. Planning and evaluating services for chronically handicapped psychiatric patients in the United Kingdom. In L. I. Stein & M. A. Test

(Eds.), *Alternatives to mental hospital treatment.* New York: Plenum Press, 1978.

Wing, J. K., & Olson, R. *Community care for the mentally disabled.* New York and Toronto: Oxford University Press, 1979.

Wooley, F. R., & Kane, R. L. Community aftercare of patients discharged from Utah State Hospital: A follow-up study. *Hospital and Community Psychiatry,* 1977, *28,* 114–118.

Part III

ATTITUDES TOWARD PATIENT RIGHTS: SOME NEW DATA

Chapter 9

THE MEASUREMENT OF ATTITUDES TOWARD THE RIGHTS OF PSYCHIATRIC PATIENTS

Steven R. Perry

The adversary process of the judicial system and new statutes from the legislative system have resulted in a number of changes in the legal status and conditions of treatment of psychiatric patients since the early 1960s. If legal reforms are to result in a significant improvement in the lives of patients, there must be effective implementation of these new laws and regulations. Ennis and Siegel (1973) describe a fundamental difficulty in that implementation.

> There is an enormous difference between the rights mental patients have in theory and the rights they have in practice. Doctors, hospital officials, and even judges frequently pay no attention to patients' "rights," preferring, instead, to do what they believe to be in the patients' "best interest." (p. 11)

The conflict between the "legal rights" and the "best interests" of psychiatric patients highlights basic philosophical differences between the legal and psychiatric professions. These philosophical differences are extensively discussed in Bloom and Asher's review in this volume of articles dealing with the interface of the mental health and legal systems.

Less than 30 of the hundreds of publications on the rights of psychiatric patients published between 1970 and 1979 were based on empirical studies; most publications were nonempirical essays. The opinions expressed in them, however, reflect the divergent attitudes held within the legal and mental health professions.

Attitudes are considered to be "relatively enduring organizations of beliefs . . . predisposing one to respond in some preferential manner" (Rokeach, 1970, p. 112). Although this study assumes no one-to-one correspondence between attitudes and behavior, two recent review articles have reported generally positive results in research on attitude-behavior interactions. Ajzen and Fishbein (1977) found that "a person's attitude has a consistently strong relation with his or her behavior when it is directed at the same target and when it involves the same action" (p. 912). Schuman and Johnson (1976) suggest that this consistent, strong relation between attitude and behavior involves a causal process, that attitudes have a causal effect on behavior, "whatever one's model of the underlying causal process may be" (p. 199).

As specific hypotheses about attitudes toward patient rights, and behaviors occurring in the context of those attitudes, are supported or rejected by empirical research, our understanding of these complex and controversial social issues will be enhanced. Resolution of the controversy concerning which specific rights are appropriately extended to the mentally ill may depend upon our knowledge of the attitudes held by those involved in psychiatric litigation and treatment.

PREVIOUS RESEARCH

Attitudes Toward Mental Illness and the Mentally Ill

Rabkin's survey article (1972) provides the best overview of attitudes toward mental illness, mental hospitals, and mental patients during the 1960s. She notes that the negative and rejecting attitudes held by most Americans were usually shared by psychiatric patients as well. The attitudes of mental health personnel varied by occupation, age, and education, with the less educated, the older, and those in lower status occupations more negative and rejecting.

Based on the studies reviewed, Rabkin concluded that attitudes were moderately related to behavior and amenable to change. But she noted that the "major problem faced by workers in this area . . . is the absence of a measuring instrument of sufficient scope" (p. 169).

Brand and Claiborn (1976) used two social distance questionnaires with a sample of 93 employers and found significantly less social distance revealed toward ex-tuberculosis patients than toward ex-convicts, marginally adjusted individuals, and ex-mental patients. In contrast, they found that there were no differences in the sales jobs offered to confederates role-playing an ex-TB patient, an ex-convict, or an ex-mental patient, an interesting illustration of the differences to be found between attitudes and behavior.

Weinstein (1979) reported that in 30 of 38 quantitative studies of patient attitudes toward psychiatric hospitalization that he reviewed, a large majority of inpatients expressed attitudes favorable toward their institution, even more favorable toward mental hospitals in general, and that their attitudes improved between admission and discharge. Social variables appeared to be less related to attitudes than psychiatric variables. Patient attitudes were more favorable toward hospitals' treatment and restriction practices than toward staff and other patients. Voluntary patients tended to have more favorable attitudes than involuntarily committed patients, rehospitalized patients were more favorable than those hospitalized for the first time, and attitudes became more favorable as time in therapy increased. He also suggested that many patients seek hospitalization to gain a temporary refuge.

Weinstein concluded that "the defenders of mental hospitals have more accurately portrayed the patient's point of view than the critics" (p. 252). This review of patient attitudes, and Brand and Claiborn's (1976) social distance study, suggest that there may be more recent changes in attitudes that run counter to Rabkin's earlier (1972) findings.

As might be expected, given improving but still negative attitudes toward the mentally ill, other studies have consistently found a considerable lack of knowledge within the mental health professions regarding patient rights (Laves & Cohen, 1973; Peszke & Wintrob, 1974; Tancredi & Clark, 1972).

Given the generally negative attitudes toward the mentally ill prevalent in this country and the lack of knowledge about patient rights among mental health personnel, attitudes about patient rights need to be understood if we are to assess the probable extent of implementation of patient rights mandated by judicial, legislative, and administrative actions. The empirical literature regarding attitudes toward patient rights is still quite limited. This review will examine studies published since 1972.

Attitudes Toward Patient Rights

Fanning, Deloughery, and Gebbie (1972) interviewed 37 staff and 82 patients at one mental health center regarding the role of patients in planning their own psychiatric care. They found that both groups supported the joint staff-patient planning of treatment, starting at the time of admission. The younger, less well-educated, and female patients tended to be more accepting of staff control of treatment issues. The authors found that the longer patients had been in treatment, the less they indicated a desire to be involved in planning. They also found that patients with inpatient experience were less interested in participating in treatment planning than were persons with only outpatient experience.

Kumasaka and Stokes (1972) conducted semistructured interviews with 30 staff psychiatrists, 11 defense attorneys, and 15 attorneys acting as officers of the court "officially remaining neutral" (p. 202). Virtually all of the psychiatrists and court attorneys thought involuntary hospitalization was an indispensible procedure, while less than half of the defense attorneys agreed. Over 60% of the psychiatrists and court attorneys thought dangerousness was a valid criterion for involuntary hospitalization, as compared with the less than 20% of the defense attorneys.

Laves and Cohen (1973) developed a 35-item Likert-style scale from New Jersey law to assess the attitudes of 66 psychiatrists, psychologists, social workers, nurses, and attendants. They found all five groups somewhat favorable toward the rights of patients, with no significant difference in amount of support among the groups. They noted that their data did not confirm Rabkin's (1972) observation that "employees of lower status tend to display more authoritarian and restrictive attitudes" (Laves & Cohen, 1973, p. 63).

Rachlin, Pam, and Milton (1975) examined involuntary hospitalization from the "standpoint of the profession, the patient, and the community, with particular reference to legal rights and civil liberties" (p. 189) and concluded that the community and the families of patients were more strongly in favor of treating more patients, for longer periods of time, in locked-ward settings, than were the mental health professionals.

Snooks (1975) studied 66 clinical social workers at agencies in five states using a Likert-style attitude scale he developed that covered 17 patient-rights issues. He found that 80% of the social workers favored patient-rights legislation, feeling it would result in better care for patients. But he also found that 70% of the sample thought attorneys intruded into mental health concerns without adequate knowledge of the realities of the treatment modalities employed.

Daugherty (1978) developed a short questionnaire to assess attitudes regarding 10 rights "guaranteed to all patients under state law, that . . . might not be supported by all ward personnel" (p. 225). They assessed the attitudes of 43 psychiatric aides and found that most of the aides supported all of these "unpopular" rights. They also noted that the rights dealing with "abstract issues or basic human necessities received unqualified support" (p. 225). The rights that might disrupt ward routine or that required responsibility and judgment on the part of patients received less support.

Kahle and Sales (1978) surveyed 316 clinical psychologists in a national study with a 125-item questionnaire on attitudes toward involuntary commitment. They found that the psychologists were in favor of involuntary commitment, but with many restrictive definitions and criteria to limit the use of commitment hearings. The respondents also favored mandatory hearings within set time-limits and due process protection in the hearings, and they endorsed rights regarding the activities of hospitalized patients (e.g., uncensored use of the mail, access to telephones). They concluded from their results that, "clinical psychologists are generally in favor of increasing the civil liberties both of individuals who are facing commitment proceedings and of individuals who have been committed" (p. 438).

As these studies indicate, attitudes toward patient rights are clearly related to occupation and role. Differences among mental health personnel are less striking than differences within the legal profession. The effects of age, sex, education, patient status and history, occupational status, and other similar variables are still unclear.

It is difficult to draw any conclusions regarding attitudes toward the rights of psychiatric patients based on the studies reviewed since most were done with ad hoc survey instruments developed to meet local circumstances, and were done with small or very limited samples. There is a clear and important need for a standardized survey instrument to assess such attitudes. The studies reviewed, while interesting and informative, point to the need for reliable baseline data for large samples from the many groups concerned with the treatment of the mentally ill. It was for this reason that the Patient Rights Attitude Questionnaire was developed. Standardization of the scale with a large national sample represents an attempt to provide a broad, reliable, and comprehensive data base on attitudes toward the rights of psychiatric patients.

A Scale for the Assessment of Attitudes Toward Patient Rights

Initial Pilot Study

The development of the Patient Rights Attitude Questionnaire (PRAQ) followed the process used by Baker and Schulberg (1967) in the construction of the Community Mental Health Ideology Scale. Nearly 100 statements were derived from the literature to encompass the many issues associated with the rights of psychiatric patients. After elimination of ambiguous and redundant items, the remaining 73 items were prepared in a Likert (1932) response format. Respondents were asked to indicate the extent of their agreement or disagreement with each statement by circling one of six symbols (AAA, AA, A, D, DD, DDD) following each item. The 73 items and several questions to elicit demographic information constituted the pilot version of the PRAQ. This questionnaire was distributed to a sample of 400 attorneys, patients, and mental health personnel in Colorado.

There were 181 pilot PRAQs returned with enough data to permit analysis (85 patients, 79 mental health personnel, and 17 attorneys). The replies were subjected to the cluster analysis procedure described by Tryon and Bailey (1970). This analysis yielded five reliable (Cronbach, 1951), adequately homogeneous (Scott, 1968), relatively independent clusters incorporating 41 of the items. The five clusters exhausted 92% of the initial communality. Two of the clusters were difficult to distinguish from each other conceptually, although their intercorrelation (.35) suggested that they were relatively independent. In contrast, the other three clusters were more easily characterized and named, though their intercorrelations were somewhat higher (see Table 9-1).

National Sample

The national sample was selected to assess the attitudes of a variety of groups-at-interest regarding the rights of psychiatric patients on the final version of the PRAQ. In July of 1978, 1,000 packets containing one or more of the 41-item PRAQs, return envelopes, and cover letters were mailed to 200 district attorneys, 200 public defender attorneys, 400 inpatient facilities, and 200 mental health centers. Each state and the District of Columbia was represented, in proportion to population, in every category, to the extent possible. Locations within each state were selected at random.

The cover letter explained the research project, requested participation, offered a copy of the results, and assured the participants of the voluntary and confidential nature of their participation. The packet sent to the psychiatric inpatient facilities included three PRAQs and requested the participation of the chief administrator, one inpatient, and one clinical staff member. The packet sent to the community mental health centers included six PRAQs and asked for the participation of the center director, two outpatients, and three clinical staff members. A letter encouraging participation, provided by the executive director of the National Council of Community Mental Health Centers, Inc., was enclosed in the packet sent to the community mental health centers.

Table 9–1 Pilot Sample, Five-Cluster Solution: Cluster Intercorrelations, Reliabilities, Homogeneity Ratios, and Explained Communalities

Clusters	Cluster intercorrelations				Scale reliability (Cronbach Alpha)	Homogeneity ratios (Scott)	Cumulative explained communalities
	B	C	D	E			
A. Protection of Constitutional Rights	.52	.40	.18	.49	.84	.32	.41
B. Protection of Due Process		−.01	−.02	.55	.84	.32	.62
C. (Unnamed)			.35	.18	.69	.25	.74
D. (Unnamed)				.16	.69	.27	.84
E. Patient's Role in Treatment Planning					.71	.30	.92

Within two months of the first mailing, replies were received from over 250 locations. A follow-up postcard yielded additional replies, and the final-response tally showed returns of 823 PRAQs (29.3%) from 368 locations. After deletion of those returned PRAQs with significant amounts of missing data, the responses for the remaining 727 subjects were analyzed.

Scale Development.

Cluster analysis of the data from the national sample showed that the five-cluster solution used with the pilot sample was highly reliable (see Table 9–2). The five-cluster solution exhausted 89% of the initial communality with somewhat higher intercluster correlations than in the pilot sample analysis. The intercorrelation of the two difficult-to-define clusters had increased from .35 to .55. Given this high intercorrelation and the conceptual similarities of these two clusters, it was decided to combine them. As can be seen in Table 9–3, the four-cluster solution was mathematically sound and resulted in clusters with conceptual coherence and identifiable themes. The names, intercorrelations, reliabilities, homogeneity ratios, and explained communality of the four clusters are shown in Table 9–3. The items and their factor loadings are shown for each of the four clusters in Table 9–4.

RESULTS AND DISCUSSION

The 727 subjects in the national sample were grouped into the nine groups shown in Table 9–5. The 31 members of the mental health worker (MHW) group included all of those subjects who checked LPN, psychiatric technician, or mental health worker on the job-classification question. The PHD group includes psychologists at all levels of training (all but three psychologists indicated some advanced degree). All members of the MD group were psychiatrists. The mean scores for the groups and for all subjects for each cluster and for the entire PRAQ are shown in Table 9–5.

The overall, one-way analysis of variance for the groups on the entire PRAQ and the four, 1-x-9 analyses of variance for the groups on each cluster showed highly significant differences between the groups. The F ratios, significance levels, and eta^2 values are shown in Table 9–5. The results of the specific comparisons tests (least significant difference procedure) are shown in Table 9–6.

When the 494 mental health personnel were grouped according to whether or not they were primarily responsible for direct patient-care, scores for the patient-care group showed less agreement with the

Table 9–2 National Sample, Five-Cluster Solution: Cluster Intercorrelations, Reliabilities, Homogeneity Ratios, and Explained Communalities

Clusters	Cluster intercorrelations				Scale reliability (Cronbach Alpha)	Homogeneity ratios (Scott)	Cumulative explained communalities
	B	C	D	E			
A. Protection of Constitutional Rights	.59	.44	.26	.52	.77	.23	.43
B. Protection of Due Process		.20	.15	.48	.81	.29	.57
C. (Unnamed)			.55	.29	.68	.25	.74
D. (Unnamed)				.30	.68	.26	.81
E. Patient's Role in Treatment Planning					.72	.32	.89

Table 9-3 National Sample, Four-Cluster Solution: Cluster Intercorrelations,
Reliabilities, Homogeneity Ratios, and Explained Communalities

Clusters	Cluster intercorrelations			Scale reliability (Cronbach Alpha)	Homogeneity ratios (Scott)	Cumulative explained communalities
	II	III	IV			
I. Protection of Constitutional Rights	.59	.52	.39	.77	.23	.43
II. Protection of Due Process		.48	.20	.81	.29	.57
III. Freedom From Restraint			.33	.79	.23	.76
IV. Patient's Role in Treatment Planning				.72	.32	.84

rights of patients than scores for the non-patient-care group, but these differences were not significant for any cluster nor for the total scores.

The results of this national survey indicate clear differences in attitudes regarding the rights of psychiatric patients for the groups studied. It is also clear that the four clusters of the PRAQ reliably measure four specific, identifiable, and coherent areas within the general field of patient rights.

Group Comparisons

In general, prosecuting attorneys expressed the least agreement and defense attorneys the most agreement with the rights of patients. Future studies with attorneys who have moved from a public defender role to being a prosecuting attorney and vice versa would be useful in exploring the stability of these attitudes in the face of changing role demands. Protection of the rights of patients may depend to a very large extent upon the continued existence of public defender programs.

The contrast in total scores for the two patient groups, with outpatients expressing far more agreement with the rights of patients than inpatients, highlights an important difference that may be a function of the inpatient experience, as suggested by Fanning, Deloughery, and Gebbie (1972). These findings also support Weinstein's (1979) observation that "more experienced" inpatients are willing to forego some civil rights for what they report as the protective and therapeutic benefits of hospitalization. It is clear that further study of the effects of the inpatient experience on the assertion of rights is critically important if the legal and administrative extension of these rights is to have practical meaning for inpatients.

Among mental health personnel, psychiatrists and mental health workers expressed less agreement with the rights of patients than did social workers or psychologists. These results are consistent with the findings reported by Kumasaka and Stokes (1972). The low levels of agreement with the rights of patients expressed by psychiatrists may be due to the larger sample size or to the use of the more comprehensive PRAQ, as compared with the data used by Rabkin (1972). The nurses occupied a middle position among the mental health personnel, with total PRAQ scores that were similar to those of the mental health workers, psychologists, and social workers. This study did not support the findings of Fanning et al. (1972) and Laves and Cohen (1973) that there are no differences among mental health personnel in their attitudes toward the rights of patients. The effect of occupation within the mental health field, clearly will need further study before any final conclusions can be drawn.

Table 9-4 Items and Factor Loadings for Each PRAQ Cluster

Scale item	Factor loading

Cluster I: Protection of Constitutional Rights

1. All psychiatric inpatients should routinely be permitted to keep and spend their own money. — .64
2. All psychiatric inpatients should be permitted to send and to receive uncensored sealed mail, to receive visitors, and to make and receive telephone calls at their own discretion. — .56
3. Except for protective restraint, such as to prevent a patient from falling out of bed, no inpatient should be restrained physically for more than a few hours without review by a patient's rights committee. — .53
4. Psychiatric patients should be allowed to examine their own medical charts or agency records. — .50
5. If inpatients are willing and able to work in a psychiatric hospital, they should be paid at least the minimum wage. — .50
6. Psychiatric inpatients are as competent as anyone else to exercise their civil right to vote. — .49
7. After a specified period of time, former psychiatric patients should have the right to have their psychiatric records destroyed. — .47
8. If involuntary hospitalization is permitted at all, it should be limited to a definite, brief period of time. — .46
9. If a psychiatric hospital fails to provide treatment to an inpatient, involuntary hospitalization is not justified. — .42
10. Requiring a willing and able inpatient in a psychiatric hospital to work, whether or not the patient is paid, is a form of involuntary servitude or "peonage" and should be prohibited. — .40
11. Statements made by an inpatient that could be incriminating in a criminal proceeding, should be excluded from hospital records and psychiatric reports. — .34

Cluster II: Protection of Due Process

1. Provisions should be made so that every prospective psychiatric patient being considered for involuntary hospitalization can be represented by an attorney. — .71
2. Mental health professionals who certify to the mental illness of any person should be available for cross examination by the prospective patient's attorney at any involuntary hospitalization hearing. — .67
3. The court should appoint an attorney for an involuntarily hospitalized patient who wishes to petition to be discharged from a psychiatric hospital and cannot afford legal counsel. — .66
4. Persons recommending the involuntary hospitalization of a prospective patient should be required to show that available, less restrictive alternatives would not be adequate. — .62

Table 9–4 (Continued)

Scale item	Factor loading

Cluster II: Protection of Due Process (continued)

5. Every psychiatric inpatient facility, public or private, should have available to patients a legally trained patient advocate whose task is to ensure that the civil rights of patients are protected. .57

6. Verbatim transcripts of relevant hearing procedures should be made available to committed patients on request. .56

7. If a psychiatric inpatient obtains legal counsel, that lawyer should be allowed (with the patient's permission) to examine the patient's medical records. .54

8. A hearing should be necessary in order to declare a hospitalized patient legally incompetent. .48

9. Prospective patients should be notified whenever the legal process of securing their involuntary psychiatric hospitalization has been initiated. .47

10. Provisions should be made so that every prospective psychiatric patient being considered for involuntary hospitalization can be represented by a mental health professional. .38

11. Decisions regarding involuntary hospitalization are best made by collaboration on the part of legal and mental health professionals representing all sides of the issue. .32

Cluster III: Freedom from Restraint

1. It is necessary to have some procedure to hospitalize persons involuntarily based on the judgment of competent mental health professionals. −.62

2. Mental health professionals are generally capable of evaluating the ability of prospective patients to make rational decisions about the necessity for treatment. −.61

3. The concept of "dangerousness" as applied to prospective psychiatric patients should be broadly defined to include any degree of judged dangerousness to oneself, to others, or to property. −.61

4. It is appropriate to use physical restraints or seclusion rooms to prevent inpatients from injuring themselves or others. −.56

5. People who are so incapacitated that they are unable to decide about treatment for themselves can often benefit from treatment in spite of their disability. −.53

6. Mental health professionals are better able to predict dangerousness of patients than are random samples of equally intelligent members of the community. −.52

7. With all the attention being paid to the rights of psychiatric patients, there is some danger that the rights of mental health professionals might be forgotten. −.50

Table 9–4   (Continued)

Scale item	Factor loading
Cluster III: Freedom from Restraint (continued)	
8. It should be possible to hospitalize a patient briefly on an involuntary basis without a court hearing.	–.48
9. Voluntary psychiatric patients should be required to remain in the hospital a minimum length of time before exercising their right to leave.	–.47
10. Inpatient's rights can be fully protected by the creation of patient's rights committees whose function is to bring problems to the attention of the staff, but who do not have the ability to bring court action against the agency.	–.39
11. As long as people are not a danger to others, they should be left alone to pursue their own goals, real or imaginary.	.37
12. When court hearings are conducted on a petition for involuntary hospitalization, prospective patients should be required to testify even if they might say some things that could demonstrate the presence of mental illness.	–.34
13. Mental illness reduces the capacity of the individual to make rational decisions.	–.33
Cluster IV: Patient's Role in Treatment Planning	
1. Psychiatric patients should be able to consult with an independent mental health professional when they have a question about the adequacy of the treatment being received.	.65
2. A psychiatric patient's informed consent should be obtained before any medical or psychological treatment is instituted.	.65
3. Psychiatric patients should be able to transfer to another available therapist or another available treatment modality without prejudicial consequences if they are dissatisfied with their current treatment program.	.63
4. Psychiatric patients should have the right to participate in planning their own treatment program.	.60
5. Persons with psychiatric disabilities should have the right to refuse treatment for their disorder.	.55
6. Involuntary hospitalization of a psychiatric patient should be permitted based solely on the allegations of that patient's family or acquaintances.	–.35

Cluster Score Comparisons

The amount of agreement with patient rights varied as the focus of the rights changed from cluster to cluster. The respondents, as a group, were most in agreement with rights related to due process in commitment proceedings and the right to participate in treatment planning. The entire sample expressed less agreement with those rights identified as basic, constitutional rights, and did not agree with those of the rights relating to freedom from restraint. All groups expressed the least agreement with the rights in this area, suggesting that, when the issue comes down to the protection of the individual versus protection of the community, there was a shared willingness to sacrifice the rights of the individual.

Protection of Constitutional Rights and Due Process.

The two attorney groups anchored the opposite poles of the score distribution on Cluster I and Cluster II. This polarization reflects the traditional adversarial relationship of prosecuting and defending attorneys. Role demands were the apparent determiners of attitudes in these two areas; protection of basic, constitutional rights and protection of due process in committment proceedings.

The two patient groups expressed strong agreement with the rights contained in these clusters. Clearly, the patients were in agreement with the protection of those safeguards that would protect them from unnecessary or arbitrary commitment.

Psychiatrists and mental health workers expressed less agreement than did nurses and social workers, with psychologists in between. It is possible that these results reflect some concern on the part of psychiatrists that the exercising of these rights may interfere with the treatment provided the patients or that commitment is primarily a medical, rather than a legal, concern. The MHWs may have been expressing their concern over the intrusion of legal issues into the day-to-day operation of the words.

Freedom From Restraint.

This cluster concerns those issues related to the restraint of disruptive individuals; the protection of the community. Here again, the public defenders expressed the strongest agreement. The district attorneys were more in agreement with the rights of the individual in this area than on any of the other clusters. While the results for the defending attorneys are consistent with their strong agreement with the rights of patients, the results for the prosecuting attorneys were surprising. It may be that the prosecuting attorneys were expressing their unwillingness to become involved in legal proceedings against disruptive psychiatrically disabled individuals.

Table 9–5   Mean Item Scores for Nine Groups
Total PRAQ and Four Clusters

Group	N	Total Score	Clusters			
			I	II	III	IV
District Attorney (DA)	53	3.47	3.11	4.59	2.76	3.62
Psychiatrist (MD)	106	3.78	3.55	4.70	2.70	4.85
Mental Health Worker (MHW)	31	3.85	3.76	4.94	2.57	4.80
Inpatient (IP)	83	4.01	4.23	5.22	2.45	4.73
Registered Nurse (RN)	56	4.03	4.08	5.07	2.55	5.23
Psychologist (PHD)	157	4.10	4.03	5.01	2.96	5.09
Social Worker (MSW)	115	4.12	4.20	5.05	2.80	5.12
Outpatient (OP)	64	4.20	4.46	5.34	2.63	5.04
Public Defender (PD)	62	4.83	4.82	5.54	4.01	5.31
All Subjects	727	4.06	4.04	5.04	2.84	4.92
F ratios (8,718)			33.02*	27.51*	13.61*	32.00*	32.61*
eta^2			.2690	.2346	.1316	.2627	.2665

*$p < .0001$.

Both patient groups expressed less agreement with their rights in this area than in the rights covered by the other three clusters. Of all the groups, the inpatients expressed the least agreement with their right to be left free from restraint. This issue appears to have been reaching the inpatients at a basic level, reflecting a concern that there be some provision for what might be characterized as *protective restraint,* even if this means some curtailment of their freedom. The in-patients may also have been expressing an acceptance of the notion that the mentally ill have significantly reduced capacity to manage their own lives and are in need of the protective functions offered by psychiatric institutions.

The social workers and psychologists were more in agreement with the rights of patients in this area than were nurses and MHWs, with the psychiatrists occupying a middle position. Examination of the results suggests that this may be an area where further study of the patient-care variable may prove the most revealing, since nurses and MHWs are the most likely to have direct patient-care responsibilities.

Patient Role in Treatment Planning.

The two attorney groups again anchored opposite ends of the score distribution on this cluster. Since the items in this cluster relate to the role of the patient in treatment planning and related issues, it is difficult to explain the reasons that would result in this great a difference in attitudes. The strong agreement expressed by the public defenders is likely a further expression of their general, strong agreement with the rights of patients. District attorneys are not usually involved in legal matters related to the issues raised by items in this cluster, thus their relative lack of agreement here may have been a simple extension of their lack of agreement with patient rights issues in general.

The outpatients expressed more agreement with the rights contained in this cluster than did the inpatients, as was the case on all of the clusters. The inpatients expressed almost as much disagreement as the prosecuting attorneys on this cluster. This result supports the findings of Fanning et al. (1972), that inpatients are less supportive of their participation in treatment planning than outpatients, suggesting a greater acceptance of a "doctor knows best" attitude.

Table 9–6   Specific Comparisons Test:[a] Nine Groups,
Four Clusters and Total Score

Items									
All	DA	MD	MHW	IP	RN	PHD	MSW	OP	PD
Cluster I	DA	MD	MHW	PHD	RN	MSW	IP	OP	PD
Cluster II	DA	MD	MHW	PHD	MSW	RN	IP	OP	PD
Cluster III	IP	RN	MHW	OP	MD	DA	MSW	PHD	PD
Cluster IV	DA	IP	MHW	MD	OP	PHD	MSW	RN	PD

[a] Least significant difference procedure. Underscoring defines the subsets of groups whose highest and lowest means do not differ by more than the shortest significant range for a subset of that size.

The psychologists and social workers expressed more agreement with the rights of patients to participate in the planning of their treatment than did the psychiatrists and MHWs. The nurses expressed their greatest degree of agreement in this area, expressing almost as much agreement as the defense attorneys. The attitudes shown by the nurses, and to a slightly lesser extent by the social workers and psychologists may have been a reflection of recognition of the contribution that patients can make in the planning of their treatment.

It is important to emphasize that, except for public defenders, overall agreement with the rights of psychiatric patients was not very great. The implications of these findings will be discussed at the end of the next chapter in connection with Freddolino's hospital studies.

References

Ajzen, I., & Fishbein, M. Attitude-behavior relations: A theoretical analysis and review of empirical research. *Psychological Bulletin* 1977, *84*, 888–918.

Baker, F., & Schulberg, H. C. The development of a community mental health ideology scale. *Community Mental Health Journal,* 1967, *3*, 216–225.

Brand, R. C., Jr., & Claiborn, W. L. Two studies of comparative stigma: Employer attitudes and practices toward rehabilitated convicts, mental and tuberculosis patients. *Community Mental Health Journal,* 1976, *12*, 168–175.

Cronbach, L. J. Coefficient alpha and the internal structure of tests. *Psychometrika,* 1951, *16*, 297–334.

Daugherty, L. B. Assessing the attitudes of psychiatric aides toward patients' rights. *Hospital and Community Psychiatry,* 1978, *29*, 225–229.

Ennis, B. J., & Siegel, L. *The rights of mental patients: The basic American Civil Liberties Union guide to a mental patient's rights.* New York: Avon Books, 1973.

Fanning, V. L., Deloughery, G. L. W., & Gebbie, K. M. Patient involvement in planning own care: Staff and patient attitudes. *Journal of Psychiatric Nursing and Mental Health Services,* 1972, 5–8.

Kahle, L. R., & Sales, B. D. Attitudes of clinical psychologists toward involuntary commitment law. *Professional Psychology,* 1978, *3*, 428–439.

Kumasaka, Y., & Stokes, J. Involuntary hospitalization: Opinions and attitudes of psychiatrists and lawyers. *Comprehensive Psychiatry,* 1972, *13*, 201–208.

Laves, R., & Cohen, A. A preliminary investigation into the knowledge of and attitudes toward the legal rights of mental patients. *Journal of Psychiatry and Law,* 1973, *1*, 49–78.

Likert, R. A technique for the measurement of attitudes. *Archive of Psychology,* No. 140, 1932.

Peszke, M. A., & Wintrob, R. M. Emergency commitment—A transcultural study. *American Journal of Psychiatry,* 1974, *131*, 36–40.

Rabkin, J. G. Opinions about mental illness: A review of the literature. *Psychological Bulletin,* 1972, *77,* 153–171.

Rachlin, S., Pam, A., & Milton, J. Civil liberties versus involuntary hospitalization. *American Journal of Psychiatry,* 1975, *132,* 189–192.

Rokeach, M. *Beliefs, attitudes, and values.* San Francisco, Calif.: Jossey-Bass, 1970.

Schuman, H., & Johnson, M. P. Attitudes and behavior. In A. Inkeles, J. Coleman, & N. Smelser (Eds.), *Annual Review of Sociology* (Vol. 2). 161–207. Palo Alto, Calif.: Annual Reviews, Inc., 1976.

Scott, W. A. Attitude measurement. In G. Lindzey & E. Aronson (Eds.), *Handbook of social psychology,* (Rev. ed.) Vol. 2, pp. 204–273. Reading, Mass.: Addison-Wesley, 1968.

Snooks, H. D. Clinical social workers' opinions on patients' rights. (Abstract). *Smith College studies in social work,* 1975, *46,* 71–72.

Tancredi, L., & Clark, D. Psychiatry and the legal rights of patients. *American Journal of Psychiatry,* 1972, *129,* 328–330.

Tryon, R. C., & Bailey, D. E. *Cluster analysis.* New York: McGraw-Hill, 1970.

Weinstein, R. M. Patient attitudes toward mental hospitalization: A review of quantitative research. *Journal of Health and Social Behavior,* 1979, *20,* 237–258.

Chapter 10

ATTITUDES TOWARD PATIENT RIGHTS:
Data From Two State Hospital Studies

Paul P. Freddolino, Ph.D.

In the previous chapter, Perry described the development of the Patients' Rights Attitude Questionnaire, and reported the major findings derived from a national sample of respondents. In his review of the literature, Perry noted that most of the previous research has examined attitudes toward mental illness and the mentally ill, with little attention to attitudes toward patient rights. Three studies that did examine attitudes toward patient rights (Laves & Cohen, 1973; Peszke & Wintrob, 1974; Tancredi & Clark, 1972) noted the lack of information concerning these rights among mental health professionals. Other studies (Kahle & Sales, 1980; Kumasaka & Stokes, 1972; Rachlin, Pam, & Milton, 1975) focused particularly on issues involved in involuntary hospitalization.

In this chapter, data from two studies of state hospital personnel are reviewed. Conclusions from these studies and Perry's work will be discussed as will their implications for the fields of patient rights and patient advocacy.

The Studies

In 1975, a study of administrators and clinical staff at six state hospitals in New York concerning a number of patients' rights issues was undertaken (Freddolino, 1977). Four of the hospitals were "traditional," large, state mental hospitals, while two were smaller and more community-oriented in their service delivery. The data included 459 self-administered questionnaires representing 60.5% of all questionnaires distributed. Structured interviews were completed with 96 additional respondents.

The instruments contained attitudinal items on patients' rights and the "medical model" of mental illness, as well as demographic items. The items relating to the medical model constitute a scale of traditionalism developed by Bardach (1972). The patients' rights items were pretested at another state hospital in New York. A coding system was developed for each open-ended item in the structured interview after all responses had been examined. The codes were then employed by other judges, with discrepancies discussed until mutual agreement was reached. The intercoder reliability rate was 0.84. Full details of the research design, instruments, and data analysis can be found in Freddolino, 1977.

Many of the same items were used in 1978 as part of an evaluation of the effectiveness of an advocacy project that offered services to patients at two state hospitals in California. One hospital provides services for the mentally ill (MI), while the other directs its service delivery toward developmentally disabled (DD) clients. The data include 529 questionnaires from administrators and staff, representing an overall response rate of 43%. Additional responses to a series of open-ended questions were collected from 133 of these respondents in an interview. Full details of the design and analysis can be found in Freddolino, 1979.

Three key patients' rights issues covered in both studies will be considered here, as well as a fourth issue included only in the California study. Some factors affecting variance in responses to these issues will be discussed.

THE ISSUES

In the discussion that follows, *propatients' rights* or civil-libertarian pole on each issue was drawn from the major themes and positions defined and advocated by Ennis (1972), Ennis and Siegel (1973), Szasz (1961, 1970), and Vail (1966), while the *antipatients' rights* pole was defined by the responses that came closest to the antithesis of the "pro" pole.

The first issue to be considered is a very basic one: *Should patients be made more aware of their rights?* The propatients' rights position would be that patients should be made more aware, while the antipatients' rights position would argue that they should not be made more aware and that, in fact, patients are already *too* aware of their rights.

The basic idea of making patients more aware of their rights received almost equal approval among both groups of respondents in New York (65.4% among questionnaire respondents, 66.7% among interview respondents). The California data revealed only slightly lower levels of support, with 63.4% of the DD staff and 56.0% of the MI staff approving. These results indicate that a majority, but by no means all, respondents appear to favor informing patients of their rights.

The next issue to be considered is probably the most controversial patient rights issue because it gets at the very basis and justification for hospitalization: specifically, *should patients have the right to refuse treatment?* Here the reference is not to psychosurgery or electroconvulsive therapy, but rather the day-to-day round of medications, group therapy, and other forms of treatment used in a mental hospital setting.

The extreme propatients' rights position on this issue is that all patients should always have the right to refuse treatment, while a slightly modified position makes an exception if a patient is overtly dangerous to self or others, or clearly psychotic. The opposing position is that no patients should have the right to refuse treatment, occasionally modified to allow the right to refuse to certain patients who are "able to comprehend."

Data from all New York respondents, and from respondents in the MI facility in California, will be considered first. In both states, voluntary psychiatric patients had the right to refuse treatment, while involuntary patients did not have this right. Data from both studies show that staff attitudes do not favor the right to refuse treatment. In the New York study, only 39.1% of the questionnaire respondents agreed that voluntary patients should always have the right to refuse specific treatment modalities while 46.5% disagreed. In the California study, only 33.2% of the MI staff agreed with the statement, while 57.3% disagreed.

Only 27.7% of the questionnaire respondents in New York agreed that involuntary patients should have the right to refuse specific treatment modalities, while 61.1% disagreed. Among staff at the California MI facility, only 15.6% of the respondents agreed with the statement, while 75.5% disagreed with this position. One possible explanation for the stronger resistance to this idea among respondents in California is that the state's mental health statute permits only a 72-hour initial retention period for involuntary patients. New York's statute permits a 15-day period. Thus, staff in California may be unwilling to grant these patients any right to refuse treatment during this brief period.

In the New York interviews, the results followed a similar pattern, but provide some important insights into how staff members view patients. The responses indicate that in spite of the distinction made in the regulations between patients on voluntary and involuntary status, staff members do not see formal status as being highly correlated with patients' actual "mental condition," or with whether or not they may be dangerous or psychotic.

Among the interview respondents, 34.4% state that patients should not have the right to refuse specific treatment modalities, regardless of status. For some respondents, voluntary and involuntary patients differ only in that the voluntary patients can and possibly should leave if they don't want to accept the treatment. However, there is again the idea that formal status and actual mental condition are not the same. Thus, 26.0% of the respondents believe that patients should have the right to refuse, but that there must be exceptions to this right, dependent upon mental condition and not formal status.

Less than a third of the respondents (29.2%) believe that all patients should have the right to refuse treatment unless they are dangerous or psychotic. Finally, 10.4% of the respondents believe that all patients should have the right to refuse treatment, regardless of formal status. These respondents often note alternative ways of dealing with patients, or other approaches that are not utilized at their facilities.

In summary, a small percentage (10.4%) believe that everyone should have the right to refuse treatment. The remainder of the respondents appear to support the idea of the right to refuse in varying degrees and with various exceptions, but usually based on the patient's perceived mental condition, which is taken not to be necessarily related to his or her formal patient status as voluntary or involuntary. Nearly 30% of the respondents identify psychosis or dangerousness as the only exception to the right to refuse treatment.

The New York interview data seem to suggest that laws that define rights according to legal status may not be seen as valid by the staff. The enforcement of these laws will require close monitoring.

In regard to the right to refuse treatment for developmentally disabled clients, data from the relevant question posed to DD staff in California indicate that 55.9% agreed that high-functioning clients should always have the right to refuse specific treatments, while 33.3% disagreed. At first glance, this appears to indicate a high level of support for this "right," but it must be noted that only a small percentage —1 or 2%—of the patients in the facility would be considered high functioning.

The third issue to be considered raises the question, *Should we spend more money on community facilities and staff?* Given limited resources, the question attempts to determine the level of support for providing services in a less restrictive environment. The data indicate that the staff of state mental hospitals are divided on this issue.

Among respondents in the New York questionnaire sample, 57.7% agreed with the proposition that a larger percentage of the state mental health budget should be geared toward aftercare facilities and staff, even if it means cutting the budget of the state hospitals, 27.9% were opposed to the idea, and 14.4% were neutral. A similar percentage (54.2%) of the New York interview sample support the proposition. A sizable group (17.7%) feels that community aftercare facilities do need more money, but they believe that the state hospitals also need more money. Thus, they oppose cutting state hospital budgets. Finally, more than a quarter (28.1%) of the respondents think that money should not be diverted from state mental hospital budgets, and, if anything, these budgets should be increased.

In the California study, 45.9% of the MI staff respondents agreed that resources should be shifted toward community facilities and staff, even if it means cutting state hospital budgets. Thirty-seven percent disagreed with the statement, while 17.1% were neutral. Among respondents in the DD facility, 36.7% agreed, 53.6% disagreed, and 9.7% were neutral. A t-test of the difference in means between the two groups reveals that respondents at the MI facility were significantly more supportive of this item, t (516) = 3.65, $p < .01$. The lower level of support among DD staff may well reflect a strong belief that community placements for the profoundly retarded—the modal client at the facility—will never be accepted by local residents or parents, and, thus, the state should concentrate on improving the quality of care found within the state facilities.

The fourth issue to be considered addresses the question, *How far should the institution go in providing advocacy resources to protect patients' rights?* Here the reference is to organized provision of advocacy services for all patients. Unfortunately, only the California study included items pertaining to this issue.

The data indicate that respondents at the MI facility strongly support the idea of making available a legally trained patient advocate in every psychiatric inpatient facility, public or private. More than three-quarters (76.7%) of the respondents agreed with this idea. It should be noted that the facility currently has such a patient advocate; however, the structure presents problems from a patients' rights perspective because the advocate is a state employee who reports to the director of the facility, with potential limitations on the advocate's independence.

The second relevant item reveals a much more divided picture of support for the notion of providing an attorney for all MI patients facing involuntary hospitalization. Here, only 39.0% agreed, while 36.3% disagreed, and an additional 24.8% took a neutral position. These responses seem to indicate support for some form of advocacy assistance, but not to the point of providing attorneys for commitment proceedings.

Respondents at the DD facility also strongly support the idea of having a legally trained patient advocate in the system. More than four-fifths of the respondents (80.2%) agreed with this item. As was the case in the MI facility, there is a patient advocate in the DD facility who reports to the director.

FACTORS AFFECTING RESPONSE

In addition to the issues already discussed, other issues were included in summary measures in both studies, and these indices were then utilized in multivariate analyses of the data. In the discussion to come, the interview summary measure is the focus of analysis for the New York data. Corresponding analyses from the questionnaire data can be found in Freddolino (1977). Detailed descriptions of all items included in the summary measures can be found in the basic references (Freddolino, 1977, 1979).

Type of Hospital.

Given the hypothesis that respondents in community-oriented (COMM) state hospitals in New York will show more support for patients' rights than those working in more traditional facilities (TRAD), an examination was conducted using univariate t-test comparisons for the nine items together with the multivariate Hotellings' T^2 statistic. The results indicate a relatively small difference in the predicted direction $T (9,85) = 3.77, p = .091$. The only two items that show significant differences suggest that the primary difference between COMM and TRAD facilities may lie in the *general decision-making role of patients seen as appropriate by the staff.* Thus, respondents in COMM facilities are more likely to approve a somewhat more active role for patients concerning the preparation of their general treatment plan— not necessarily how it will be implemented—and in deciding whether or not they are "ready" to be released. But there is no significant difference between respondents at the two types of hospitals in their attitude toward patients' rights to refuse specific treatment modalities (such as drugs) in the context of everyday ward life. Both groups are opposed to this idea.

Profession.

Analysis of the New York interview data strongly suggest a three-tiered relationship between profession of the respondents and their support for patients' rights. Support for patients' rights shows no statistically significant differences among nurses, psychologists, and psychiatrists. Therapy aides (or psychiatric technicians) clearly show the lowest level of support, while social workers reveal the highest level.

The California results are divided. Among staff at the DD facility, psychologists clearly show the highest levels of support and psychiatric technicians the lowest levels, with other professions in the middle. At the MI facility, however, no statistically significant differences among professional groups are evident.

Traditionalism

A 10-item scale developed by Bardach (1972) was used to measure respondents' attitudes on a number of "ideological cleavage" issues in mental health. The items are intended to measure the extent of agreement with tenets of the *medical model,* a common term among mental health workers. The hypothesis was that those respondents who showed high levels of support for tenets of the medical model would be low in support for patients' rights. Analyses of the data support this hypothesis. The correlation coefficient relating traditionalism and patients' rights ideology in the New York study is $-.39$, significant at the .01 level. In the California study, the correlation is $-.42$, significant at the .001 level. The multivariate analyses revealed the same strong negative relationships when profession is taken into account.

Patient Care Responsibilities

There is conflicting evidence concerning differences in attitudes between staff in predominantly direct patient-care positions, compared to staff in principally administrative and/or supervisory roles. Unlike the national survey described by Perry in the previous chapter, all respondents in the New York and California studies work in state mental hospitals and no other types of facilities. The use of interviews in New York also provided a rich source of data concerning the complex patient rights issues. The New York interview data clearly indicate significantly higher levels of support for patient rights among staff without direct patient care responsibilities T (9,85) = 5.38, p = .002.

The significant differences in resistance to patients' rights between staff with and without patient care responsibilities can be attributed to differences in both the structurally given demands of the positions they occupy, and staff conceptions of how these demands must be met (Levinson, 1959). Staff without patient care responsibilities generally occupy positions that demand interaction with two principal groups—other staff and people outside the hospitals. For staff without patient care responsibilities, a sense of accomplishment and fulfillment does not require close working relationships with patients. It *does* require some measure of compromise on patients' rights issues with advocates or administrators. For staff with patient care responsibilities, however, patients form an important part in their role definition. Spending time with patients is demanded by the very nature of their positions in the organization, and how they deal with patients is an important component of their own role definition.

In the New York study, the dimension of patient-care responsibilities provided the most potent independent variable to explain variance in individual responses to patients' rights issues in the interviews. In California, however, no differences appeared among questionnaire respondents at the MI facility. The differences that occurred among DD staff were inconsistent, leaving no clear indication of the actual impact of this characteristic. One possible explanation for these conflicting results is that the forced-choice questionnaire items did not elicit as much variation in responses as the open-ended interview items utilized in the New York study.

CONCLUSIONS

These two studies indicate some important divisions among staff in state hospitals concerning patients' rights. While there is strong support for the basic idea of informing patients of their rights, analyses of specific issues reveal attenuation of this support. For example, staff in both studies do not support present statutes that grant voluntary patients the right to refuse treatment. The implication is that changing the laws regarding patients' rights will not necessarily affect daily life on the wards. Vigorous monitoring by groups with real power may be necessary to insure that legislative and judicial changes are implemented. This need for monitoring may be even more critical in those private facilities that have few outside groups reviewing their activities.

Analyses of factors affecting responses produce some important insights. For example, even staff in the community-oriented state hospitals—those expected to show higher levels of support for patients' rights—seemed to support only general rights, and they were as resistant as their colleagues in more traditional facilities on specific issues, such as the right to refuse treatment. Although the evidence is not conclusive, psychologists and social workers seem to be less resistant than other mental health personnel. Support for patients' rights is directly related to low levels of support for the traditional medical model of mental illness. Finally, there is some indication that staff in administrative and supervisory positions are less resistant to extending patients' rights than direct patient-care staff, perhaps because their jobs do not require direct control of involuntarily committed patients on a daily basis.

SUMMARY AND IMPLICATIONS

The studies reported here, in Perry's research, and in the research literature reviewed, show how complex the controversial issues regarding the rights of psychiatric patients have become. The formulation of the Patients' Rights Attitude Questionnaire (PRAQ) reported by Perry is an important step in the development of a tool for investigations in this area. The use of open-ended questions reported here provides additional insight into these complex questions. Sufficient research has been done to permit some general observations to be made with confidence.

Most of the earlier research had examined attitudes toward mental illness and toward the mentally ill, with little direct examination of the attitudes toward the rights of psychiatric patients. The studies painted a picture of generally negative but improving attitudes toward the mentally ill.

Those studies that examined the rights of patients presented a fairly consistent pattern of "information deficiency" on the part of mental health professionals regarding legal and procedural protection of the rights of patients. Recent legislation and judicial decisions, as well as new administrative regulations in mental health systems, have increased the amount of information to be learned. None of the work described here or in Perry's chapter addressed this issue directly, but it seems safe to state that the rights of patients cannot be protected without some knowledge of these developments on the part of mental health service providers. Nothing in the literature to date can let us feel sanguine about current levels of knowledge, and it can only be hoped that the expansion of advocacy services will lead to an increase in providers' knowledge of the rights of their patients.

The few studies described in the literature that included attitudes regarding the rights of patients unfortunately utilized fairly small samples and *ad hoc* survey instruments, making their comparability and generalizability problematic. Perry and I both sensed a strong need for reliable baseline data on attitudes toward patient rights, and each of us independently had begun work seeking to address this need. Perry sought to unravel some of the complexity involved in the topic by deriving groups of specific issues as mathematically distinct and logically coherent entities. He developed the 41 forced-choice item PRAQ that could "capture" the significant aspects of the range of attitudes regarding the rights of psychiatric patients. The PRAQ was then used with a national sample of attorneys, mental health personnel, and psychiatric patients.

The PRAQ is divided into four distinct clusters and the results indicate that there was highly significant variation in the attitudes of respondent groups for each cluster. There was also significant variation among cluster means, indicating varying levels of support for subsets of rights. For example, the set of items regarding provision of due process to patients involved in involuntary commitment proceedings received fairly strong prorights support, while the items relating to freedom from restraint for disturbed individuals were the least supported. When it came down to individual rights versus community protection, respondents were more willing to restrict the rights of the individual. Examination of all four clusters showed that the mean scores for only one cluster represented a clearly positive attitude; two were mildly positive, and one represented a slightly negative attitude. These findings will give little comfort to those who would like to see the mental health system open to significant advances in the protection of the rights of patients.

The data reported in these chapters demonstrate that attitudes of a variety of interest groups—professionals and consumers—can be measured, and the differences that emerge generally confirm expectations. The legal profession is clearly split along role-influenced lines, with those attorneys who are most likely to defend current or prospective patients supporting the rights of their clients, while prosecuting attorneys are most protective of the community. Continued support of public defender programs will clearly be a strong force in the continued expansion and protection of the rights of psychiatric patients. Interest was expressed for research with attorneys who have changed roles to see if the role change from defender to prosecutor, or vice versa, effects attitudes. It would also be appropriate to examine the function of attitudes in this area as a possible predictor of the choice of legal work preferred by law students and by newly practicing attorneys.

The patient/consumer groups included in the national sample are not strong supporters of the rights of patients. This may be a reflection of the generally negative and rejecting attitudes held by most Americans as was noted by Rabkin (1972). Or it may be an expression of a felt need for societal intervention when their behavior becomes potentially life threatening. The two patient groups varied in their responses to different aspects of the patients' rights area measured. The generally lower levels of support for rights espoused by the inpatient group may reflect the effects of their status as "occupants" of a total institution as discussed by Goffman (1961). Inpatients tend to have low levels of self-esteem, and thus would be less likely to support their own rights. The out-patients may be better able to locate themselves, physically and psychologically, in the community, and thus be less likely to experience the negative effects of "patient" status. Studies of individuals who have changed from outpatient status to inpatient status, and the reverse, could help us better understand the effects of patient status on their attitudes regarding their rights. In a similar fashion, studies that examined the effects of length of treatment, type of treatment, and type of treatment facility could offer further insight into these complex phenomena.

The responses of the patient groups point to an important implication for the field of patient advocacy. It may well be that efforts to protect the rights of patients, and especially efforts to assist patients to be more assertive in regard to their rights, may be facing insurmountable obstacles, so long as the patients remain within the confines of a total institution. It may be that assertive, self-protective behavior is impossible to achieve in an inpatient setting, given the role requirements for patients placed on them by staff—particularly by the administratively powerful psychiatrists and the practically powerful psychiatric aides.

Results from the New York study reported in this chapter showed that the staff working in traditional hospitals and in more community oriented hospitals were not significantly different in their support for patient rights. Both groups work in inpatient settings, and it may be that the role demands for control of patient behavior inescapably constrain the formation of prorights attitudes. In a sense, the staff of inpatient institutions may be as trapped by the "total institution" as the patients who reside there. Support for the rights of patients threatens the very structure of the power relationships that keep such institutions functioning.

The responses of the psychiatrists suggest another facet of this issue. In all the studies conducted, this group tended to express negative attitudes toward the rights of patients, despite their high status and high level of education, factors that might lead one to expect a more prorights attitude. The very real power of psychiatrists in the mental health system carries with it the burden of legal responsibility for the effects of their decisions. This burden increases their vulnerability and may explain their nonsupport of the extension of the rights of the group they are required to control. Furthermore, the psychiatrists are the representatives of the medical model and strong support for the medical model was found to be related to low level of support for patients' rights.

The mental health groups studied were less clearly divided than the attorney groups, but they showed significant variation in attitude, depending on the specific issues under consideration. Among mental health personnel, social workers and psychologists are the most likely to be supporters of the rights of patients. This may reflect their rejection of the medical model of mental illness in favor of more behavioral or humanistic models of treatment. Perhaps also the greater emphasis on *treatment* (*therapy*)—rather than legal issues of commitment, or considerations related to the reduced patient control responsibilities of social workers and psychologists—permits greater recognition of the rights of patients without the threat of any challenge to their authority. It is obvious that considerably more research will be required before the reasons for the differences in attitudes among personnel within the mental health field can be explained satisfactorily.

The basic thrust of the data presented is that the variation in support for the rights of patients found in the groups studied all occurs within a mildly negative to mildly positive range, with the exception of the defense attorneys who are far more supportive than all other groups. None of the other groups studied could be described as enthusiastic in their support of patient rights. If this is the case, then changes mandated by courts, legislatures, and administrative centers can be seen as running counter to significant components of the mental health system. It is likely that resistance to the extension of the rights of patients will be strong, even in those facilities, and among those groups of professionals, where we might expect support.

There is strong indication that resistance to patients' rights may be structurally inherent in the system of inpatient mental health treatment. Although the present data do not permit assessment of actual staff behavior, the resistance shown in both traditional and community-oriented facilities, among all types of staff, would seem to suggest that staff reactions to the extension of patients' rights are not being recast into overly positive activity. It may be that extension of patients' rights can only be brought about by forcing the organizational structure to shift toward outpatient treatment. The data reported earlier suggest that outpatient consumers are more supportive of their own rights, and the move to less restrictive outpatient settings may enhance these positive feelings. Furthermore, the decreased demand on staff to "control" patients in the outpatient setting may make it easier for them to be more supportive of patients' rights as well.

As noted, there is no absolute correspondence between attitudes and behavior. Nevertheless, studies of attitudes provide important insights into the culture of organizations, and reveal important areas of controversy. As various legislative and judicial strategies are exercised in the movement to protect and extend the rights of patients, the types of studies reported above point to the need for monitoring the implementation of these strategies. Staff support for patients' rights is far from unanimous, and the assumption that simply changing the "rules" will change behavior seems untenable, given the findings reported to date. Close monitoring by groups with power to compel compliance is definitely required.

It is my hope that this review of the relevant research will help others to focus their efforts in the study of patients' rights, and that interested and concerned readers will note that in many areas, the rights of psychiatric patients remain controversial. As our ability to measure attitudes in this arena improves, we may be better able to design appropriate supplemental programs to increase staff awareness of rights, and to assist in monitoring implementation of legislative and judicial mandates for the betterment of all patients.

REFERENCES

Bardach, E. *The skill factor in politics: Repealing the mental commitment laws in California.* Berkeley, Calif: University of California Press, 1972.

Ennis, B. J. *Prisoners of psychiatry: Mental patients, psychiatrists, and the law.* New York: Harcourt, Brace, Javanovich, 1972.

Ennis, B. J., & Siegel, L. *The rights of mental patients: The basic American Civil Liberties Union guide to a mental patient's rights.* New York: Avon Books, 1973.

Freddolino, P. P. *Patients' rights ideology and the structure of mental hospitals.* (Doctoral dissertation, The University of Michigan, 1977). *Dissertation Abstracts International,* 1978, 38, 6978A. University Microfilms No. 78–04, 701.

Freddolino, P. P. *Assessing advocacy services for the mentally disabled: An evaluation of the Mental Health Advocacy Project.* Washington: American Bar Association, 1979.

Goffman, E. *Asylums.* Garden City, N.Y.: Doubleday Anchor, 1961.

Kahle, L. R., & Sales, B. D. Due process of law and the attitudes of professionals toward involuntary civil commitment. In P. Lipsitt & B. D. Sales (Eds.), *New Directions in Psycholegal Research.* New York: Van Nostrand Reinhold, 1980.

Kumasaka, Y., & Stokes, J. Involuntary hospitalization: Opinions and attitudes of psychiatrists and lawyers. *Comprehensive Psychiatry,* 1972, *13,* 201–208.

Laves, R., & Cohen, A. A preliminary investigation into the knowledge of and attitudes toward the legal rights of mental patients. *Journal of Psychiatry and Law,* 1973, *1,* 49–78.

Levinson, D. J. Role, personality, and social structure in the organizational setting. *Journal of Abnormal and Social Psychology,* 1959, *58,* 170–180.

Peszke, M. A., & Wintrob, R. M. Emergency commitment—A transcultural study. *American Journal of Psychiatry,* 1974, *131,* 36–40.

Rabkin, J. G. Opinions about mental illness: A review of the literature. *Psychological Bulletin,* 1972, *77,* 153–171.

Rachlin, S., Pam, A., & Milton, J. Civil liberties versus involuntary hospitalization. *American Journal of Psychiatry,* 1975, *132,* 189–192.

Szasz, T. *The myth of mental illness.* New York: Hoeber-Harper, 1961.

Szasz, T. *The manufacture of madness.* New York: Harper & Row, 1970.

Tancredi, L., & Clark, D. Psychiatry and the legal rights of patients. *American Journal of Psychiatry,* 1972, *129,* 328–330.

Vail, D. J. *Dehumanization and the institutional career.* Springfield, Illinois: Charles C. Thomas, 1966.

Part IV

EPILOGUE

Chapter 11

THREE LINGERING ISSUES IN PATIENT RIGHTS

John Monahan

There are easier acts to follow than the excellent contributions that Bernard Bloom and Shirley Asher have orchestrated in this volume. The temptation is strong to merely make again the major points that the authors have already made. Perhaps an epilogue should be like an after-dinner conversation: a mellow recounting of once-told tales to leave everyone feeling warm and glad they made the trip. Patient rights and patient advocacy, however, are not topics given to being wound down. They are, by their very nature, fighting phrases, to be discussed with rolled-up sleeves, ice-cold beer, and at least an occasional pound on the table. So, I will shamelessly take advantage of this rare opportunity to have the final word, and will plunge us back into the quick of the debate.

I would like to consider three issues that have been alluded to but not fully drawn out by the chapters in this volume. The first is the structural context in which the topics of patient rights and patient advocacy arise; the second is the likely consequence of achieving the *ultimate* patient right—the right to refuse involuntarily hospitalization itself; and the third concerns the violation of rights proportedly sanctioned by the widespread adoption of the dangerousness standard of civil commitment.

THE STRUCTURAL CONTEXT OF PATIENT RIGHTS

The single most important distinction in the area of patient rights and patient advocacy, it seems to me, is that between rights to be free from interference in one's life—what will be called *negative rights,* since they tell others what they can *not* do to us (cf. Stone, 1975, p. 15)—and rights to have access to resources that society possesses—what will be called *positive rights,* since they entail an affirmative giving of goods or services. This distinction may parallel that of Bloom and Asher between *civil* and *clinical rights* (this volume). These two classes of rights, I believe, have much less in common than meets the eye. Indeed, the achievement of the one may hasten the demise of the other.

Negative rights include all forms of guarantee against state interference in an individual's decision-making. Rights to refuse treatment, to court hearings, to confidentiality of information (see Noll & Rosen, this volume), to the provision of attorneys, to send and receive uncensored mail, and to periodic reviews are all negative rights. They either tell the government what it cannot do to a patient, or they mandate one branch of the government (e.g., the public defender's office) to protect the patient against the excesses of another branch (e.g., the prosecutor's office).

Positive rights include all forms of guarantee that resources will be forthcoming to an individual who might benefit by them. Rights to treatment, to be paid minimum wage for labor in an institution, to enjoy certain living standards, and to have the state provide alternative treatment settings with as few restrictions as the patient's condition will allow (see Barrow & Gutwirth, this volume) are examples of positive rights. They tell the government how large a portion of the goods and services under its control must be allocated to the care of mental patients.

An index of the relative attention given to negative and to positive rights in the scholarly literature can be gleaned from the fact that of the 41 items in Perry's (this volume; see also Freddolino, this volume) Patients' Rights Attitude Questionnaire, only two ("If patients are willing and able to work in a psychiatric hospital, they should be paid at least the minimum wage," and "If a psychiatric hospital fails to provide treatment to an inpatient, involuntary hospitalization is not justified") refer to positive rights. The other 39 refer to freedom from state interference in patient decision-making.

Positive rights differ from negative rights along one crucial dimension: positive rights cost money. It costs virtually nothing to give a patient the right to send uncensored mail, make phone calls, receive visitors, or refuse intrusive treatments. These are all essentially rights to be let alone, and leaving someone alone is, among other things, free. To be sure, there may be indirect costs involved in granting negative rights, as occurs when a treatment that would have resolved a patient's difficulties cannot be forced upon him or her, and the patient then relapses and incurs further mental health processing. But these costs are not immediate, are often borne by other social agencies (e.g., welfare agencies) and are given to severe inflation by those trying to justify the denial of negative rights. Positive rights, on the other hand, are expensive by their very nature. If one has a right to have an individual treatment plan drawn up, somebody has to pay a mental health professional to do it. If one has a right to a high staff-to-patient ratio, the checks of the additional staff have to be signed.

Patient advocates have argued for both positive and negative rights, with very different reactions from the mental health system. Patient rights groups arguing for negative rights—for rights that reduce the discretionary power of professionals to impose treatments or deny privileges—are often viewed as pariahs by the mental health establishment. Us-versus-them mentality prevails.

Patient-rights groups advocating positive rights, on the other hand, are often viewed as coreligionists by the mental health elites. They are seen as potentially powerful allies in the perennial fight for a larger share of the public pie. The things that the proponents of positive rights want—more staff, better facilities, more programs—are the same things that most mental health professionals want. Stories can be heard of mental hospital administrators yearning to be sued for abrogating their patients' "right to treatment," disgorging reams of damaging evidence to their patient-advocate "adversaries," and rejoicing when "losing" the suit, because the result is that the state must then augment the mental hospital budget.

While there have been some significant victories for the proponents of positive rights (e.g., *Wyatt* v. *Stickney,* 1972), it would appear that patient advocates have been much more successful in securing negative rights and of having negative rights actually implemented. Part of the reason for this is no doubt due to the fact that, in demanding negative rights, patient advocates can appeal to the tradition of individualism that runs deeply in American law and in American society. A parade of horrors along the lines of *One Flew Over the Cuckoo's Nest* can be marshaled to make even the least sympathetic legislator experience a temporary attack of libertarianism. The choice is often simply put: What do you value most, liberty or health? Images are painted of Patrick Henry battling Marcus Welby, and the preferred resolution is clear.

Those arguing for positive rights have to tap a different emotional well. They must appeal not to individualism but to a sense of community, a sympathy for those less able or less fortunate. We are asked not to affirm our commitment to liberty, but to share our standard of living. It is the Golden Rule, rather than the Bill of Rights, that must be invoked as authority.

The bedrock problem of the proponents of positive rights is that we, as a society, judging by our actions rather than our rhetoric, simply do not want to foot the bill for them. The history of positive rights, as I read it, is largely one of evasion, noncompliance, interminable delay, and, finally, when pressed, dumping the many to provide improved service to the few that remain. For example, a court rules that the state must pay the minimum wage to mental hospital patients who perform services for the institution. Rather than providing the funds, however, the state simply terminates the work programs (Bloom & Asher, this volume). The positive right to be paid is made meaningless by the lack of opportunity to work.

Indeed, at least some advocates of negative rights have recognized the reluctance of the state to provide positive rights and have exploited it to their advantage:

> They believe that the number of individuals incarcerated makes standards of the type imposed [in *Wyatt* v. *Stickney*] too expensive to implement. They anticipate that a state, rather than upgrading its institutions, will recoil at the cost and abdicate its responsibility. Convinced that asylums are no more effective than prisons, they welcome this abdication; it would bring, at the very least, a drastic reduction in the number of people incarcerated for mental illness. (Rothman, 1973, quoted in Scull, 1977, p. 154)

The only consistent explanation, of which I am aware, to account for the relative success of obtaining negative rights for mental patients and the relative failure to gain or implement positive ones is the structural approach of Andrew Scull (1977).

Scull believes that many of the negative rights given to mental patients in recent years have as their primary function the "enabling [of] the state to disguise neglect as humane concern for the rights of the deviant" (p. 155). The issue of patient rights has served as *ideological camouflage* (p. 152) to allow the state to cut back on the spiraling costs of mental hospitals. Until the middle of this century, Scull states, it was simply less expensive for a capitalist state to store what he refers to as "social junk" in "monasteries for the mad" than it would have been to create the extensive support services necessary to sustain them in the community. "However," he notes, "with the advent of a wide range of welfare programs providing just such support, the opportunity cost of neglecting community care in favor of asylum treatment . . .

rose sharply" (p. 135). The newfound interest of the state in recognizing the negative rights of mental patients, therefore, is a function of the fact that such rights are compatible with the overriding need of the state to process "nonproductive" citizens in the cheapest way possible. Since the rise of the welfare state, it is now cheaper to maintain disordered persons in the community than in the hospital. To recognize positive rights, however, would be to incur costs that could reduce or eliminate the savings produced by community care.

As support for his position that fiscal rather than therapeutic or libertarian concerns motivated the move toward community care, Scull notes that the actual outcomes associated with granting patients and potential patients a wide variety of negative rights has not been the increase in dignity and autonomy its advocates claim. Rather, according to Scull, it has been to deinstitutionalize patients into "newly emerging 'deviant ghettoes,' sewers of human misery and what is conventionally defined as social pathology within which (largely hidden from outside inspection or even notice) society's refuse may be repressively tolerated" (p. 153). Even those who do not share Scull's conceptual framework agree that the care deinstitutionalized patients receive "is often illusory; they may have less community and less care where they live than they had in their state hospitals where at least food, clothing, shelter, and the presence of other people were routinely available" (Rabkin & Zitrin, this volume; see also Morse, 1978, pp. 639–640).

I present Scull's (1977) radical critique of patient rights and community mental health as an alternative heuristic for understanding the structural framework within which these topics arise. It is not a perspective in which I am well-versed or entirely comfortable. It is also not a perspective that lends itself to "action recommendations" short of massive social restructuring of a kind that the American people give no sign of accepting. But policy usefulness is not the touchstone of scholarly explanation. Macrosociological analyses of patient rights and patient advocacy seem to me to be among the highest research priorities in the field.

THE ULTIMATE PATIENT RIGHT—THE RIGHT TO REFUSE HOSPITALIZATION

The "ultimate conclusion" (Klein, 1976, p. 8) of the civil liberties approach to patient rights is the right to refuse commitment itself, which would be synonymous with the abolition of involuntary mental hospitalization. Proponents of abolition claim that several things would follow from it:

(1) People who wanted treatment would seek it voluntarily, free from fear of being "transferred" to involuntary status.

(2) The criminal justice system would be applied to those people who have demonstrated their danger by performing illegal acts: they would be arrested.

(3) We would all learn to be more tolerant of the harmless eccentricities of our fellow citizens.

(4) Behavior that we do not wish to tolerate but is not illegal would be dealt with by informal social controls, e.g., divorce, rather than commitment, of a bizarre spouse.

I believe that the truth-to-falsity ratio of each of these claims is low. By examining the most extreme case of patient rights, we may be in a better position to put other patient rights issues into perspective.

Voluntary Treatment

I know of no evidence that the existence of civil commitment deters anyone from voluntarily seeking therapy, and no reason to believe that the abolition of civil commitment would bring forth the timid. On the contrary, according to Klein, "there are people who, precisely because of severe mental illness, will not accept treatment voluntarily."

> For example, some depressed people believe they are unworthy of help. There are also paranoid people who reject treatment on such grounds as that the psychiatrist "is a CIA agent who will plant a tape recorder in my head." And, perhaps most significantly, there are numerous extremely passive people, including many elderly, who simply will not seek treatment on their own. If they are not treated involuntarily—and here I think the concept of "involuntariness" is largely metaphysical—we know by recent experience that many of them will wander aimlessly through our blighted inner cities, subject to a host of dangers. (Klein, 1976, p. 8)

The leading approach to deciding when, if ever, to override a person's "voluntary" refusal of treatment emphasizes the notion of *competence* (e.g., Stone, 1975; Roth, 1979). A person may be mentally disordered and still competent to refuse commitment. Stone (1975) proposes two "tests" for determining competence: the patient or prospective patient must give a *reason* for refusing treatment, and that reason must not be related to mental disorder. "I am a Christian Scientist" or, "The stigma of being in a mental hospital outweighs the benefits of the therapy" may be competent refusals, while "Martians must be free" would be an incompetent refusal. If one assumes that a population exists that is both mentally disordered and incompetent to make treatment decisions, then reliance upon the availability of "voluntary" treatment in the absence of civil commitment is a policy option riddled with internal contradictions.

The Criminal Justice Alternative

According to Szasz (1978), many people committed as dangerous could and should be subject to criminal arrest instead. "Disordered" people wandering in traffic, for example, should be dealt with through the criminal law: "When people act like this they are asking for attention. They want to make trouble. The only way to deal with it is by punishing them" (p. 58).

What percentage of the people committed as dangerous could be subject to arrest if civil commitment did not exist? One recent study (Monahan, Caldeira, & Friedlander, 1980) interviewed police officers after they had petitioned someone for civil commitment. The officers were asked if they could have made a legal arrest rather than initiate a commitment, and, if so, why they chose to commit. In 30% of the total commitment cases (39% of those whose grounds for commitment included danger to others) the police believed they could have made a legal arrest, but in less than half these cases did the officers seriously consider filing charges. The reasons given by the officers for choosing not to arrest those susceptible to it were evenly divided between variations of a legalistic "no intent or motivation to commit a crime" due to mental illness—a form of *presumptive insanity defense*—and variations of a paternalistic "in need of help not incarceration."

The proponent of abolition could retort that the fact that most people being committed as dangerous could not be arrested simply reflects the overinclusive manner in which dangerousness has been operationalized. But the fact that in half the cases where a legal arrest *could* have been made, the police did not do so because they believed the "offender" lacked the *mens rea* necessary for criminal conviction is more problematic. If the police are accurate in this perception, and if commitment were abolished, half of those arrested for what was formerly called "dangerous" behavior might be adjudicated not guilty by reason of insanity and returned to the mental health system as "criminal" rather than "civil" commitments (see Pasewark & Pasewark, this volume). The people denied entry to the mental health system through the front door would simply be sent around the back. In this regard, Bonovitz and Guy (1979) found that a narrowing of Pennsylvania's commitment criteria resulted in substantial increases in admissions to inpatient jail psychiatric facilities, usually within one week of arrest. You can change the name of the game, but you cannot avoid playing it so long as "responsibility" is a necessary prerequisite for imposing punishment and disordered people are seen as lacking it (Monahan, 1973).

Increased Tolerance

It is frequently argued that mental hospitalization is often imposed on persons who are "deviant" only in the sense that they offend our esthetic sensibilities. They are people who speak in uncommon idioms, hold atypical values, or have been the victims of some capricious or perhaps even malevolent "labeling" in the past. If commitment were abolished, the argument goes, we would simply have to tolerate a wider range of behavioral variability, much as we have learned in the past few decades to be more tolerant of people of different races and different lifestyles. Indeed, we might even be enriched by the experience.

I know of no reason to believe, however, that I or anyone else is prepared to "tolerate," much less "accept" many of the behaviors that precipitate civil commitment (see Rosen, Cowan, & Grandison, this volume). On the contrary, the response of society to those denied commitment would doubtlessly be similar to the response of society to those people released from commitment to community care as part of the deinstitutionalization movement. We will tolerate them, but not in *our* neighborhoods. We will literally impose them (by the location of halfway houses and board-and-care homes) on the inner-city poor who are powerless to resist. Indeed, if they do resist, we will chide them for being "uncharitable and reactionary" (Rabkin & Zitrin, this volume). When a politically naive mental health administrator does attempt to locate a community treatment facility in an upper-or middle-class neighborhood, the protests "are scarely the reaction one would expect from those becoming more 'tolerant' of the presence of deviance" (Scull, 1977, p. 99). A great deal of insight into the dynamics of mental health law can be achieved by pondering the fact that ideological opposition to civil commitment is inversely proportional to the number of released or potential mental patients living on one's block.

Informal Controls

Thomas Szasz (1963) believes that most situations that result in commitment relate to a person's functioning in the family. When a

family member begins to act erratically or unacceptably, the family has
three options:

1. A relative may request the failing member to alter his behavior
   —by asking, begging, coercing, self-sacrificing, and so forth.
2. He may sever the relationship—by emotional withdrawal, separation or divorce, running away and "disappearing," and so
   forth.
3. He may enlist medical or psychiatric help and secure involuntary hospitalization of the failing member. (p. 153)

Szasz (1963, 1978) believes that the elimination of the third option would increase families' reliance upon the first two. To Szasz, the
choices are clear: "Which should we prefer, *the integrity of the family or
the autonomy of the individual?* Commitment laws favor the former. I
suggest that we favor the latter" (1963, p. 154, emphasis in original).

Szasz recognizes that the abolition of commitment would transform the nature of the family in society. Commitment "ensures the
maintenance of family relationships, loyalties, and responsibilities as
positive moral values. Our whole system needs the safety valve that
commitment laws provide. Without it, our traditional ideas about the
duties and rights of family members would have to be reexamined,
reassessed, and changed" (1963, p. 154).

It is highly uncertain, however, whether society is willing to reex-
amine, reassess, and change its notions of what constitutes the responsibilities of family members to one another. It is also unclear, to me
at least, whether the arguable gain in "autonomy" occasioned by di-
vorcing an acutely depressed and possibly suicidal spouse or parent is
always preferable, as a matter of policy and of morality, to the preservation of family integrity allowed by a brief period of involuntary
treatment. Marcus (quoted in Roth, 1979, p. 1121) has put it well:
"You can degrade people by taking care of them and you can degrade
people by not taking care of them, and I see no simple answer to such
questions."

I am unconvinced, therefore, that the abolition of civil commitment could be as benignly accomplished as its proponents claim. The
costs of abolition to the would-be patient whose incompetent refusal
of treatment was honored, to his or her family and significant others
whose lives would be significantly affected, to the criminal justice system, which is ill-equipped to deal with those who lack criminal intent,
and to society, which would have to redraft its norms of social responsibility, are not so easily dismissed.

There is one other argument in opposition to the abolition of civil commitment that is of a political rather than a moral nature. Joel Klein (1976) in an extremely lucid paper that I have never seen cited, argued that achievement of the right to refuse commitment would preclude achievement of positive rights such as the right to treatment.

> Involuntary patients arguably have a constitutional right to treatment, as several courts already have held. Thus, once a patient is committed, his lawyer can use the courts to insure that treatment is provided. . . . On the other hand, it seems extremely unlikely that voluntary patients will soon be found to have a constitutional right to treatment. Rather, when indigent, they must accept whatever services a state provides—usually significantly less than needed. In short, the irony is that people who want mental health treatment frequently cannot get it, while those who do not want it sometimes can. I cannot overemphasize that in the absence of involuntary commitment it will be extremely difficult to force the state to provide decent mental health care. (p. 8)

In other words, if the government involuntarily details a person for treatment, it may be constitutionally obligated to follow through and provide that treatment. If, on the other hand, the treatment is not forced but is a matter of "choice," the government is likely to respond: "So you want mental health care at the public's expense. All right, go stand in line behind the people who want us to pay for their medical care and their social security and their school lunches and their urban renewal. We'll see what we can do." And what they can—or will—do is very little.

PATIENT RIGHTS AND THE DANGEROUSNESS STANDARD

If there has been any national trend in the area of involuntary hospitalization in the past decade, it has been to replace or augment the standard of "need for treatment" with that of "danger to self or others." Forty-eight of the 51 American jurisdictions now phrase their commitment statutes in terms of dangerousness (Schwitzgebel, 1978). Ironically enough, the patient advocates who objected so vociferously to the biases and vagaries inherent in the judgment of "need for treatment"—thus hastening the arrival of the dangerousness standard as an alternative commitment criterion—have recently come to see "dangerousness" as equally problematic (Rabkin & Zitrin, this volume). Wilkins (1974) and Steadman (this volume) have aptly termed this new patient rights issue "the right not to be a false positive," that is, the right not to be falsely predicted to do harm. Several beliefs appear to gird the position of those who see the dangerousness standard as a major affront to patient rights.

(1) Research has proved that mental health professionals are extremely inaccurate at all forms of violence prediction.

(2) The dangerousness standard transforms the primary role of the mental health professional from one of a healer of psychic pain to that of an agent of social control.

(3) Eliminating the dangerousness standard as a matter of policy would result in a substantial reduction in the number of persons subject to commitment.

Each of these beliefs, in my opinion, is misguided.

The Empirical Issue

It is unquestionably true, as Steadman (this volume) has stated, that "There is not a single piece of empirical evidence that accurate predictions under any circumstances are made by clinicians." Yet his following sentence is equally accurate: "There may be many instances in which they are quite accurate but they have yet to demonstrate empirically they can [accurately predict]." While there have been several studies of the accuracy of clinical prediction in the context of long-term hospitalization, there has yet to be a single investigation of the accuracy of the clinical prediction of violent behavior in short-term "emergency" contexts. And brief emergency commitment is becoming the rule rather than the exception for involuntary hospitalization, with the vast majority of committed patients being released within approximately two weeks of admission (Spensley & Werme, this volume).

The absence of evidence regarding the validity of clinical predictions in short-term "community" contexts is not the same as evidence of the absence of such validity. There are a number of reasons why one could expect predictions made in close situational and temporal contiguity to the acts they forecast to be superior to the kinds of long-term, hospital-to-community predictions that have been studied. In any event, the empirical basis for the short-term emergency commitment of the "dangerous" mentally ill is an open question, rather than the dead issue one may presume it to be. Further, it is a question that, for legal and ethical reasons, may never be directly answered. Society simply may be unwilling to sanction an experiment in which people believed to be imminently violent are set free so that researchers can see if they actually hurt someone (Monahan, 1977, 1978).

The Professional Issue

After years of being blasted as empirically incompetent to predict violent behavior, and crypto-fascists if they even tried, some mental health professionals have made a counterattack. They have not only outflanked their critics by *agreeing* that accurate prediction is factually impossible and politically improper, but have gone them one better by asserting that the prediction of violence and subsequent interventions to avert it are not—and, in fact, never were—within the purview of the mental health professions. It was the legal system that asked the psychiatrist and psychologist to give opinions regarding violence potential for use in civil commitment and other proceedings. If mental health professionals naively acquiesced, they have now discovered that this incursion into forecasting the future was a mistake. It was a mistake not simply because research allegedly showed the effort to be fruitless or because political rights were trampled, but because in the process the mental health professional gave up his or her essential role as a healer of psychic pain and became an agent of social control. Engaging in the prediction of violence to others "tends to relegate psychiatry to the very role for which it has been criticized, that of valuing societal rights above those of the individual," whereas, "Our sole aim should be to ensure the welfare of our patients." Thus, "The prediction of danger is not within medical competence and under no circumstances should be" (Peszke, 1975, pp. 826, 828).

Professionally, I believe that it would indeed be nice if mental health personnel could leave their current "police power" roles (i.e., their roles as protectors of community safety rather than of the individual client) to those who were sworn police officers and could focus exclusively on promoting their clients' welfare. But it is not clear to me that this is either possible or desirable. Do not all "human service" professions have a social protection component to them? Teachers, for example, surely view themselves primarily as transmitters of knowledge and culture whose role is to improve the welfare of their students. Yet they frequently function as disciplinarians whose tasks include expelling those whose conduct is detrimental to the learning of others, and acting as society's gatekeepers by withholding diplomas needed for jobs and further education from those who do not meet socially defined standards of academic performance. It is as the agents of society, not for the welfare of the individual pupil, that teachers perform these functions.

Likewise and more to the point, nonpsychiatric physicians perform a variety of social-control functions with little adverse effect on their primary help-giving role. They can initiate the involuntary detention of persons who, through no fault of their own, carry contagious diseases. They are bound in many states to report to the police whenever they suspect child abuse to have occurred.

While one would hope that the community-protection role of mental health professionals would be minimal relative to their helping functions (as it is with teachers and physicians), it does not seem to me to be unreasonable of society to demand that a limited "police power" function remain (cf. Roth, 1979).

The Policy Issue

Since California began the trend toward the dangerousness standard in 1969, the vast majority of the published attention given to commitment standards has been given to dangerousness *to others,* with much less emphasis upon the companion standards of dangerousness *to self* or *grave disability* (which is best understood as a passive form of danger to self). This may reflect the fact that all but the most dogmatically libertarian of the critics of commitment find sequestering the suicidal easier to justify than what is plainly preventive detention of those who would harm others.

One gains the impression that the critics of the dangerousness standard believe that if it were banished from consideration, the population of those subject to commitment would plummet, or, at the very least, "The elimination of the dangerousness standard would alter the composition of the hospitalized population and reduce the rate of criminal activity among discharged mental patients" (Rabkin & Zwerling, this volume).

On the contrary, however, there is reason to believe that eliminating danger to others from the scope of civil commitment would have very little effect on the number of types of persons subjected to it. Warren (1977) found that only 4% of the people committed in one jurisdiction were committed solely as dangerous to others. Ninety-six percent were dangerous to self or gravely disabled (often in combination with danger to others). Monahan et al. (1980), in another California county found only 2% solely dangerous to others. The Teknekron Corporation (1978), in a study of 813 persons subject to emergency commitment in seven California counties, found that only eight were subsequently committed for a two-week period as dangerous to others. To the extent these data allow for generalization, therefore, dangerousness to others could be *completely eliminated* as a criterion and 96–99% of the people being committed would still be committable on the *parens patriae* grounds that they will actively (suicide) or passively (grave disability) harm themselves.

Regarding short-term emergency commitment, therefore, I am less certain of the empirical inadequacy, less confident of the professional inappropriateness, and less convinced of the policy importance of the dangerousness standard than those who criticize it in the name of patient rights.

REFERENCES

Bonovitz, J., & Guy, E. Impact of restrictive civil commitment procedures on a prison psychiatric service. *American Journal of Psychiatry*, 1979, *136*, 1045–1048.

Klein, J. Legal doctrine at the crossroads. *Mental Health Law Project Summary of Activities*, March, 1976, 7–10.

Monahan, J. Abolish the insanity defense? Not yet. *Rutgers Law Review*, 1973, *26*, 719–740.

Monahan, J. Strategies for an empirical analysis of the prediction of violence in emergency civil commitment. *Law and Human Behavior*, 1977, *1*, 363–371.

Monahan, J. Prediction research and the emergency commitment of dangerous mentally ill persons: A reconsideration. *American Journal of Psychiatry*, 1978, *135*, 198–201.

Monahan, J., Caldeira, C., & Friedlander, H. Police and the mentally ill: A comparison of committed and arrested persons. *International Journal of Law and Psychiatry*, 1980.

Morse, S. Crazy behavior, morals, & science: An analysis of mental health law. *Southern California Law Review*, 1978, *51*, 527–654.

Pezke, M. Is dangerousness an issue for physicians in emergency commitment? *American Journal of Psychiatry*, 1975, *132*, 825–828.

Roth, L. A commitment law for patients, doctors, & lawyers. *American Journal of Psychiatry*, 1979, *136*, 1121–1127.

Schwitzgebel, R. Survey of state civil commitment statutes. In A. McGarry, R. Schwitzgebel, & P. Lipsitt (Eds.). *Civil commitment and social policy*. Boston, Mass.: Harvard Medical School, 1978.

Scull, A. *Decarceration: Community treatment and the deviant—A radical view*. Englewood Cliffs, New Jersey: Prentice-Hall, 1977.

Stone, A. *Mental health and the law: A system in transition*. Washington, D.C.: Government Printing Office, 1975.

Szasz, T. *Law, liberty, & psychiatry*. New York: Macmillan, 1963.

Szasz, T. Nobody should decide who goes to the mental hospital. *Co-Evolution Quarterly*, Summer 1978, 56–59.

Teknekron, Inc. *Improving California's Mental Health System: Policy Making and Management in the Invisible System*. Report to the California Assembly Permanent Subcommittee on Mental Health and Developmental Disabilities, Berkeley, Calif., 1978.

Warren, C. Involuntary commitment for mental disorder: The application of California's Lanterman-Petris-Short Act. *Law and Society Review,* 1977, *11,* 629–650.

Wilkins, L. Current aspects of penology: Directions for corrections. *Proceedings of the American Philosophical Society,* 1974, *118,* 235–247.

Wyatt v. Stickney, 344 F. Supp. 373 (M.D. Alabama), 1972.

NAME INDEX

SUBJECT INDEX